100 THINGS
MICHIGAN STATE FANS
SHOULD KNOW & DO
BEFORE THEY DIE

100 THINGS
MICHIGAN STATE FANS
SHOULD KNOW & DO
BEFORE THEY DIE

Michael Emmerich

TRIUMPH
BOOKS

Library of Congress Cataloging-in-Publication Data

Emmerich, Michael.
  100 things Michigan State fans should know & do before they die / Michael Emmerich.
    pages cm
    ISBN 978-1-60078-789-8
    1. Michigan State University—Football—History. 2. Michigan State Spartans (Football team)—History. 3. Michigan State University—Basketball—History. 4. Michigan State Spartans (Basketball team)—History. I. Title. II. Title: One hundred things Michigan State fans should know and do before they die.
  GV958.M5E66 2013
  796.0430977427—dc23
                                                2013015887

This book is available in quantity at special discounts for your group or organization. For further information, contact:
  Triumph Books LLC
  814 North Franklin Street
  Chicago, Illinois 60610
  (312) 337-0747
  www.triumphbooks.com

Printed in U.S.A.
ISBN: 978-1-60078-789-8
Design by Patricia Frey
Photos courtesy of AP Images unless otherwise indicated

This book is dedicated to the memory of Eric Telman,
devoted Spartans Fan

Eric Telman, 1982–2011

Contents

Acknowledgments

Few Division I colleges offer equal measures of drama, success, and fan support in both football and basketball. In fact only two schools have won multiple major championships in both sports. Florida is one. Michigan State is the other.

For that reason this book includes both MSU basketball and football, offering Spartans fans a blended taste of the rich and always entertaining history of two of college sports' most successful programs. MSU may not stand among the absolute elite in either sport, but at various points in the history of both football and basketball, Michigan State has been a highly relevant and dominant force.

For years I edited sports books written by other capable authors. This is my first attempt at switching hats. I can appreciate better now the virtues and trials of starting with a blank page instead of one filled with the carefully chosen words of someone else. Stacked high in my office are numerous books by other authors who have written about Michigan State sports. Each and every book proved essential. Without them this book would have had more holes than a typical UM argument about its historical greatness. I'm indebted to the many first-rate authors who staked a claim to this topic before me.

Oh, and about Michigan. I plead guilty to bouts of hyperbole and overstatement—but just a little. The Michigan State-Michigan rivalry is similar to many Flagship U-State U feuds. But few other so-called second fiddle schools in the country must contend with an adversary as smug, dismissive, and, yes, successful, as the one in Ann Arbor. So I have a little fun with Michigan while still stating the truth.

Many thanks to Mitch Rogatz and Tom Bast at Triumph Books for helping make this book happen and to my editor, Jeff

Fedotin, who made significant improvements to all aspects of the book. I can't overstate how wonderful my family has been while I labored to write this book, which consumed more time than I ever imagined. My wife, Becky, never hesitated in her support. She didn't even wince when I asked her to read the final manuscript, which included oblique complaints about Duke, her beloved alma mater. Becky's positive and constructive feedback and patience proved invaluable, and it's just one more reason why I'm one lucky guy.

No one has been a stronger advocate of this book than my 10-year-old daughter, Hannah. She even helped me type some of it. Her enthusiasm throughout kept me moving forward through thick and thin. I suspect Hannah will be the book's best and most tireless promoter. How blessed I am to have a daughter who cares so much, and a special thanks to my brother, Tom, as well.

I'd also like to acknowledge my loving parents, who moved our family to the doorstep of the MSU campus when I was three. The first organized football game I saw live was with my father on November 11, 1967 at Spartan Stadium. Michigan State lost to Indiana 14–13. I became a steadfast fan of college football that day—and decided afterward my dream was to attend...Indiana. What can you say? I was a shameless frontrunner. That dream faded eventually replaced by a more sensible one. Ultimately I received a degree from Michigan State and long have followed the Spartans' fortunes avidly.

Magic

Earvin Johnson called a press conference to announce his college choice. Today every high school player with a decent jump shot and 40-inch vertical leap does that. In 1977, however, such grand gestures were reserved for the truly grand. Looking back, though, maybe Johnson should have announced his choice of college on the top of the Lansing state capitol building. That would have better symbolized his standing in the history of Michigan State sports.

The first thing to know about Johnson: His contributions cannot be described by scanning the stat sheets. Johnson's name is mostly absent among the all-time record holders at Michigan State. The second thing: He is the single greatest athlete to ever wear a Michigan State jersey.

And he almost said no to the Green and White, his boyhood favorite. Johnson starred at Lansing Everett High School, and the chatter about him started his freshman year and only grew exponentially as he matured. After a 36-point, 18-rebound performance during his sophomore year against favored Jackson Parkside, Johnson earned a new moniker—"Magic." The nickname given to him by local media personality Fred Stabley Jr. stuck because the skills Johnson exhibited on the basketball court defied a better description. He could handle the ball as well as or better than any guard. He commanded the floor, directing, cajoling, and encouraging his teammates and demoralizing his opponents with game-changing assists, scores, steals, and rebounds. As a passer he had few equals, possessing a preternatural vision of the court that enabled him to make the impossible pass possible. (MSU coach Jud

Heathcote said he played as though he had a "big eye in the back of his head.") Magic could also shoot and finish with either hand, once dominating an AAU game with his left hand because of an injury to the middle fingers of his dominant right hand. But what really caused scouts and basketball junkies to salivate, besides the delicious package of skills, was Johnson's size. He stood 6'9". No frame of reference existed for a kid like Johnson. The combination of skills and size was unprecedented. It was in a word—magical.

Magic won a state title at Everett, and Michigan State recruited him hard. So did Michigan and every other major college. At the end, though, it came down to MSU and UM, which at the time owned infinitely more cachet. Johnson appeared to be leaning toward the Spartans until MSU fired its coach, Gus Ganakas. Magic adored Ganakas and had deep reservations about his replacement, Jud Heathcote. "I didn't really know him," Johnson wrote in his autobiography. "I saw the way he yelled at his players and I didn't like it." Despite having recently accepted the head coaching position at Wayne State, former MSU assistant Vernon Payne persuaded Johnson that underneath Heathcote's rough exterior resided a "terrific coach and excellent teacher."

A week before Johnson's decision, Jay Vincent, Magic's prep school rival and a blue chipper himself, committed to MSU. Johnson mulled over his decision, weighing the numerous plusses of Michigan against the strong tug of his childhood favorite. At his press conference, he started by asking the throng of reporters—some from as far away as New York—if they had any questions. Then he blurted out that he had decided to attend Michigan. He paused just briefly—long enough for MSU fans to gulp hard—then finished his sentence with "State." "The Wolverines were on national TV and this and that," he said. "But I like the underdog school."

Magic helped turn the tables, and UM receded into the background while MSU bolted into the headlines. It had been more than a decade since Michigan State had upstaged the Wolverines in anything. Now all the talk among Michigan sports fans, especially starting in January, listed in the direction of Earvin Johnson and his MSU Spartans.

Johnson's debut against Central Michigan underwhelmed. Perhaps succumbing to nerves for the only time in his collegiate career, Magic scored just eight points and committed eight turnovers to offset his eight assists. The Spartans survived thanks to fellow freshman, Vincent, who came off the bench to score 25 points in 24 minutes. Magic wiped away all doubts in the next two games at the Carrier Classic in Syracuse, New York. He performed so spectacularly that the tournament named him MVP, even though the Spartans had lost to the host team of Syracuse, one of only three games the Spartans would lose to non-conference foes in Johnson's two seasons.

Like a frozen turkey thawing in the refrigerator, Johnson's doubts about Heathcote started slowly melting. Magic discovered his coach shared his fierce competitiveness and almost pathological disgust of losing. But Johnson was used to being the alpha male. So was Heathcote. Clashes were inevitable—but surprisingly infrequent.

They understood each other, knew when to push and when to back off. Once when Johnson committed a few turnovers, Heathcote pulled him from the game. "I didn't come here to sit," Johnson snorted in the direction of his coach. If another player had complained in a similar fashion, Heathcote would have responded sharply, probably apocalyptically. He said nothing to Johnson, who checked back in a minute later. "Earvin and I have strong personalities," wrote Heathcote in his autobiography, *Jud.* "But I think we made a great combination because we both wanted the same thing."

Magic transformed the entire MSU program. No one worked harder than Johnson in practice. No one desired to win more. No one cared less about personal stats and individual glory. "In those days, they'd bring the stat sheets in right after the game," Heathcote said. "And Earvin wouldn't even look at them. He'd say, 'I'll look at it in the morning. We won the game. That's all that counts.'"

What counted for Magic was involving his teammates, which in turn meant the team succeeded. He made them look good and made them better. They found gears they didn't know they had, skills that had been dormant. "Earvin made things easier for everybody he played with," Greg Kelser said.

Johnson acted as a surrogate coach. He guided, directed, scolded, and praised his teammates. And they responded with an eagerness to please instead of scorn. "He had a way of telling other players what to do and having them accept it," Heathcoate said. "And if he had the ball on the break and didn't hit you, he'd always give you a wink or a nod and say he'd get you the next time. It made you run just a little harder."

Fans marveled at Johnson's rare talent. His repertoire included no-look passes, supernal court vision, timely scoring, and rainbow lobs for alley-oop dunks, which were usually triggered by a nod of his head to Ron Charles, Kelser, or Vincent. But anyone who saw him play remembers something else. Johnson loved the game of basketball. He didn't let the inevitable troughs and frustrations of the game keep him down for long. And his smile, which grew to match his size-14 shoe after big plays, and enthusiasm infected his teammates and the spectators who watched him. "He was the Pied Piper of college basketball," broadcaster Dick Enberg said. As the Spartans rose to prominence, Johnson embraced the attention. The press sought him out, and he complied with cheerful and entertaining interviews that only further burnished his reputation.

Throughout his college career, a cadre of scouts questioned whether he had the athletic ability—vertical leaping was not his forte—and shooting touch to be a superstar as a professional. At MSU Johnson scored in a variety of ways. Because he usually had the ball in his hands and pushed it relentlessly, he got to the free throw line often. He still holds the MSU single-season record for free throws made and attempted and shot 81.6 percent at the line for his career, seventh best in school history. His shot, however, fell far short of textbook. He cradled the ball as if he were about to shot put it, and his jump shot had very little jump in it. Few complained though. Awkward looking as the shot may have been, it usually found its target.

Magic's collegiate career ended after his sophomore year in the 1979 NCAA championship game where he met Larry Bird for the very first time. The Spartans beat Bird's Indiana State Sycamores 75–64 to earn Michigan State's first national championship in basketball. That hatched a rivalry that would dominate the NBA during the league's golden era of the 1980s. Magic's NBA career ended temporarily in 1991 after he contracted HIV though he returned later to win the MVP of the All-Star Game in 1992. Currently Johnson is co-owner of the Los Angeles Dodgers. Since his retirement from basketball, he also has owned and operated a number of successful businesses, and many serve underrepresented populations of Los Angeles.

"He was the greatest passer in basketball history and arguably the greatest player," Heathcote wrote. "Earvin did what only a few have ever been able to do: Make everyone else on his team play better than they actually were."

Tom Izzo

Born in the Upper Peninsula mining town of Iron Mountain, Michigan, to a family of self-made men and women, Tom Izzo inherited the can-do gene from his ancestors. He played high school football and basketball at Iron Mountain where he missed a free throw with :02 left in the regional finals to send his school packing. Unrecruited and unappreciated, he walked on at Northern Michigan University, roomed with his high school friend Steve Mariucci, and became a third-team Division III All-American in basketball. He coached at Ishpeming High School, then as an assistant for his alma mater, and finally—for a pay cut—as the third assistant for Jud Heathcote at MSU in 1983. Other than a brief stop at Tulsa, he has been at Michigan State ever since.

He worked his way up the chain as an assistant, establishing himself as a bulldog recruiter and sounding board for victims of Heathcote's tirades. Heathcote retired in 1995 with a national championship among his many credits. Upon his departure he insisted MSU replace him with Izzo. Two years plus into Izzo's head coaching tenure Heathcote's advocacy of his top assistant appeared more like cronyism than genius. The Spartans came up empty in their pursuit of an NCAA tournament bid in Izzo's first two years. Then came a loss to mid-major Detroit in December of 1997 that lit up talk radio with calls for Izzo's dismissal. Two weeks later, the Spartans ventured into West Lafayette, Indiana, as a heavy underdog to meet conference favorite Purdue. They departed with a convincing victory that changed the program—forever. Now 16 years later, everyone thanks Heathcote for what many believe is the greatest gift the university has ever received.

Izzo belongs in consideration as the greatest college basketball coach of all time. Other coaches have won more games, conference championships, and national championships. Today's college game, however, is about getting into the tournament and doing well when you get there. It's how the general public remembers—and judges—the sport. And few, if any, can compete with the quality of Izzo's NCAA overall tournament resume.

Only three coaches have made more consecutive tournament appearances than Izzo (Mike Krzyzweski, Lute Olson, and Dean

Izzo's Impressive Numbers

The following numbers are a few thoughts to consider about the incomparable Tom Izzo, the greatest ambassador for Michigan State University in at least a half a century:

- Seven Big Ten championships
- 209–95 Big Ten record
- No finishes in the conference below .500
- 16 consecutive NCAA Tournament appearances
- 11 Sweet 16s
- Seven Elite Eights
- Six Final Fours
- Two Finals appearances
- One National Championship
- 439–178 overall record

Smith), demonstrating that Izzo has avoided the dips that bedevil most programs. Only six coaches have a better overall tournament winning percentage (Wooden, Roy Williams, Coach K, Larry Brown, John Calipari, and Billy Donovan), suggesting that Izzo knows something about the secret sauce of avoiding upsets and advancing. Finally, only five coaches have more Final Fours to their credit (Wooden, Coach K, Smith, Williams, and Rick Pitino). Two others are tied with Izzo at six (Adolph Rupp and Denny Crum).

Izzo gets into the tournament almost without fail—regardless of circumstances. He wins consistently, losing only three times to a lower seed (and one of those occurred in the Final Four) and he advances to the promised land at a remarkably high rate. (Only John Wooden has a higher percentage of years coaching to Final Four appearances.)

Now let's consider context. The coaches listed above won at the following schools: UCLA (Wooden), North Carolina (Smith, Williams), Kentucky (Rupp, Pitino, Calipari), Kansas (Brown, Williams), Duke (Coach K), Louisville (Crum, Pitino), Arizona

Coach Tom Izzo, who has led Michigan State to six Final Fours and 11 Sweet 16s, crouches during the 2013 Big Ten Tournament.

(Olson), and Florida (Donovan). One doesn't have to stretch credulity to argue that all of these schools enjoy natural advantages over Michigan State. Five of the eight schools emphasize basketball, pouring considerable resources, time, and treasure into the sport. Football is an afterthought, forever competing for the leftover scraps. Basketball tradition stretches back through multiple generations, and fan support borders on the intense, if not insane. Of the three remaining schools, Florida and Arizona enjoy status as the flagship university in their states, which usually results in a resource advantage. It's also relevant to note that Olson and Donovan each appear only once on the above lists. As for UCLA, well, for years California has beckoned young men seeking a better life.

As for MSU, it is a football school in a state that prefers the gridiron to the hardwood. It had very little basketball tradition before the 1970s. It is not the flagship school in its home state, competing endlessly for attention and respect among the in-state media and its own residents. Its chief rival, Michigan, is a behemoth in college sports, and at the time of Izzo's hire, this behemoth's basketball program was a cultural phenomenon, devouring nearly every inch and second of basketball coverage in the state. Where does Izzo measure up now? The only two coaches, other than Izzo, who appeared on all three lists (consecutive tournament appearances, winning percentage, and Final Fours) are Wooden and Krzyzweski. Coach K, who has coached 20 more years than Izzo, and Wooden, who won multiple national championships, probably top Izzo for college coaching Zeus. But if you consider the context of Izzo's accomplishments, does that change the calculus at all for you? Does that narrow an already thin gap? It's something to think about for sure.

Biggie Munn

Clarence "Biggie" Munn, named the head coach of Michigan State on December 14, 1946, took a moderately successful program eternally overshadowed by its in-state rival and accomplished what only the most blinkered Spartans fan could imagine: dominance over Michigan and the rest of college football.

Munn was an All-American at Minnesota in track and football, playing for the legendary Fritz Crisler. In 1931 he was named the Big Ten MVP as a lineman. He eventually went into coaching, following Crisler to Michigan in 1938 where he would serve as a key assistant. They were wildly successful there, restoring dominance over the Spartans, who had beaten them four straight times, and rebuilding the Wolverines into a national power once again. Eight years later, Munn, who enjoyed a cordial but hardly warm relationship with Crisler, left to assume head coaching duties at Syracuse. Meanwhile, John Hannah, president of Michigan State College (MSC) since 1941, had a grand vision of where he wanted to take his school. Football was a key part of it. Losing to Michigan was not. That drove Hannah to Munn, who had built a strong program at Syracuse, knew the landscape of the Midwest, and owned valuable intelligence on arch foe Michigan.

Munn's first order of business: restore the green and white colors to the Spartans uniform, which had been changed to black and gold under Charlie Bachman. His second: reshape the offense.

Biggie developed the Michigan State Multiple, an offense based on speed and deception. It usually started with the backs in a T formation, but just before the snap, they would shift into a variety of different formations, depending on the alignment of the defense, the down and distance, etc. The offense could attack one area of the defensive line from 14 different offensive variations. "I don't see how a college team can be taught so much offense. Even the pros don't do it," wrote a reporter in Portland, Oregon, after watching Munn's offense in action.

Munn also experimented with spreading out his ends, a primitive precursor to the spread offenses of many decades later. All the movement and unusual formations kept defenses endlessly puzzled and allowed Munn to recruit players based on their quickness, speed, and agility. Size was only a secondary matter to him.

A strong proponent of the two-platoon system (substitution rules relaxed considerably until 1953), which allowed for defensive and offensive specialists, the Spartans roster bubbled with Munn prototypes. "It was a pleasure to watch 175-pound guards and tackles play big college football by using speed, quickness, and desire to overcome the natural advantages of the 220-pound opponent," Munn wrote in *Sports Illustrated.* He regularly used 50 or more players in one game, sometimes doubling that of his opponent.

Munn sweated the small stuff too, fussing about every detail, leaving nothing to chance. He scripted his first three plays,

Two Coaching Legends Who Almost Ended Up at Michigan State

Three times Michigan State attempted to woo Knute Rockne to East Lansing. The most serious happened in 1920 when Rockne reportedly signed a lucrative contract to coach the Aggies. But the deal eventually fell through. MSC made another run at Rockne in 1930 to no avail.

Seventy-four years later MSU thought they had an agreement with another coaching giant, Tom Osborne, coach of multiple national champions at Nebraska. This time the offer was in the seven figures. Osborne almost accepted it. Then five years later in 1999, Osborne, who had been retired for two years, was ready to say yes to MSU until his doctor counseled against it.

demanded his team perform its assignments with precision, and drilled his players tirelessly. He also had an eye for talent.

The Munn era started slowly with a 55-point loss to Michigan. After questioning his own abilities and indulging in a smidge of self-pity, Munn scraped his crushed ego off the Michigan Stadium turf and recommitted himself to the job. He always credited running back George Guerre, who had praised Munn to a group of MSC supporters, for helping him rally.

Soon, almost immediately in fact, the Spartans started winning. By 1950 with Munn's players and system entirely in place, the goal shifted a bit from a desire to win to an urgent need to be the best in the land. A 28-game winning streak that ended in 1953 convinced many that Munn had accomplished just that. So did the 1952 national championship, the 1953 Big Ten title, and the 1954 Rose Bowl championship.

At the end of the 1953 season, Munn turned 45 years old. Many wondered what would be next for him and his Spartans. Another long winning streak? More Rose Bowls and national championships? But what happened next surprised everyone as much as the Spartans' rise to brilliance. Munn retired. Rumors had surfaced about that during the Rose Bowl and intensified in the days following. Munn became the athletic director, replacing Ralph Young, and elevated his assistant Duffy Daugherty to head coach.

That ended seven years of near-perfection. Munn won 54 games and posted a .867 winning percentage. He produced 18 All-Americans. In 1959 Munn entered the College Football Hall of Fame.

Buck Nystrom, who played for Munn near the end of Biggie's tenure, reflected on the keys to Munn's success in an interview with Steve Grinczel in 2012. "Probably his strongest suit was that he had a great personality for motivating players. He could motivate you pretty strongly particularly when you got into the Michigan game," Nystrom said. "He always had some kind of psychological effect that he would incorporate during the week. He had that rough, gruff voice, and the two words that you learned from Biggie were 'demand' and 'confront.' He would demand that you worked hard and performed well and all of those kind of good things. But if you didn't do it the right way, he'd confront you and get on your butt. You had a little scare in you when you played for him, but he had a good way of doing it. He didn't do it in a vicious way."

Munn, as Nystrom indicated, had a knack for inspiring those around him. His mind percolated with ideas and ways to gain an edge, which he adeptly communicated to his team. "Biggie had a very strong personality," said tackle Don Coleman in a 2010 *Detroit Free Press* interview. "When he spoke it was like God talking. He demanded respect from his players and gave it right back."

Yet at times he could become myopic and easily irritated. He had his devoted friends and advocates and he had his inveterate enemies even within the MSU community, who found his ego overgrown and his temper too quick to ignite. But no one could argue with the success he achieved. His favorite aphorism about sports and life was placed on buildings all over campus and neatly summed up his world view: "The difference between good and great is a little extra effort." Munn died at the age of 66 in 1975, leaving a legacy unmatched by any Spartans coach and few in his profession—his little extra effort having made all the difference.

The Game of the Century

"They were Notre Dame and Michigan State, the two best teams that ever met by the quirk of a schedule at the end of a season to play for it all." These are the closing words of author Mike Celizic's book, *The Biggest Game of Them All*. That Celizic could devote an entire book to one football game suggests in itself the magnitude of the game and its lasting effect. It also explains why the 1966 game between Michigan State and Notre Dame caused reams of copy to be spilled and spawned hundreds of stories passed down from multiple generations.

The No. 1-ranked Fighting Irish entered 8–0, and the No. 2-ranked Spartans were 9–0. The Irish's only loss the year before came against the Spartans, which had probably cost them a national championship. MSU suffered a loss in the 1966 Rose Bowl to deny it a consensus national championship. Both teams returned many starters and highly regarded newcomers and viewed the 1966 season as their chance at redemption. Both schools' rosters overflowed with marquee names and superior, once-in-a-generation athletes. A staggering 17 first team All-Americans would take the field for Notre Dame and Michigan State. An 18th All-American, Nick Eddy, sat on the sidelines.

Anticipation for the collision between the two ancient rivals started building sometime in late October. The Spartans began the year No. 2, and the Irish were No. 6. As the scores rolled in week after week, college football fans and media alike began looking ahead to the November 19 game in East Lansing. On November 12 the Spartans and Irish each won handily, enabling them to now join the rest of the college football world in focusing on November 19. The Spartans win wrapped up another Big Ten title, the first time in 11 years a Big Ten team had repeated as champion.

The press dubbed it "the Game of the Century" almost immediately. It would be the biggest college football game anyone could remember since Army and Notre Dame played to a 0–0 tie in 1946. "If ever there were to be another event to leave the nation as transfixed as on Pearl Harbor, 1:30 PM Saturday should qualify," *The Washington Post*'s William Gildea wrote. Fans desperate for tickets resorted to all means of insanity, overpaying by hundreds of dollars (thousands in today's money). One fan even offered to sell part of his business in exchange for tickets. The press devoured 745 credentials to attend the game, filling every hotel and spare bedroom in town. Spartans coach Duffy Daugherty, who relished the attention, held press conferences every day of the week to satisfy the reporters hungering for information. Notre Dame's Ara Parseghian did the same as a cascading swell of reporters overwhelmed South Bend. The madness extended beyond the Midwest. Strict rules governing how many times a school could appear on national television limited the broadcast to a few regions of the country. Fans protested. One in the South even filed a lawsuit, causing ABC executives to agree to show the game on tape delay in the South and Northwest. More than 30 million television viewers tuned in.

Students took an unscheduled holiday. Bonfires and rallies outnumbered pop quizzes and lectures. Many professors canceled classes. Banners hung from dorm room windows, buttons adorned sweaters and jackets, and cheeky slogans decorated cars. "Even the Pope has no hope," read one. "Hail Mary Full of Grace, Notre Dame's in Second Place," read another. The latter elicited numerous complaints from viewers of ABC, which had shown the sign on its evening news.

The Irish were made small favorites and most outside of East Lansing agreed. "Notre Dame is, I believe, bigger and stronger physically than Michigan State," said Daugherty, aiming to be as objective as possible. "But we may have more quickness." To ease tension Daugherty halted practice on Thursday and ordered relay races.

The evening before the game, Eddy, the Irish's brilliant running back, slipped exiting the train in East Lansing and reinjured his shoulder. Eddy would not play, a definite blow to the Irish. That night in East Lansing, Bubba Smith found himself in trouble when an overzealous police officer arrested Smith for unpaid parking tickets. MSU athletic director Biggie Munn, annoyed at both Smith and the police, showed up to free Smith.

Gray clouds, hanging thick and motionless, greeted the 80,000 fans lucky enough to have tickets. That morning the Spartans made their traditional walk from the on-campus hotel. Fans and well-wishers jostled each other to get a look at their heroes. Emotion overwhelmed many of the players. A few even cried. An official who worked the game, future NFL referee Jerry Markbreit, compared the mood on campus to that of a Super Bowl. "It was the most highly charged pregame atmosphere I'd ever experienced," he said.

On Notre Dame's second possession, Terry Hanratty kept the ball on a draw and took a few steps forward. MSU linebacker Charlie Thornhill met him abruptly. He twisted Hanratty right into Smith, who then drove the quarterback to the ground. Hanratty popped up, but he knew something wasn't right. After an incompletion, he walked to the sidelines—and never returned. He had separated his shoulder. Coley O'Brien replaced Hanratty. "That didn't help us any," Smith said. "It just let them put in that O'Brien, who's slippery and faster and gave us more trouble. The other guy just sits there and waits, and that's what we wanted."

The pressure showed on both teams in the early moments. Before he left the game for good, Hanratty misfired badly on three of his four passes. The Irish also failed to get off a punt because of a bad snap. For their part the Spartans fumbled and committed three penalties, which kept stalling drives. In the waning moments of the first quarter, the Spartans finally found daylight. Quarterback Jimmy Raye hit a streaking Gene Washington for 42 yards on a route that had been open the previous possession. Nine running plays later, Spartans back Regis Cavender, playing for the injured Bob Apisa but struggling through his own shoulder injury, scored on a four-yard run. The Spartans used two tight ends to batter away at an Irish line not used to giving up touchdowns.

Up 7–0 the Spartans forced the Irish, now playing without center George Goeddeke, who had left the game with an ankle injury, to punt again. Michigan State moved the ball into Irish territory once more. Raye busted loose for a 30-yard gain and then found Washington open for a 17-yard pass completion. The drive stalled there, bringing on Dick Kenney, who made a 47-yard field goal to put the Spartans up 10–0. The Irish responded just before the half. Notre Dame returned the kickoff 46 yards to set up a 34-yard touchdown pass from O'Brien to Bob Gladiuex.

The Spartans entered their locker room in a foul mood, peeved that they had allowed Notre Dame to cut into a 10-point lead. Daugherty didn't have time to fret, though, He was busy hatching a plan to exploit the patched-up Irish offensive line. He moved Smith directly over Tim Monty, the inexperienced underclassman who had replaced Goeddeke at center. The Irish were more upbeat. They only trailed by three despite the loss of their quarterback, center, and running back. And All-American receiver Jim Seymour had yet to catch a pass.

The third quarter featured more of the same: violent collisions and yards yielded stubbornly. Finally after Smith nullified a Spartans fumble recovery with an off-sides penalty, the Irish managed to move the ball to the Spartans 18-yard line. Three plays produced seven yards as the third quarter wound down. The Notre Dame field goal kicker, Joe Azzaro, had attempted only two field goals all year (both makes). But Parseghian sent Azzaro into the game, and he calmly booted a 28-yarder on the first play of the first quarter to tie the score at 10–10.

After a series of empty possessions by both sides, Raye threw an interception at the Spartan 49 that Tom Schoen returned to the Michigan State 18. The Irish ran one up the gut for little gain. On second down MSU's Dick Hoag broke free and with Smith's help tackled back Dave Haley for an eight-yard loss. A pass incompletion brought forth down. What would have been a 34-yard field goal became a 42 yarder. Azzaro missed it. A late gust of wind knocked the ball just wide. With disaster avoided, Spartan stadium exhaled.

The Spartans picked up a first down by inches then had to punt. Deep in his own territory, Daugherty thought about going for it, but the negatives triumphed in the battle waging in his mind. Schoen signaled for a fair catch at the Irish 30, but the ball slipped out of his grasp. Fourteen different hands, 12 of them belonging to six Spartans surrounding Schoen, desperately reached for the ball. It bounced determinedly into the hands of Schoen. Disaster avoided, Irish edition.

There remained 1:24 on the clock. The Irish had timeouts remaining. They only needed around 55 yards to get into field goal range. Parseghian didn't care. He hated gambling and liked to control the odds. The Irish had battled all day and without a handful of key performers. Moreover, they still had another game to play against USC; the Spartans did not. Tie today and beat heavy underdog USC next week, and Parseghian figured the national championship would be his. He weighed the factors and made the call.

Six running plays later, the game ended, 10–10.

"Sissies!" "Cowards!" The Spartans taunted and screamed at the Irish offense. "We couldn't believe it," George Webster said. "When they came up for their first play, we kept hollering back and forth, 'Watch the pass, watch the pass.' But they ran. We know the next one was a pass for sure. But they ran again. We were really stunned. Then it dawned on us. They were settling for tie." A few of the Irish disagreed with Parseghian's decision, including O'Brien. But defying their coach? None would have ever considered it.

Spartan Stadium, which had throbbed all day, fell dead silent. Most fans milled around as if waiting for the game to resume and for a winner to be declared. The national media seemed split on what they had just seen. Some could understand playing for a tie especially given how difficult moving the football had been. (Neither team gained more than 300 yards.) Others complained that Parseghian had sold out and that history would penalize him. "Tie, tie for old Notre Dame!" chided *Sports Illustrated* that week.

The game marked the end of the brilliant careers of many Spartans: Webster, Smith, Thornhill, Washington, Jess Phillips, and more. Twenty-one Spartans earned All-Big Ten honors, 11 earned first team, five earned second team, and five earned honorable mention. "If we had won that game," said Thornhill in Celizic's book, "we would have gone down in history as the greatest football team ever." The next week they watched Notre Dame dismantle USC 51–0 and eventually claim the national championship, validating in part Parseghian's decision to play it safe at the end of the Spartan game.

For MSU the Game of the Century also meant the end of an era, the climax of an almost 20-year run when Michigan State elbowed its way into the ranks of the sport's elite. Daugherty never again recruited as well as he had before because the schools in the South ended their ban on black athletes in 1966, which for the most part ended Michigan State's pipeline to southern black athletes.

A Magical Championship

The Final Four, a term only recently in vogue at the time, found its muse in 1979 as a result of two supercharged, charismatic figures and one cosmic matchup.

The Spartans, 21–6 overall, 13–5 in conference, and co-champs of the grueling Big Ten, were just thankful to be free of conference play. "If we make the NCAA tournament, that's the way we will play," said MSU assistant Dave Harshman after the Spartans throttled Kansas in the middle of the season. "People in the Big Ten are better prepared to play us because they've seen this group for two years. It will be new to everyone we play in the tournament."

As the No. 2 Mideast seed behind No. 1 Notre Dame, the Spartans needed three wins to advance to the Final Four in Salt Lake City. Lamar coach Billy Tubbs and his brassy and sassy charges talked about sending the whole state of Michigan home. Magic and his boys sent them packing instead, rolling to a 95–64 victory that resembled a pregame layup drill. "Johnson is a man among boys," declared Al McGuire during the broadcast. But starter Jay Vincent suffered a stress fracture during the Lamar game that hampered him the rest of the tournament. Ron Charles replaced him in the starting lineup against LSU and enjoyed the best game of his career, scoring 18 and collecting 14 rebounds in the Spartans' 87–71 victory.

The two easy wins sent the Spartans to the regional final to meet Notre Dame. The Irish, considered the region's favorite, featured a roster of six future NBA performers, including Bill Laimbeer, Kelly Tripucka, Orlando Woolridge, and Bill Hanzlik. "Notre Dame goes at you with nine players," Heathcote said. "And we come at you with two."

Heathcote, though, had adeptly noticed during scouting sessions that Notre Dame didn't usually put a man back on defense for the opening tip. So Greg Kelser tipped the ball to Johnson, who flipped it to a streaking Mike Brkovich, who jammed it home. Then Terry Donnelly stole the inbounds pass and scored on a layup. Within a matter of seconds, the Irish trailed by four. "It was an avalanche from there," said Notre Dame coach Digger Phelps. The Spartans lead climbed gradually and settled at 11 after 20 minutes. Play had been chippy at times. During one sequence Hanzlik drew a charge on Magic and—loud enough that he could be heard courtside and on TV—mocked him and his name, saying "Not today, Irwin."

In the second half, the Spartans pulled away. They were sparked by Vincent, whom Heathcote inserted early in the second half to test his foot and help spur a suddenly stagnant offense. Vincent, limping noticeably, pump-faked Laimbeer and then drove around

"Shoes" Huffman

Leading by 28 against Lamar in the opening round of the 1979 NCAA Tournament, Heathcote emptied his bench. In went Jamie Huffman. He'd seen action in five games all year. Soon after entering the game, he reached for an offensive rebound and lost his shoe. The Spartans hurried back on defense. But Huffman didn't follow. For two changes of possessions he stayed put, struggling to get his shoe back on. Heathcote screamed. The NBC crew howled in laughter. "For the rest of your life," Al McGuire said, "you're going to be known as 'Shoes.'" Dick Enberg followed: "Attaboy, Shoes Huffman." To the delight of McGuire and Enberg, Huffman eventually scored a basket, his only bucket of the year. After the game the crew interviewed him—and a legend of a different kind was born.

him for a basket. Heathcote pulled Vincent shortly after that, but from that point, Michigan State, quicker and more athletic than Notre Dame, hit the Irish with a blitz of fast breaks, lobs, and dunks to build an 18-point lead en route to an easy 80–68 victory. Kelser had six dunks himself during this stretch. Special K finished with 34. Johnson had 19 points and 13 assists. "If Notre Dame would have beaten us, it would have won the championship," said Heathcote years later.

Interest in Magic and his Spartans climbed steadily throughout the tournament as did the fascination with 31–0 Indiana State led by Larry Bird, a 6'9" magician himself. Bird owned a reliably accurate jumper that had more range than a nuclear warhead. He passed cleverly and possessed a presence on the court matched only by Johnson. "Let me tell you, Larry Bird is a hell of a basketball player," said Oklahoma coach Dave Bliss after his Sooners lost to ISU in the Midwest Semifinal.

But before Magic-Bird could become a reality, each school had to beat its opponent in the semifinals. Much of the attention actually centered on Indiana State's opponent, DePaul, coached by Ray Meyer, and the Spartans' opponent, the University of

Pennsylvania. "All of the interest was in Penn upsetting St. John's and keeping Lou Carnesecca from reaching the Final Four and the fact that Ray Meyer had made it to the Final Four with DePaul," said Malcolm Moran, who covered the Final Four for *The New York Times*. Incredibly the Spartans headed to Salt Lake City as probably the least compelling of the four stories.

Michigan State ended Penn's moment in the sun quickly and mercilessly. The Quakers scored first, prompting the Penn students to engage in their traditional littering of the court with toilet paper. Then the Spartans scored 30 of the game's next 36 points. The heavily partisan MSU crowd roared as Michigan State cruised to a 50–17 halftime lead. The scrubs accounted for many of the second half minutes as the Spartans coasted to a 101–67 victory. Johnson scored 29 and Kelser 28. Penn coach Bob Weinhaur, who had never seen MSU play live or on TV, expressed awe. "Earvin Johnson and Gregory Kelser are two of the most outstanding, dominating basketball players I have ever come across in my coaching career," he said.

Late in the Penn game, the Michigan State fans started chanting, "We want Bird." The Indiana State fans responded, "You'll get Bird." Bird scored 35 points on 16-of-19 shots, earning the respect of the Spartans who stayed to watch the game. The game went to the wire, but Indiana State survived, advancing when DePaul's Mark Aguirre's fadeaway, 19-footer fell short at the buzzer.

The national media had descended on Salt Lake City in unprecedented numbers, overwhelming the NCAA with requests for credentials. They had come to write one story. Now they were gradually awakening to one of the best stories college basketball had ever seen. "If Indiana State with Larry Bird meets Michigan State with Earvin Johnson in the finals and the result isn't the biggest TV rating ever for a college basketball game, then either we, the press, aren't doing our jobs or this country's sports fans are beyond salvation," wrote Bob Ryan in the *Basketball Times*.

Magic Johnson celebrates Michigan State's 1979 national championship victory, which came against an Indiana State team led by Larry Bird.

The Spartans had a day to prepare for Indiana State. Heathcote put Earvin on the scout team to imitate Bird. Magic went off, scoring at will and helping the scout team beat the first team regularly. Heathcote fumed. He also decided the Spartans would stay in their base defense (the matchup zone). But he tweaked it by putting two men on Bird no matter where he was on the floor. That meant the other three would have to cover four.

The day before the game, NBC started promoting the David and Goliath storyline. Little Indiana State with a relatively unknown superstar against Big Ten bully Michigan State and its somewhat better known superstar. Dick Enberg, the play-by-play man for the NBC broadcast, called it, "Truth strangling fiction." Millions of sports fans tuned into the game. The momentum that built during the regionals when all four regional finals set TV ratings records continued through the semifinals of the Final Four. Then it reached its zenith for the championship final. The game notched a 24.1, the highest television rating for a college basketball game ever—then and now.

Heathcote's defensive scheme handcuffed Bird, who picked up his second foul with seven minutes left in the first half. He made only three baskets the remainder of the game. Meanwhile the Spartans built a nine-point lead in workmanlike fashion. Bird had started the game on Kelser, who was quicker and beat Bird a few times off the dribble to either score himself or dish off for easy baskets. A Johnson to Kelser alley-oop pushed the lead to 11. With five minutes left in the half, Johnson picked up his third foul, and Kelser would do the same with only seconds remaining before intermission. Bird's free throw put the Sycamores down by nine going into halftime.

The Spartans padded their lead in the second half. With the Sycamores collapsing on Johnson and Kelser, the Spartans started feeding guard Terry Donnelly, who had averaged only six points a game on the season. During halftime, Heathcote, suspecting ISU would overplay his two stars, told Donnelly, suffering from an injured back and high fever, he would need to hit some jumpers. Donnelly did just that. He buried three straight, all from at least 15 feet, to give the Spartans a 48–32 lead.

With 15 minutes to play, Kelser picked up his fourth foul and left the game. Indiana State now made its run, keying on Johnson and taking Donnelly's uncontested jumpers away. The Sycamores dared sharpshooter Brkovich, who was struggling from the outside all game, and Vincent, moving around like a bike with a flat tire, to beat them. Eventually, they cut the Spartans lead to six with nine minutes left. Heathcote promptly reinserted Kelser, who immediately nailed a 14-footer. The lead held stable for the next five minutes, and then the Spartans went to their spread offense.

Moments later with Kelser holding the ball at the top of the key, Johnson beat his man on a backdoor cut. Special K hit him with a perfect pass. Johnson, not renowned for his leaping ability, sprang up and over Bob Heaton, jamming the ball through the hoop. The Spartans bench went berserk. The game had its signature play, and the lead grew to 10. The final basket of the game came on a Magic to Kelser no-look, full-court sling that Kelser dunked with a flourish at the buzzer. The final: Michigan State 75 Indiana State 64.

The Spartans won every game of the tournament by double digits, averaging a victory margin of 20.8, the third highest in history. Johnson scored 24 points, pulled down seven rebounds, and had five assists. He was named the Final Four MVP. Donnelly pitched in with 15 points, going a perfect five for five from the floor.

The game itself had failed to live up to the hype engulfing it. "It was an electric moment to be there, but I think everybody was waiting for something that just never happened," said *Sports Illustrated*'s Bruce Newman in *When March Went Mad*. "It was supposed to be this colossal showdown, and it ended up being almost a blowout."

Spartans fans, though, couldn't have been happier. More than a thousand greeted the players at the Lansing Airport, and another 10,000 waited for them at Jenison Field House. More than 15,000 fans endured a dreary, rain-soaked day to attend the following day's parade saluting the Spartans. The 1979 championship is credited for accelerating the popularity of college basketball and the NCAA Tournament.

Duffy Daugherty

If Biggie Munn's coaching era represented a pivotal history, Duffy Daugherty's coaching era represented a good story. Munn was the monarch who built a great empire. Daugherty was the author whose engaging plots and vivid characters spread the influence of the empire far and wide.

Daugherty, who succeeded Munn in 1954 as head coach of Michigan State, was all color in an era of black and white. He replaced a legend and became an even bigger legend. He won national championships. He recruited and coached players whom college football fans of any age or generation would recognize instantly. He disarmed his critics and flattered his friends with a wit quicker than 4G. He became a go-to quote for national stories about trends in college football. He even appeared on the cover of *Time* magazine. During his tenure as head coach, Michigan State football was all that—and a bag of chips.

Daugherty eschewed clichés and platitudes throughout his coaching career. But his upbringing was a cliché from central casting. The son of a miner turned small business owner in the rolling hills of Pennsylvania, he grew up in fairly modest circumstances. Small but scrappy, he played center on his high school football team. In 1937, four years after graduating from high school, Daugherty enrolled at Syracuse University. There he met Munn and played against Michigan State in 1938. Daugherty earned two letters as a guard and was named captain of the 1939 Orangemen. During World War II, he served in the army, spending much of his time in Papua New Guinea, where the Australian soldiers he met exhibited a gallows humor that he found appealing and tactically useful. After the war Munn hired Daugherty as an assistant at Syracuse, and Duffy followed Biggie to Michigan State in 1946.

Daugherty coached the interior line at MSC where he continually produced top-notch lines and linemen. "Duffy's Toughies" they were called. One of his linemen, Ed Bagdon, won the Outland Trophy for interior lineman, the only Spartan to ever earn that honor.

After the 1954 Rose Bowl when Munn unexpectedly stepped down as head coach of Michigan State to become the school's athletic director, he named Duffy as his successor. Daugherty had Paul Bunyan-sized shoes to fill, but, as he said on the eve of his first game, no one needed to worry about him: "I want to tell fans right now that they can save their sympathies...There's no one...who has a better job than mine."

There were probably better jobs in 1955. A slew of graduation losses resulted in an unfamiliar and uncomfortable losing season (3–6). Smoke rose from the athletic director's office, but before anyone could up pick up pitchforks and knives, Daugherty's next team finished 8–1 and second in the Big Ten. They also earned a trip to Pasadena, California because of the league's no-repeat rule, which eliminated conference champ Ohio State. Duffy was named Coach of the Year by his fellow coaches, and the Spartans finished No. 2 in the national polls.

Daugherty proved to be a tireless and resourceful recruiter. He ran crisp practices and deftly kept his team loose and engaged, relying on stories and humor to get his point across. Optimistic to a fault, he never took himself or the game too seriously, managing to find the proper balance between being a decent human being and winning football games. "With Duffy the more a person needed, the more he gave them," said his former player and assistant George Perles.

The winning continued under Daugherty, including additional split national championships. Mixed into the banner seasons, however, were a few 3–5–1 and 4–5 clunkers. Injuries and just plain bad luck played a part. But the up-and-down cycle drove Munn batty. It also led to a nasty rift that culminated in a shouting match in the office of president John Hannah. Just when Munn had enough, Daugherty would rescue himself with a big year or two.

None were bigger than the Big Ten and national championship years of 1965 and 1966, Daugherty's only two conference titles and the seasons that define his coaching career. Composed of players that spanned the country from Hawaii to Virginia, Daugherty's most famous two teams enraptured college football with mold-busting players up and down the roster especially on defense.

For two years college football fixed its gaze on East Lansing. Everyone wanted to talk to Daugherty. He happily obliged, regaling the press and fans with thought-provoking ideas about the sport (he favored a football playoff of eight teams, for instance), a seemingly inexhaustible trove of stories, and an inimitable sense of humor. The Spartans would finish physically and mentally thrashing an opponent, and then afterward Daugherty would drain the room of tension with an amusing anecdote here or a well-timed joke there. It was a perfect stew and it made him a national treasure.

Daugherty called it quits in 1972, ground down by a string of mediocre seasons. His career record finished at 109–69–5. His winning percentage trailed Munn's and John Macklin's. But he won more games than any other Spartan coach, earned parts of four national championships, finished in the Top 10 of at least one poll seven times, had a winning record against both Michigan and Notre Dame, guided his team to two Rose Bowls, coached 29 different first team All-Americans, and did it all with a magnetic personality that pulled the college football world toward him and Michigan State. He may not have been the best coach in Michigan State history, but he was without a doubt the Spartans' most unforgettable. "Anytime a player or coach is remembered by his first name, you know how important he has been to the sport," said Bobby Bowden, Florida State's record-breaking coach, upon learning of Duffy's death in 1987.

One Shining Moment

On an October day in 1999, Michigan State basketball hopes, which had been through the roof about the upcoming season, fell from the rafters. During practice Mateen Cleaves, the leader and nerve center of the Spartans, suffered an injury, which the doctors diagnosed as a stress fracture a week later. The injury put Cleaves on crutches and out of the lineup until at least January. "This is a huge blow," said Izzo, who had scheduled nonconference foes North Carolina, Kansas, Arizona, and Kentucky to challenge his Cleaves-led, No. 3-ranked, national championship contender.

Cleaves made the best of the situation, putting on his assistant coach's cap and ramping up the leadership. He immediately challenged fellow senior Morris Peterson, saying, "It's time for you to take over and be the All-American you know you are." Cleaves assumed a prominent role on the bench, peppering Izzo with suggestions during games, and offering advice for his teammates. He also became the Spartans' most vociferous cheerleader, responding with a one-footed hop to every Spartan dunk, steal, and rebound.

The Spartans battled tough during the preconference season. Losses to Texas, Arizona, and Kentucky were offset by a road upset of North Carolina and a solid 12-point win against No. 5 Kansas. The game at Carolina opened eyes. Few expected MSU to win the road contest—especially after Texas had beaten MSU by seven in the San Juan Shootout. But thanks to an inspired effort by Peterson, the Spartans controlled the game from start to finish, eventually building a 17-point lead. Peterson torched the Tar Heels for 31 points (on just 18 shots), six rebounds, and five steals. "When I think back to Scott Skiles, Steve Smith, and Shawn Respert, we've had some great performances in the last 15 years," said Izzo in *Green Glory*. "But what Morris did ranks up there with the best I've seen as an assistant or a head coach."

It had been an emotional few days in North Carolina. The night before the game, Cleaves walked into the Smith Center. Looking up at the championship banners, he broke down as the weight of his injury finally overwhelmed him. North Carolina coach Bill Guthridge was overwhelmed by something else. "When they get Cleaves back," he said, "I can't imagine how good they'll be."

A week later MSU knocked off fifth-ranked Kansas by 12 in the Great Eight in Chicago. Four Spartans—Charlie Bell, A.J. Granger, Peterson, and Andre Hutson—scored in double figures. MSU owned the boards and in general pushed the Jayhawks around. Kansas coach Roy Williams complained obliquely about the physical nature of the game. "They blemish your every little pimple," he said.

An 11-point loss to Arizona and a two-point loss to Kentucky on the road didn't surprise. Jason Richardson's jaw-dropping, reverse-slam, put-back against Arizona did. Then Peterson passed up a shot in the closing seconds against Kentucky, and Izzo started aching for the return of Cleaves. That ache became a knifing pain when the Spartans lost to Wright State, a mid-major nobody of the highest order. The Spartans shot 32.7 percent from the field, including 20.8 percent in the second half, and lost 53–49. Michigan State had their uh-oh moment.

The brutal nonconference schedule had stretched the Spartans, a schedule Izzo never would have created had he known he'd be without Cleaves. But the tough schedule without Cleaves had its long-term benefits. Bell became more assertive. So did Granger. And Peterson grew more comfortable as the primary offensive weapon. But the Spartans' hopes of a championship rested on the return of Cleaves. "When [Cleaves] wasn't there," said Izzo, "defenses could stay home in the half court because they knew that we were more of a perimeter team. We thrive on second-chance opportunities, but we weren't getting them with the frequency we wanted without Cleaves."

Cleaves made his season debut as the Spartans opened Big Ten play at home against Penn State. At the 15:08 mark of the first half, Cleaves entered the game. Within a minute he scored his first basket. Later in the half, he delivered a perfect alley-oop pass to Peterson. The Breslin Center quaked even stronger than when Cleaves first checked in. "He didn't look like somebody who hasn't played in three months," said Penn State coach Jerry Dunn, who watched his Nittany Lions fall 76–63.

With Cleaves back in the fold, the Spartans returned to pushing the basketball like Showtime, rebounding as if they had three arms, and playing suffocating man-to-man defense. They won seven of their first eight conference games. MSU knocked off ninth-ranked Indiana at home when Peterson, unlike at Kentucky, attempted and made an NBA-range three to send the game into overtime. It was Izzo's 100th win as a coach.

Nine days later Ohio State ended MSU's 21-game conference win streak, topping the Spartans 78–67 in Columbus, Ohio. The Buckeyes outrebounded and out-toughed the Spartans, mortal sins for Izzo. "We need to get rid of that pretty boy attitude and get back to playing with a meat-and potatoes attitude," he growled. To hammer home his point, Izzo unfurled shoulder pads and football helmets at the next practice. The players donned them for the War Drill, Izzo's famous no-holds-barred, anything-goes rebounding free-for-all. "That might have been the best thing we did," said

Izzo in *Green Glory*. Northwestern paid the price. The Spartans clobbered the Wildcats 69–45, rebounding 42 of the game's 51 missed shots.

Four more wins followed, including one at Michigan. The crowd at Crisler aimed barb after barb at the Spartans, implicating the players for the riots that broke out in East Lansing after the Spartans lost to Duke in the previous year's Final Four. Unruffled, MSU steamrolled the Wolverines 82–62. UConn fell next on national television to the tune of 85–66. "We've played Duke, Arizona, Syracuse, St. John's, and Texas," said UConn head coach Jim Calhoun, "Clearly this is the best a team has played against us. No one has come at us with that kind of energy." Illinois coach Lon Kruger, whose Illini had been thrashed a week earlier by the Spartans 91–66, had similar thoughts. "We were a little awed and intimidated by how physical [the Spartans] were."

Needing a win on the final day of the regular season to finish 13–3 and guarantee a share of the Big Ten title, the Spartans humiliated Michigan on senior day 114–63, the worst defeat in Michigan basketball history. "It was an incredible day," said Izzo. "It just seemed like every guy, who took a shot, made the shot." As the game went deeper, it became apparent that Cleaves had a shot at breaking the Big Ten single-game assist record. Izzo left Cleaves in the game longer than he would have normally under these circumstances to let him make a run at the record. Ultimately, Cleaves picked up his record-breaking 20th assist, and Bell scored a career-high 31 points as the beneficiary of all those passes. Many Michigan fans accused Izzo of running up the score and skewered him for an alleged lack of class. No one else, including the usually pro-UM local media on hand, agreed. As Cleaves cut down one of the nets after the game, he shouted, "We will win a national championship."

The Spartans gutted out three wins in the Big Ten Tournament, including a 76–61 beatdown of Illinois in the championship game, to earn their second consecutive conference tournament title. "Michigan State is the type of team that can make you look tired after a full week's rest," said Wisconsin's Dick Bennett after MSU beat his Badgers for the third time on the season.

The Spartans appeared to be peaking. They entered the NCAA Tournament as one of the favorites, earning a No. 1 seed in the Midwest after top-ranked Cincinnati lost their best player, Kenyon Martin, and were ousted in the Conference USA Tournament. That seed was more important than usual because if they could survive the first weekend, the Spartans would get to play in Auburn Hills, an hour drive from campus.

The Tournament was a bumpy ride. Twice the Spartans trailed at half, and twice they trailed in the final 10 minutes. At one point they fell behind by 14 points. The Spartans played undue minutes of the tournament walking a tightrope.

They breezed in the first round, parlaying a 20–3 opening salvo to win 65–38 against Valparaiso. The Crusaders' offensive output was the second fewest points in the history of the NCAA's first two rounds. "They did a great job denying our penetration and making us take off-balance shots," lamented Valpo guard Lubos Barton. The Spartans followed Izzo's script perfectly against the Crusaders. In the next round, a few of the guys started wandering from it.

The first bump came against Utah, which shot 56.6 percent in the first half, including 40 percent from three. The Utes' hot shooting, aided and abetted in Izzo's view by lackadaisical Spartans defense, put them up 35–32 at the half. MSU had failed to fight through the numerous Utah screens designed by Utes head coach and mastermind Rick Majerus. The Spartans' fast break offense sputtered despite MSU's decided advantage in speed and quickness.

The players, heads slumped, tip-toed into the locker room at half, preparing for the coming tempest. "I just grabbed a drink and sat down because I knew I was gonna get chewed out," said Peterson, whose lethargic effort on both ends of the floor represented the most glaring problem. Cleaves and Granger came around to exhort Peterson to pick up his play. Then Izzo entered. He looked at the chalkboard and kicked it until it collapsed. Pivoting toward Peterson, Izzo unloaded. "You're not playing like an All-American," he yelled. "You're not rebounding, you turned the ball over before the half was done, you're not running the floor. Basically, you stink." Peterson never said a word.

The Spartans returned to the floor and promptly fell behind by six. Now it was Cleaves' turn. He ranted like a man unjustly sentenced to death. "Mateen has been vocal before," said Peterson. "But it was like a demon came out of him." Cleaves' fury had the desired effect. The Spartans rallied and won 73–61. Cleaves, who Majerus dared to shoot by sagging off of him, had a game-high 21 points, five assists, and only one turnover. The win didn't follow the script, but it put the Spartans into the Sweet 16 for a third straight year. And this time they would be playing in front of a friendly crowd.

The Spartans won the Midwest regional by defeating 26–5 Syracuse and 32–4 Iowa State. Both the Orangemen and the Cyclones presented daunting challenges. Both led the Spartans with 10 minutes remaining in the game. If the Spartans hadn't been playing in front of a mostly partisan crowd, who knows what would have happened? "The atmosphere of those two games were just indescribable," said Granger in 2008. "I always explained it to people that you were literally a foot or foot and a half away from somebody, and you couldn't hear the other person. It was so loud in there that you couldn't hear because it was shaking the fluid in your ears."

After they trailed Syracuse by 10 at the break, the locker room once again resembled a scene from *12 Angry Men*. This time, however, Cleaves, scoreless and with three turnovers himself, delivered the message before Izzo even made it to the locker room. "I don't know what went on in there, but I heard he had one of them by the throat," Izzo said.

Peterson heated up, burying five threes. He gave Cleaves his patented look after knocking down the first one. "It was a gameface you don't often see," said Cleaves about Peterson's countenance. "I know enough to give him the ball and just get out of the way." When Bell banked in a three with 5:35 remaining to give MSU its first lead, the Spartans closed on 17–0 run to win 75–58. Peterson ended with 21 points, and Granger added a career-high 19. "It was one of those days that everybody was hot," Granger said. "You could see it in their faces. They were wondering when we were going to miss."

Iowa State posed numerous threats, starting with All-American Marcus Fizer, a 6'8" jack-of-all-trades mismatch. The Cyclones featured Jamaal Tinsley, a near-replica of Cleaves, at point guard. Iowa State dominated the boards in the first half, outrebounding the Spartans 19–8. "Nobody's done that to us in five years," Izzo said later. Despite this anomaly, MSU led 34–31 at the half.

With 5:49 remaining the Cyclones led, using two made free throws following an Izzo technical to put them up seven. In the huddle Izzo grew impatient. "Look at Mateen. Look at A.J. Look at Pete," he yelled. "They've got five minutes left right now. Don't tell me you can't give it up for five more minutes." Out of the timeout, Granger hit a three. After Fizer banked a shot in, Peterson hit another three. The Spartans defense stiffened, forcing a string of empty ISU possessions. Eventually with 2:52 left, Bell hit a 16-footer to give the Spartans a one-point lead. Then after another scoreless Cyclone possession and an MSU timeout, the Spartans salted the game away with a gorgeous Cleaves to Peterson alley-oop dunk. The final score ended 75–64, a misleading double-digit margin victory due to Larry Eustachy's double-technical. Peterson and Granger paced the scoring with 18 each. Andre Hutson added 17 and more importantly held Fizer to just 15. "I don't want to put too much pressure on Izzo," Eustachy said. "But that's the best team in the country."

Tears flowed freely immediately after the game, as one by one each Spartan clipped a piece of the net. They'd already made school history by returning to the Final Four in back-to-back years. But this year they had their sights set much higher.

It turned out the Spartans were the only No. 1 seed to advance to the Final Four. It also turned out they would meet Wisconsin in the semifinals, the same Badgers whom they had beaten three times already. Wisconsin had finished sixth in the Big Ten and were a No. 8 seed in the tournament. MSU entered as the heavy favorite just as Duke had the year before. The Spartans knew the score. Lose to Wisconsin and the whole season would go up in smoke. Publicly MSU pushed back against this idea, but privately they harbored similar thoughts. "If we do all we can and lose, I'll be able to live with and appreciate all we've accomplished," Izzo said. "But would it bother me for the rest of my life—or at least until we win one? Yeah."

The only team to beat Wisconsin since February 12 had been MSU. The Badgers grind it out, half-court style, which forced opponents to play defense for 30-plus seconds, could be frustrating, an emotion many fans probably felt after watching the first half of the semifinal. The Spartans led 19–17. Defense ruled. Or was it lack of offense? Whatever it was, few enjoyed it, including the players. "Whenever you play Wisconsin, it's going to be ugly," Cleaves said. Both sides suffered long droughts. The Spartans denied Wisconsin the open threes that were the lifeblood of the Badgers offense. MSU never found a rhythm.

Silence, borne out of vexation and embarrassment, reigned in the Spartans locker room at the half. "We kind of had a little kiss and hug," said Izzo. Things opened up in the second half as Peterson, whose grandmother had died that week, scored 10 points in a 13–2 Spartans run that put the game out of reach. "His grandmother carried some of those shots for him," Cleaves said. MSU's 53–41 victory proved once again how it could beat an opponent at any pace or style. In the championship game, the Spartans would prove that point emphatically.

Upstart Florida defeated North Carolina to advance to the championship game. The 29–7 Gators preferred an up-tempo game. They pressed you full court, trapping everywhere. They rained three pointers. The more the talk centered on Florida's desire to run and MSU's ability to contend with it, the wider the Spartans' grin grew. They felt as if they were setting up a trap. When allowed, MSU loved to run.

The Spartans destroyed the Gators' full-court press. Using all five players to shred it, MSU forced Florida's coach, Billy Donovan, to abandon the press before halftime. "There was no doubt we could run with them," Bell said. "We were insulted when we heard people say we couldn't run with Florida. But we showed that's our game." Its press in tatters, Florida fell back into a half-court defense and dared the Spartans to beat them from three. That failed too. With Cleaves nailing three three-pointers, the Spartans went up 43–32.

Out of the half, the Gators trimmed the Spartans' lead to six. Then on a fast break layup, Cleaves tumbled to the ground after Florida's Teddy Dupay fouled him hard—perhaps with malice, perhaps not. In any event Cleaves immediately grimaced and grabbed his ankle. "It's broke," he cried. "It's broke." Helped to the bench, he eventually limped to the locker room. It appeared the Spartans would have to finish the game without their leader. "We're going to war!" shouted Izzo in the huddle. "They took out our leader."

Cleaves spent four minutes in the locker room, pleading with the trainer to patch him up. "I told the trainer he would have to amputate my leg to keep me out of this one," Cleaves said. During his absence the Spartans actually extended their advantage as the bench players rose up. Seldom-used Mike Chappell, a transfer from Duke who had struggled with his shot all year, hit a three and a twisting put-back to increase the lead to nine. "This is a night when we had a lot of guys do a lot of things," Izzo would say later. "I don't know what we would have done without some of those subs."

With 12 minutes remaining, Cleaves hobbled back to the bench reminiscent of Magic Johnson's triumphant return against Ohio State in 1979. Izzo put him back in. Cleaves hobbled around on the court, providing more spiritual guidance than anything else as the Spartans continued to add to their lead. Peterson scored 15 of his 21 points during this stretch. The inevitable drew closer. As the seconds evaporated on the clock, Cleaves started hopping on one leg as he had done on the bench during December. When the buzzer sounded and Michigan State won 89–76, Peterson dropped to his knees and sobbed. Magic, sitting behind the Spartan bench, shouted out, "You're a champion, baby."

MSU had one other matter to attend to. After receiving the National Championship trophy, the Spartans grabbed hold of each other and sang along to "One Shining Moment," the CBS ode to March Madness that capped every NCAA tournament. It was also Cleaves' favorite song. While the song swelled on the arena's big screen, the sweet tears of victory streamed down Cleaves' face. He and his Spartan teammates had indeed shone brighter than anyone in 2000.

The Spartan Marching Band

Founded in 1870 as a 10-member student brass band created by Civil War veteran Ransom McDonough Brooks, the Spartan Marching Band is one of the oldest college marching bands on record.

It has grown in lockstep with the college, mushrooming in size and complexity over the decades. In 1885 Michigan Agricultural College, an early name of MSU, created a military department. In response the band morphed into a Cadet Corps, adding gray and black braided trim uniforms and performances during military drills and public concerts. The leader of the band, student I.E. Hill, played first cornet.

A little more than two decades later, MAC created a full-time position for band conductor. Chemistry professor A.J. Clark assumed the job in 1907, increasing the band from 25 members to 60 and performing at school functions, including athletic events for the first time. The band became known as the MAC Touch-down Band.

When the MAC "Aggies" beat Ohio State in an upset in 1912, the men in football uniforms were not the only East Lansing folks who impressed the Buckeye faithful. "Never had there been a band on Ohio Field that can compete with the Michigan Aggie," wrote a local scribe in a Columbus, Ohio, newspaper. Earlier in 1907 the band had impressed another unsuspecting fan, president Theodore Roosevelt, who visited MAC in 1907 to celebrate the school's semi-centennial.

In 1927 the newly-renamed Spartan Marching Band came under the direction of Leonard Falcone, the John Hannah of Michigan State band history. A famous horn soloist, Falcone nurtured the band through an explosive growth period when its membership rose from 60 members to 144 and its role as ambassador of the college increased exponentially. After a fund-raising drive helped the band gain its...uh...independence in 1952, it broke ties with the ROTC. Green and white replaced khaki as the band's colors, and a few more frills dressed up the uniform, which changed again in 1964 when white overlays with a block "S" were added to a darker green sleeve and trouser.

In the 1960s Falcone, with the help of assistant band director William Moffit, introduced "Patterns in Motion," a distinctive marching style, featuring ever-changing patterns that became internationally known. It heavily influenced college marching bands throughout the U.S. The new style inspired another signature Spartan Marching Band maneuver, spinning of the block S, which the band performed at halftime for years. "Spinning the S" is now part of the band's pregame routine.

The first women—twirler Beth Mlynarek and saxophonist Lynne Charbonneau—joined the Spartan Marching Band in 1972. The last four decades have seen three new band directors, a few more tweaks to the uniform, the inclusion of a color guard, and constant tinkering with "Patterns in Motion."

The Spartan Marching Band has performed in four Rose Bowls, two world fairs, one World Series, and in front of five U.S. presidents. It has performed throughout the country and Tokyo, Japan. It has entertained Spartans football fans at every home game since the turn of the previous century. Gameday without the Spartan Marching Band stimulating the soul and goosing the juices would be like ribs without the sauce.

1952: Champions at Last

By 1952 Michigan State had nearly completed its rise from college football striver to college football nobility. To finish its ascent, Michigan State needed a national championship as recognized by a majority of major selectors. The previous undefeated year had teased with national championship awards from a few lesser polls.

But a smattering of lip-biting and close wins prevented the major polls from getting behind the Spartans' cause.

To achieve its football nirvana in 1952, MSU needed to again go unbeaten but with more authoritative victories. And all of this would have to be accomplished without three key graduating seniors: All-American do-everything lineman Don Coleman, big-game quarterback Al Dorow, and another All-American, Bob Carey.

No one, though, needed to weep for MSU. Munn's recruiting sizzled, and he had assembled a roster the envy of any in college football. "There may be more formidable individuals on other teams," said Ben Schwartzwalder, coach of Syracuse, "but as a combination the Michigan State outfit can't go wrong. I have never set eyes on a stronger college group." One big question mark, and perhaps the difference between a national championship and something short of that, was quarterback. Tom Yewcic, the junior back involved in the famed "Transcontinental Pass" from the season before, returned, but he had little experience at the position. "I had 20 days of training as a quarterback," he said in a 2013 interview. "I had never touched the ball in my life as a quarterback." But eventually he won the job.

Yewcic was backed up by the appropriately named Willie Thrower, the first African American quarterback at MSC and in the Big Ten. Thrower was from New Kensington, a small west Pennsylvania coal town that Munn had mined for an abundance of talent, including current Spartans Dick and Harry Tamburo, halfback Vince Pisano, and lineman Joe Klein. The backfield, a multilayered group of runners with versatile and complementary skills that enabled Munn to keep his backs fresh, consisted of two groups, dubbed the light "ponies" and the big "elephants."

The lines were anchored by two Pennsylvanians, future All-Americans Frank Kush and Dick Tamburo. The Spartans also excelled in the classroom. Thirteen MSU players made the honor roll. "Today's football is a game of chess—at high speed," Munn said. "Dullards only mess up the works." Defensive back Johnny Wilson, the senior class president, was a Rhodes Scholar candidate.

Installed as preseason No. 1 team by the AP and in its last years as an independent, MSC kicked off the season at Ann Arbor, the fourth straight year the Spartans had to play their rivalry game on the road. Michigan State, perhaps out of habit, fell behind. Trailing 13–0, Don McAuliffe, one of the elephant backs, stunned the 97,000 at Michigan Stadium with a 70-yard touchdown. He dodged three defenders and outran the rest, doing his best impersonation of the fleeter pony backs. The Spartans seized control of the game, scoring three more touchdowns. The 27–13 win moved local reporter Charles Capp to write in the *Grand Rapids Herald* : "Magnificent Michigan State, the Rocky Marciano of football, got up off the floor twice this beautiful afternoon and clearly proved its right to be considered the nation's number one team." On another positive note, Yewcic demonstrated that he could handle running the offense. "The big preseason question mark on the Spartans potential greatness this year was Yewcic," wrote the *Detroit Free Press*. "He can hardly be called a question mark now."

Feisty Oregon State, who had nearly ended the Spartans' winning streak the year before in East Lansing, came next in Oregon. Once again the Beavers made the Spartans sweat to the end. MSU ultimately prevailed 17–14 on a do-over, last-second field goal by Gene Lekenta. On the first attempt, which Lekenta missed, the Beavers jumped offside. "When you're riding a winning streak, the pressure builds up," Munn said. "It is increasingly difficult to keep winning."

The narrow victory margin, the act of providence needed to secure the win, and the Spartans' general struggles against an unranked opponent failed to impress the AP voters. They dropped MSC to No. 2 in the polls, elevating Wisconsin to number one. That didn't sit well with the Spartans, who steamrolled Texas A&M 48–6 in their home opener. They rolled up 592 yards of offense split almost evenly between the air and ground. The no-doubt-about-it performance pleased the pollsters, and they promptly voted the Spartans back into the top spot.

The Spartans appeared galvanized by the blowout. They rolled both Syracuse and Penn State by a combined score of 82–14. Munn's multiple formations and waves of backs continued to vex defenses. "Biggie would start the big backs, and they'd play until we began to sees signs the defense was wearing down," said Dorow in 2004 about the way Munn used his backs. "Then the coaches played the smaller backs, and they all had great speed. We'd run sweeps left and right and then trap up the middle and, of course, pass. But Michigan State could really keep on running the ball at you."

The Spartans' own defense yielded points and yards more sparingly than Munn doled out compliments. Coach Ray George of Texas A&M, who had been beaten soundly by the Spartans weeks earlier, proclaimed the Spartans "one of the finest college football teams" he'd ever seen, singling out their remarkable depth as a central reason.

The winning streak stood at 20 games. The Spartans held a firm lead in the AP and UPI polls. College football orbited around the star glowing brilliantly in East Lansing. Sportswriters from across the nation lined up for press credentials. Red Barber, Van Patrick, Lindsey Nelson, and renowned sports scribes became regulars in East Lansing. Red Smith and H.G. Salsinger also made appearances.

Ten years had passed since the Spartans faced Purdue, usually a tough out for Michigan State. Not surprisingly Purdue shoved a rod into the fast spinning wheel that had been the Spartans offense, limiting MSC to only two touchdowns. Doug Weaver saved the day with an interception at the Spartans' four-yard line to preserve a 14–7 win.

Another trip to Indiana, this time to Bloomington to face lowly Indiana, offered an excellent chance to pad MSC's lead in the polls. The Hoosiers proved the perfect patsy. They couldn't stop Billy Wells, who gashed them for 135 yards and two touchdowns, nor Don McAuliffe, who also scored two touchdowns—one on a 57-yard touchdown pass. The 41–14 drubbing of Indiana brought around the last of the AP skeptics, and the Spartans surged in the polls.

The third Indiana school in a row, Notre Dame, arrived in East Lansing with a 5–1–1 record, No. 6 ranking, and the usual roster of college football glitterati such as future Heisman winner halfback John Lattner and All-American quarterback Ralph Guglielmi. Thanks in part to seven Irish turnovers, the Spartans won comfortably 21–3. The defense sparkled, limiting Lattner to only 65 yards rushing. Dick Tamburo recovered three fumbles. McAuliffe, Thrower, and Evan Slonac starred on offense. The impressive win represented Munn's third in five games against legendary Notre Dame coach Frank Leahy, who would lose only 13 games in his entire career. "Notre Dame was primed to score an upset," said Munn a few weeks later when asked about the season's toughest game, "and their squad was stronger than generally rated."

The win buried the Spartans' competition. With a commanding lead in first place votes, MSC faced Marquette, its last hurdle to the school's 24th consecutive win—and a likely national championship. The Spartans cleared it as if they were wearing jet packs. All 60 MSC players saw action in the 62–13 win, the largest margin of victory since the streak began. Playing on a muddy field, MSC still managed to gain 601 yards, mixing in a flotilla of big plays and five interceptions. "I'm old fashioned enough to know that 50 to 60 percent of football is a matter of heart," said Munn, discussing weeks later the secret sauce of the Spartans' success. "We were successful because everyone on the team wanted to be good, and they never ceased improvement."

The Spartans finished 9–0. Georgia Tech (then in the SEC) finished 11–0. The Spartans received 171 more first place AP votes and 434 more total AP votes than the Yellow Jackets. Their 207 first place votes set a record for the most ever in the AP poll. In the UPI poll, the Spartans received 32 of 35 first place votes. The two biggest, most respected polls agreed: the 1952 Spartans were national champions. Six Spartans earned first team All-American honors, and Munn was named "Coach of the Year."

10 Mateen Cleaves

"One of the greatest leaders the game of college basketball has ever seen," intoned CBS broadcaster Jim Nantz in reference to Mateen Cleaves as he started to hop up and down with his wounded ankle in the closing seconds of the 2000 NCAA championship game. The Spartans had just dispatched Florida, who crumbled as so many Spartan opponents had done in Cleaves' four years as a Spartan. Stylistically, he rarely impressed. But Cleaves, an unembroidered warrior and leader who left a legacy few Spartans athletes could match, was a central reason the Spartans stood on the mountaintop that evening.

Cleaves starred in both football and basketball at Flint Northern High School. A quarterback and safety, he could have played major college football. Izzo, a football guy at the core, loved that about him. It helped the two develop a strong relationship and made MSU Cleaves' favorite school—even when his recruitment took a few odd turns. The strangest and scariest occurred on his official visit to Michigan. Cleaves suffered a back injury in a rollover accident on the freeway the night of his recruiting visit to Ann Arbor. He was a passenger in the Ford Explorer driven by UM's Maurice Taylor, who fell asleep at the wheel as he, some of his teammates, and Cleaves returned home at 5:10 AM from a party. The injury put Cleaves in the hospital for weeks, led to an NCAA and FBI investigation into wrongdoing in the Michigan basketball program, and helped change the balance of basketball power in the state.

Cleaves, a McDonald's All-American, committed to MSU in March of 1996. He started his press conference by jokingly stating his intention to enter the NBA draft. After a few beats, Cleaves mimicked Magic Johnson (who did the same thing at his school selection press conference) by saying he actually planned to attend the University of Michigan (pause) State. The reaction to Cleaves' announcement, perhaps the most celebrated recruit to sign with MSU since the 1970s, aped Johnson's as well. MSU fans let their imaginations run wild. "Everybody loves Michigan with the hype and fame and the baggy shorts and all that," he said. "But State was always in my heart. And I fell in love with Coach Izzo."

Initially, many wondered if the recruiting gurus had misfired. Not fully recovered from his back injury, Cleaves struggled mightily his freshman year. Slowed by the extra pounds he carried from inactivity due to the injury, Cleaves couldn't guard to Izzo's standards, suffered from a shot flatter than a prairie, and appeared to have been robbed of the superior athleticism he exhibited in high school. Fans and media were quick to dismiss him. Just another false prophet, they said. But Cleaves kept fighting, and Izzo never lost faith.

A year later Cleaves silenced his critics and grabbed hold of the team for good. The pivotal moment may have been January 31, 1998. Off to a surprisingly fast start in the Big Ten, the Spartans trailed heavy underdog Northwestern at the half. Cleaves had scored only two points and played miserably. He shuffled

Point guard Mateen Cleaves, the consummate team leader, dribbles the ball during a 65–38 victory against Valparaiso in the first round of the 2000 NCAA Tournament ultimately won by the Spartans. (Getty Images)

disconsolately off the court. Izzo met him immediately. They exchanged words. Then Cleaves stormed out of the locker room. A few moments later, he returned. "Hey guys, that was my fault," he told his teammates, accepting blame for the Spartans' lousy first half. That proved something to Izzo about Cleaves' character. Then he returned to the floor and scored 32 points, leading the Spartans to a disaster-avoiding overtime win. That proved something to his teammates.

Things started to gel for Cleaves and the Spartans that season. They went on to win the Big Ten and play in the Sweet 16. Cleaves, who averaged 16.1 points a game, was named MVP of the Big Ten and a first team All-American. Off the court, however, there were a few hiccups. Cleaves, along with Andre Hutson, was arrested for an alcohol-related misdemeanor. Izzo benched both players for the first half of a critical late-season game against Wisconsin. With a valuable lesson learned, Cleaves put the episode behind him and returned to the business of pursuing MSU basketball history.

Cleaves started the offense from his point guard position promptly and fluidly. He engineered the fast break expertly, making the right pass at the right time. His jump shot lacked artistry, looking more like a rabbit scurrying into its hole than a beautiful arcing rainbow. And he only averaged a hair below 12 points his last two years. But in a tight spot or a big moment, he usually found the net. "He was one of the great shot clock guys," said Izzo in *Green Glory*. On defense Cleaves rarely allowed opposing guards to penetrate, sealing off the perimeter as if he wielded a glue gun. Those were just a few of his tangible contributions. As for the fuzzier, more abstract stuff? Cleaves was the man.

He worked harder than anyone else in practice, which helped establish good team wide practice habits. Winning mattered to him the way breathing does to everyone else. Soon enough, his teammates started feeling the same way. If the team needed a kick in the rear, Cleaves would usually beat Izzo to it. He would administer tough love that helped turn a teammate and a game around. During the rehab of his stress facture in his senior year, Cleaves never abandoned the team. He sat on the bench for all 13 games he missed, dispensing advice, offering criticism when necessary, and praise if deserved. Cleaves was the quintessential leader. "Mateen was a superstar who sacrificed for the good of the program," Izzo told *Green Glory*. "[He] knew winning was the most important thing. When other seniors played for NBA contracts, he took four or five shots. He knew defense was more important than offense and knew toughness and leadership meant more than glitz and glamour." As a tribute to Cleaves, Izzo gave his son a second middle name: Mateen.

The two-time Big Ten Player of the Year and three-time, first team All-American was drafted by the Detroit Pistons with the 14th overall pick. His game, however, was not well-suited to the NBA, a league that treasures individual accomplishment and skills. He hung around the NBA for a few years until retiring to become a television analyst.

The 1954 Rose Bowl

Flanked by the luminescent San Gabriel Mountains on one side and the seductive beaches of the Pacific on the other and teasingly located only a few miles from the glamour of Hollywood, the Rose Bowl was the ultimate destination. And the Big Ten had been sending its champion to play there since 1947. So when the Big Ten athletic directors selected the Spartans over the Illini—with whom Michigan State had tied for the title in 1953—MSC let loose. Spontaneous celebrations sprouted all over campus and Michigan. Around 15,000 fans headed to California to soak up the experience and watch the Spartans play UCLA, who was 8–1 and ranked fifth in the AP poll.

Planned festivities and unplanned distractions ruled the week. A visit to Disneyland, a beef-eating contest at the famed steakhouse Lawry's, VIP dinners with Bob Hope and Bing Crosby, and a tour of a movie studio all competed with practice time. Running back Billy Wells even took actress Debbie Reynolds on a date. A few Spartans also rushed to a fire at a nearby hotel to help evacuate the guests. Munn schmoozed the West Coast press as no other Big Ten coach had, allowing them to watch a few practices, something previous Big Ten coaches had forbidden the West Coast media to do. The local Southern California press delighted in writing stories about the small stature of the Spartans players, one calling them "midgets." "This must be the first college football team in history that has over-exaggerated its height and weights in its listed roster," wrote the *Los Angeles Mirror*.

On the day of the game, the sun cast a brilliant glow on the annual Tournament of Roses parade that morning and throughout the afternoon. No one would describe the No. 3-ranked Spartans start as brilliant as they fell behind 14–0 in the first 20 minutes of the game. UCLA dominated the start statistically as well, out-gaining the Spartans 154 yards to 56, intercepting a pass, and recovering two fumbles. Millions watching on television probably buried the Spartans after the first third of the game. However, in its last 33 games—32 of which had ended as victories—Munn's team had fallen behind 14 times and come back to win.

Enter Ellis Duckett.

With five minutes remaining in the first half, Duckett lined up on the left side as UCLA punter Paul Cameron set to punt from his own 10-yard line. His path clear because of a road-grading hit by Hank Bullough on the Bruin blocker protecting Cameron, Duckett charged at the punter. Duckett left his feet, stretched his arms as high as his anatomy would allow, and knocked Cameron's punt to the ground. Without stopping, Duckett continued toward the ball, scooped it up, and burst into the end zone. The score cut the Bruins lead in half. The crowd gasped in wonder at the exquisite skill and superior athleticism displayed by Duckett. And they could sense the shift in momentum, which moved seismically in favor of the Spartans. UCLA head coach Red Sanders had never had a punt blocked in his first five seasons at the school. The play was no fluke. "It was one of several kick rushes we worked hard on after studying the movies," Munn said.

At halftime Munn handed a note to the team's captain, Don Dohoney. "Get off the floor in '54," Dohoney read aloud. The players responded with a laugh, then charged out of the locker room, and took control of the game. Two long, ground-obsessed drives resulted in touchdowns—one by LeRoy Bolden and one by Wells. UCLA regrouped, though, and managed to score again, but the extra point failed, leaving the Bruins down 21–20. After an exchange of punts, Wells, enjoying quite a week, destroyed any Bruin hopes of a comeback by returning the UCLA punt 62 yards for a touchdown. The extra point made it 28–20. The Spartans iced the game with a Bobby Matsock interception in the waning seconds. After the game Munn, overcome with emotion, locked himself and his players in the locker room and wept.

Wells, nicknamed the Menominee Meteor, was the Most Outstanding Player of the game. He gained 80 yards and scored two touchdowns. His punt return for a touchdown shattered the Rose Bowl record. The national press gushed about the gritty comeback by Munn's undersized men. "They've got bigger things in crackerjack boxes than what Michigan State put on the field yesterday. But never was anything crammed with more heart and hustle than those little green-shirted guys from East Lansing…they were battered and beaten, physically and numerically, in the first half, then gamely rebounded…to soundly thrash UCLA," wrote Bobby Hunter in the *Los Angeles Times*.

12 George Webster

Why was George Webster once voted as the greatest Spartan football player of all time by MSU fans? Don't bother checking the MSU record book. You won't find him listed anywhere. Perhaps the best way to find the answer is to ask the dozens of college football players who lined up against him—in practice or in games.

Webster grew up in Anderson, South Carolina, 17 miles from Clemson, the college he rooted for as a child. In 1963, however, neither Clemson nor any other school south of the Mason-Dixon line handed out scholarships to black athletes. That meant Webster had to look elsewhere. He chose MSU over Minnesota, likely succumbing to one of the great practitioners of the art of persuasion, Duffy Daugherty. Four years later he had redefined the limits of what one individual could do on the football field.

Daugherty had created a position he called roverback, a cross between a safety and linebacker. At 6'5" and 218 pounds, Webster had the ideal physique and skills for the position. But he could also rush the passer, a rare quality for someone who had the ability to cover receivers, take on offensive linemen, and stuff running backs.

He was listed as a defensive back, but that was for purposes of the gameday program only. Against Michigan in 1964 during Webster's third collegiate game, he displayed his rare combo of talent. On five consecutive plays, Webster tackled the Michigan back for a 1-yard gain; ran down field to knock a back out of bounds after a 10-yard run; knocked the ball loose for an incompletion on a pass attempt; slammed through the line to bring down a ball carrier for a two-yard loss; and chased down the runner on a screen play three yards shy of a first down. The sequence drew oohs and ahs from the hostile UM crowd, praise from his coach, and national attention. (He won *Sports Illustrated*'s Player of the Week award). If he hadn't already, Daugherty quickly decided to build his defense around Webster, a once-in-a-generation, mold-shattering talent.

Taciturn and well-mannered off the field, Webster didn't talk a lot on it either. But his hits looked anything but polite. "He doesn't tackle people. He explodes them," Daugherty said. Bill Jauss, writing in the *Chicago Daily News*, compared Webster to another celebrated defensive star. "Webster hits ball carriers," he wrote, "the way the Bears' Dick Butkus does." Plenty of opponents who lost collisions with Webster had to be helped off the field. A few of his teammates insist that Purdue quarterback and All-American Bob Griese quivered under center at the sight of Webster during the Spartans' two wins against the Boilermakers.

Webster combined his size, speed, tenacity, and bottomless energy with exceptional football instincts. Vince Carillot, his defensive backfield coach, said in *They are Spartans* that Webster had "the knack of being where the offense is going to try to go with the football." Opponents marveled at his ability to seemingly be everywhere and to come from anywhere.

In his junior year, the Spartans were the top-ranked defense in the nation. Daugherty named Webster the captain of the defense for his senior year. He didn't say much, speaking with economy. If he had something to say, however, "by gosh, everyone listened," said Don Japinga, the previous season's captain, in *Stadium Stories: Michigan State Spartans*. Years later Webster tried to defer credit to his teammates for the success of the 1965 and 1966 defenses. But that never rang true with those who knew best. Offering the ultimate compliment, Daugherty called him "the greatest football player I ever coached." The year after Webster graduated, his No. 90 was retired by Michigan State, one of only four Spartans football jerseys ever retired.

Remarkably, Webster was hobbled throughout his career by bad knees and other various ailments. He fought through them in college, but they eventually caught up to him in the AFL and NFL after the Houston Oilers drafted him fifth overall. Webster won Rookie of the Year in 1967, made the All-Pro team in 1968, and enjoyed a few more years of success with the Oilers, Pittsburgh Steelers, and New England Patriots before injuries forced his retirement in 1976.

Webster died in 2007 after a long series of health ailments. "[Webster] is one of the top three or four players I've ever been associated with," Hank Bullough, a former MSU defensive assistant at MSU, told *The Detroit News.* "He was snake-like. He could hit like a cobra. When he stung you, it was, bam. I mean, he could bend you over backward."

Rose Bowl Immortality

Nothing went according to plan during 1954 in Duffy Daugherty's first year as head coach of the Spartans. Leroy Bolden, one of the few stars returning from Biggie's last season, collided with the goal post in the Spartans' first game against Iowa and damaged his knee. It never fully healed, severely limiting his effectiveness and contributing mightily to the Spartans' first losing season in 13 years. MSU lost four of the six games by a combined 17 points. Former coach Biggie Munn, now the athletic director, panicked. One day he barged into a coaches meeting to air his concerns. Duffy told him to get out. Munn left seething, and the relationship between the two would be changed forever.

Duffy, though, displayed a sunnier outlook than most for 1955. A promising group of newcomers highlighted by quarterback Jim Ninowski, halfback Walt Kowalczyk, and linebacker Dan Currie joined a solid group of returning veterans whose strength rested on the line. Guard and captain Buck Nystrom and tackle Norm Masters appeared poised for breakout years. Quarterback Earl Morrall flashed the skills that would earn him All-American honors by the end of the year.

Taking the field for the first time as students of a university instead of a college, Michigan State University squeezed by lowly Indiana 20–13. Then the Spartans dropped a close game to

Michigan 14–7. MSU outplayed the Wolverines, dominating statistically. A glimmer of hope arose as a strong test awaited: Notre Dame.

The Paul Hornung-led Fighting Irish hadn't been scored upon in their first three games. In warm-ups the day before the game, Hornung had sneered—loud enough so the Spartans could hear it while they yielded the practice field to the Irish—that "Notre Dame would teach the Spartans a thing or two about football." Instead Michigan State schooled the Irish, putting up 21 points while holding Notre Dame to seven. It marked Daugherty's first signature win, returned the Spartans to national prominence, and propelled them to six more convincing victories.

On the final day of the season, the Spartans played Marquette in East Lansing while Michigan squared off against its rival Ohio State. The Buckeyes were 5–0, and Michigan was 5–1 in the conference. The Spartans wanted Michigan to lose, though not just for the usual reasons. A Michigan loss would send the Spartans to the Rose Bowl (because Ohio State, which had played in the Rose Bowl the year before, was ineligible to repeat by Big Ten rules). For the 40,000 or so fans who sat in Spartan Stadium that day, their attention was divided between the game on the field and the game they listened to on their transistor radios. But they left in a brightened mood as both Marquette and Michigan went down to defeat. The Spartans could celebrate another trip to the Rose Bowl.

Few complained about how the Spartans backed in. MSU, No. 2 in both major polls, stood higher in the rankings than unbeaten and No. 9-ranked Ohio State. The Spartans had outscored their final seven opponents 209–42, and many believed this Michigan State team might be the best to ever play in the Rose Bowl.

Moreover, for the reporters covering the game, Michigan State—both under Munn and now Daugherty—represented a breath of fresh air. The year before, Woody Hayes, as just about every Big Ten coach before him, had banned West Coast reporters from attending practice. Daugherty welcomed them, saying: "If I didn't feel I could trust the newspapers, it would be a pretty poor reflection on both our professions. The job of a sportswriter is to write, so I figure my job's to help him." At a large media event, he even grabbed the loudspeaker and walked the press through a selection of Michigan State's plays—to the consternation of his assistants, who nearly choked when Daugherty included a couple put in just for the Rose Bowl.

One issue bedeviled the Spartans: the winning streak to end the season had taken a health toll. Five starters were either out or nursing an injury, so Daugherty scaled back practices and reduced their intensity. On the plus side, Clarence Peaks, a back with game-changing ability, was cleared to play after missing the second half of the season. Offense, however, wasn't really the concern. Morrall had that under control. Daugherty worried about halting UCLA's single wing offense, which put a heavy emphasis on the run and could chew through time of possession and bodies.

After trading jabs with Jack Benny on the comedian's Sunday television show the night before the game, Daugherty returned to his hotel for final preparations. The next morning dawned as just another perfect day at the perfect college football bowl venue. More than 100,000 fans sat shoulder-to-shoulder and witnessed a magnificent college football game.

Morrall, steady all year, unbuckled a bit in the first half, throwing two picks. One led to a UCLA touchdown; the other led to a missed field goal. After the missed field goal, the Spartans moved 79 yards for their first touchdown on a Morrall to Peaks short pass just before the half. Failed opportunities and defense continued to reign until early in the fourth quarter when the stalemate ended on a play Duffy had shared with the media. Morrall lateralled the ball to Peaks, who feigned a run, pulled up, and threw a pass to John "Thunder" Lewis. Lewis caught it at midfield and streaked

Three Things MSU Would Rather Forget

1. MSU football has been put on probation three times—in the early 1950s, mid-1970s, and mid-1990s. The less said the better.

2. Tony Mandarich was a first team All-American at offensive tackle in 1987 who helped lead MSU to the Rose Bowl. An amazing physical specimen, he weighed 316 pounds, stood 6'7", ran the 40 in under 4.7, and was a *Sports Illustrated* cover boy. NFL scouts drooled. The Packers drafted him No. 2 overall in the 1989 draft. He was a complete bust, hounded by rumors of steroid use. In 2008 Mandarich admitted to using illegal substances starting in college.

3. In 1917 the Aggies went winless, finishing 0–9 under Chester Brewer, who had returned to coach MAC. It is the only time in 113 years that Michigan State did not record a win. They were outscored 179–23 and shut out five times. Most of the school's best players were in military training camps.

untouched into the end zone for a 14–7 Spartans lead. UCLA responded with a quick score, tying it up with six minutes left, and it stayed that way until seven seconds remained.

Then State had the ball on UCLA's 24-yard-line.

In came a sub with the kicking tee. Morrall grabbed No. 89 and told him to kick a field goal from 41 yards. But the usual kicker, Jerry Planutis, did not wear No. 89. That number belonged to end Dave Kaiser, the backup kicker who had never made a field goal in college. Daugherty and Morrall decided to play a high-stakes hunch, going with a new guy rather than the experienced kicker, who missed his previous attempt.

Kaiser lined up and took a practice swing with his leg. But for some reason the snap came at the same time. Kaiser recomposed himself quickly, pulled his leg back for the real thing, and kicked it square on. As it soared through the goal posts, the almost 5,000 Spartans fans at the Rose Bowl rose at once to celebrate. No one celebrated more than Kaiser, a transfer from Notre Dame. "I wasn't sure I made it until the official near me," he said, "raised his arms, and then Buck Nystrom swarmed all over me."

The most famous field goal in Spartan history, which many fans and reporters—including Kaiser's father—initially thought had been nailed by Planutis, capped an incredible game. A reporter from the *International News Service* effused, "It was as good a football game, college or pro, as a fan could wish to see. A storybook finish that even Hollywood could not have duplicated with a script."

14 Kill, Bubba, Kill

Tall enough that he could reach the bar of the goal post without a step stool and strong enough that he could probably bring the whole thing down with one swift blow, Charles "Bubba" Smith and his 6'7", 290-pound physique could draw anyone's attention. What he could do with it on the football field, however, took everyone's breath away.

Smith was Michigan State's most famous athlete until a kid who could perform magic on the basketball court showed up 12 years later. Like many of his Spartans teammates, Smith grew up in the South, forbidden to play at his local school (in his case, Texas) because of his race. Unlike many of his teammates he did not choose Michigan State. His father, a successful high school football coach in Beaumont, Texas, chose it for him. Smith wanted to attend UCLA. Southern California fit his outsized personality. But his father had developed a good relationship with Duffy Daugherty through the coaching clinics sponsored by Michigan State, and he

A consensus All-American in 1965 and 1966, Bubba Smith would become the only Spartans football player ever to be drafted No. 1 overall by the NFL.
(Getty Images)

trusted and respected the Spartans coach. Without ever meeting Duffy or hearing his enticing sales pitch, Smith headed to East Lansing in 1963, grumbling all the way.

The cold weather, the preponderance of white faces, and a coach he'd never met all made for a toxic atmosphere that left Smith miserable. Smith chafed at the rules Daugherty implemented—especially one prohibiting the black players from dating white women. It was one of the few instances in which Daugherty created separate rules, though Daugherty eventually relaxed that policy. All the players—black and white—ate together, roomed together, and did as much as possible together. On the football field, Smith adapted slowly. He spent much of his sophomore year on the bench, watching a talented team underachieve at 4–5.

By his junior year, Smith had figured a few things out, started to see the wisdom of most of Daugherty's decisions, and began to excel on the football field. He played defensive end where he usually enjoyed a significant weight and size advantage over his opponent. The Spartans defense coalesced around him and teammate George Webster, another man of revolutionizing skill and ability, to create one of the most dominant defenses college football has seen. Smith spearheaded a defensive line that allowed few breaches while Webster erased whatever slipped through. Fans started chanting, "Kill, Bubba, Kill," before key third downs or obvious passing plays, an intimidating chant he readily acknowledged inflamed him even more. Students around Michigan State's campus started wearing buttons with that slogan. Smith "changed things. He was 6'7", 295, and he could run. You didn't have many guys like that," said Hank Bullough, his defensive line coach.

During the heavenly run of 1965 to 1966 when the Spartans went unbeaten in the Big Ten and claimed shares of national championships, Smith represented the essence of those sublime teams. Every national story about the Spartans seemed to start with him, usually referencing his mega size and unnatural ability. Not overly demonstrative off the field, Smith was nonetheless an immensely popular figure on campus. He even joined a Jewish fraternity. Occasionally he'd say something provocative or controversial—such as the time he suggested Daugherty tried to control him.

But in the course of time, Smith grew to adore his coach and love his school. "It was the greatest time of my life," he said, admitting that his professional football career did not compare to his time in college. Daugherty also grew to love Smith. "Bubba was Duffy's favorite," George Perles told the *Detroit Free Press*. "Whenever Bubba came back, he and Duffy would hug each other."

In 1966 Smith recorded 30 tackles for the entire year (10 for loss). If ever the hoary cliché about statistics not being the true measure of someone's worth applied, it was in the case of Smith. While Smith occupied two or three blockers, his teammates rambled unblocked toward exposed quarterbacks and frustrated halfbacks. He earned consensus All-American honors in 1965 and 1966. At the time, he and Webster were the only Spartans in history to accomplish that. Smith was drafted No. 1 overall by the Baltimore Colts, the only Spartan in history to go number one in the NFL draft. He played in two Super Bowls and two Pro Bowls. When Smith retired due to injury in 1976, he arguably became more famous. He found a home in Hollywood, where his ocean-sized presence helped him make a smooth transition to acting. Smith appeared in a series of memorable beer commercials and film comedies—most notably the *Police Academy* series. He died in 2011, five years after his number was retired by Michigan State.

2009 Final Four

The economy crashed. The stock market dropped faster than a slain bull in Pamplona, Spain. The U.S. fretted about the future. In Detroit two of the largest automakers faced extinction. Against this backdrop the MSU basketball team began practice in October, aiming to finish the season at the Final Four located in a reeling Motor City. "Ford Field," wrote Tom Izzo on the dry-erase board on the first day of practice.

Coming off a strong season in which they had won 27 games and advanced to the Sweet 16, the Spartans were back in the national championship conversation. Although All-American Drew Neitzel graduated, the Spartans returned every other key member of the team: versatile wing Raymar Morgan, defensive stalwart Travis Walton, quickly improving big man Goran Suton, lightning quick point guard Kalin Lucas, and oft-injured but tenacious big man Delvon Roe. The bench spilled over with talent and depth as well: wing Durrell Summers, off guard Chris Allen, power forward Marquise Gray, freshman wing Draymond Green, and guard Korie Lucious.

Izzo tends to do his best work when he has a deep team. The 2008 to 2009 Spartans were that and then some. The Big Ten media agreed, selecting MSU to compete with Purdue and Wisconsin for the conference crown. By the second week of the season, Izzo was cursing those predictions. At the Old Spice Classic in Florida, the fifth-ranked Spartans tumbled, losing 80–62 to unranked Maryland. Playing without Suton and forced to limit Roe's minutes because of injury, MSU succumbed to Maryland's pressure and 15 missed free throws. "I don't think I've ever seen anything like that in my career," Izzo lamented about the Spartans' troubles at the line. At 4–1 and still without their best rebounder in Suton, the Spartans headed to Ford Field to meet No. 1 North Carolina. It was no contest. The Tar Heels beat the stuffing out of MSU 98–63. Izzo called North Carolina "maybe the best team we've played since I've been here." Losing games in November and December had become an MSU basketball tradition, usually triggering sky-is-falling proclamations from fans and media. But Izzo chalked up the defeat to excessive early-season travel and North Carolina's brilliance. "You didn't see our real team tonight, but our real team might have lost by 20," he said. The national media was less forgiving. They dumped MSU stock as fast as most Americans had abandoned their own securities. The Spartans slipped almost entirely out of the national championship discussion.

Izzo knew better. He hit the reboot button, and the Spartans surged thanks in part to the return of Suton and the rapid improvement of Kalin Lucas. MSU won its next 11 games. They knocked off fifth-ranked Texas in Houston when Summers, whom Izzo had been driving hard in practice, nailed a three pointer with less than 20 seconds left. After opening the Big Ten season 3–0, MSU beat defending national champ Kansas 75–62. Lucas scored 22, continuing a four-game stretch in which he had averaged more than 20 points and three assists a game. "Morning, noon, and night I've been coming in to get a lot of shots up," Lucas said. "I've just been shooting and shooting and shooting even before and after practice."

The Spartans sprinted to a 5–0 start in conference play, the school's best since 1978 and finished by winning 10 of their final 13 games. Despite two head-scratching losses at home to bottom dwellers Northwestern and Penn State and a mysterious virus that sidelined or limited Morgan for much of January and February, the Spartans romped, winning the conference by four games. Lucas was a unanimous selection as Big Ten Player of the Year, and Suton led the league in rebounding.

The Spartans, though, had their usual troubles in the Big Ten Tournament, losing in the semis to Ohio State. The loss forfeited any hope of receiving a No. 1 seed. MSU entered the NCAA Tournament as a No. 2 seed instead. The year had been dominated by talk of the Big East—Connecticut and Louisville in particular, and Louisville ended up in the Spartans' region. Even as a high seed, MSU was an afterthought and given little chance to survive the region.

Walton was the Big Ten's Defensive Player of the Year, but he never showed much offensive game until the second round of the 2009 tournament. USC, which chose to leave Walton wide open, had the Spartans on the ropes numerous times. But the Trojans failed to close the deal because Walton kept making those wide-open shots, scoring a career-high 18 points. "I was shocked that he did make some of those shots," Izzo said.

The 74–69 win put the Spartans into the Sweet 16, Izzo's eighth, to face third-seeded Kansas. Lucas completed an old-fashioned, three-point play to put MSU ahead for good with 48 seconds left. "At the end of the shot clock," Walton said, "he wanted the ball in his hands." The Spartans had trailed by 13 in the first half before clawing their way back. "I'm really, really proud of the way our guys fought back when they could have died a few times," Izzo said.

The media narrative that Louisville, who had just destroyed Arizona 103–64, was the class of the region continued to swell. That meme was a difficult one to knock. The Cardinals had won the Big East regular season title, conference tournament title, and held the No. 1 overall seed in the NCAA Tournament. But by Sunday evening their emotions—and dignity—were in shreds. Unable to record a single fast break point off of a turnover or successfully adjust to the Spartans' relentless, physical defense, Louisville unraveled, losing 64–52 despite playing in front of a highly partisan Cardinals crowd in Indianapolis. "They were the better team," Louisville star Terrence Williams said. "They were quicker than us, their defense was more physical, and we couldn't turn them over like we wanted to." The Final Four trip would be Izzo's fifth and MSU's seventh all time. "Detroit, here we come," shouted Izzo afterward. "It's as big a win as our school has had because we're going to Detroit, and that's been a dream and a goal since they announced where the Final Four was in 2009."

Another Big East beast awaited them in the Final Four: 31–4 Connecticut and 7'3" center Hasheem Thabeet. But in the week preceding the Final Four one theme predominated: Economically-ravaged Detroit could put its despair aside for one weekend and rally around the home state Spartans. "It almost seems like divine order that Michigan State is playing in Detroit," former MSU star Greg Kelser said. "If Michigan State wins it all, my God, I don't know if it could get any more surreal than that."

Native Detroiters Summers and Lucas answered hundreds of questions about what a win would mean for the city. MSU shoot-arounds and practices drew unprecedentedly large and boisterous crowds, which cheered every layup and made jumper as if each one clinched a championship. The largest crowd in Final Four history turned out for the game. In front of 72,456 fans and many wearing Spartans colors, MSU blitzed the Huskies 82–73, stunning UConn with unexpected quickness, fastbreak proficiency, and tenacity—plus a few timely threes. Lucious nailed three threes in a span of 90 seconds in the first half. Morgan, wearing a mask to protect a broken nose, rechanneled his old self and scored 18. Lucas pitched in a game-high 21 with many coming on transition layups and slippery penetration. And Summers rattled home a huge fast break dunk. "I hope we were a ray of sunshine, a distraction for them," Izzo said.

Many started to believe that 31–6 MSU could complete the fairy tale run. But they would have to do it against 33–4 North Carolina, the same UNC team that hammered the Spartans by 30 in early December and had been the prohibitive championship favorite. The championship game, only the third in MSU history, proved a painful reminder that Hollywood endings are just make believe. Carolina strangled the Spartans, extinguishing almost immediately any MSU fantasies of winning. The Spartans fell behind 34–11 and never threatened, losing 89–72. "The best team won," said Izzo. "That's an easy statement to make."

16 Gang Green and the 1988 Rose Bowl

Emboldened by a new resolve, the Spartans entered 1987 burning with optimism. The core of the defense returned: Mark Nichols, Travis Davis, Tim Moore, Kurt Larson, Harlon Barnett, Todd Krumm, Ed Budde, Jim Szymanski, and Rob Stradley. So did safety John Miller and all-world linebacker Percy Snow, the two leaders of the defense. Driving them every day in practice was Nick Saban, the defensive coordinator who loved to be hated and could see potential disaster where others saw a job well done.

The offense didn't lack for talent. Running back Lorenzo White came back for his senior season after an injury-plagued junior year. The offensive line included preseason All-American Tony Mandarich and Pat Shurmur. The receiving corps had playmaker Andre Rison. Bobby McAllister and his bazooka arm replaced record-setting quarterback Dave Yarema. "I've never been on a team that won it all—not in college, not in high school, and not in youth football. Making it to the Rose Bowl as a senior will be one of the best things that has happened to me, one of the best Christmas presents I've had," Stradley said in August of 1987.

Christmas came early in the form of MSU's affirming 27–13 opening victory against USC, the first night game in MSU history.

The second largest crowd in Spartan Stadium history, 77,992, witnessed it. Then came two blowout losses and with them strong winds of doubt. Ninth-ranked Notre Dame whipped the Spartans 31–8. The Fighting Irish's Tim Brown returned two punts for touchdowns and just missed a third, launching his Heisman Trophy bid. Florida State rolled MSU the next week. Former legendary MSU coach Duffy Daugherty died in Santa Barbara, California, on the eve of the game. But Michigan State couldn't win one for Duffy, falling 31–3. An agitated Spartan Stadium crowd booed.

Big Ten play opened next. MSU, gripped by malaise, fell behind at Iowa 14–7 at the half. Perles "went bonkers" on his team. "Smoke was coming out my Lithuanian ears when we went into that goofy pink locker room at halftime," Perles wrote in his autobiography. "That was probably the most upset and most vocal I'd ever been in any halftime in my entire career…I just raved and ranted and tore into them." The tirade succeeded. MSU rallied for 12 unanswered points to win 19–14. Michigan State pounded the Hawkeyes with run after run for 236 yards. McAllister completed only two passes all game. The Spartans defense made its first statement of the year, holding Iowa to negative yards rushing. The season had reached its crossroads: Michigan.

The Spartan secondary picked off seven of Wolverine quarterback Demetrius Brown's passes. Safety John Miller accounted for four of them. White handled the scoring, picking up both Spartans touchdowns and rushing for 185 yards in MSU's 17–11 victory, the Spartans' first win against Michigan in East Lansing since 1969. UM kept passing, even though UM linemen pleaded with Schembechler to remove Brown. But Michigan had no other choice. The Spartans' defense throttled the Wolverines running game, limiting Michigan to 93 yards rushing. Perles had now won two of the last five games in the rivalry.

The Spartans stood 3–2 but without a loss in the Big Ten. The embarrassing defeats of September seemed forever ago especially after the Spartans abused Northwestern 38–0. The Wildcats struggled to top 100 total yards. Michigan State started 3–0 in the conference for the first time since 1966. Tantalizing thoughts of Pasadena, California started creeping in. *The Lansing State Journal* asked its readers to come up with a nickname for the burgeoning defense. Not happy with the entries, the paper settled on "Gang Green," a name that has stuck over time.

The pursuit continued in Illinois. In a hard, steady rain, the Spartans fell behind early, then rallied to tie the score, and had a chance to win it on a field goal, which John Langeloh missed. The 14–14 tie, however, didn't change the landscape of the Big Ten race. Beat Ohio State, and the Spartans still controlled their destiny.

On the first play from scrimmage in Columbus, Ohio, the Buckeyes scored on a 79-yard pass. Nichols quickly huddled the defense before the extra point and swore that the Buckeyes wouldn't score again. They didn't. Gang Green crushed the Buckeyes into tiny bits, holding them to 68 yards total, which allowed the Spartans to come back and win 13–7. McAllister rushed for 83 yards and passed for 61. The scent of roses grew stronger. Win their next two, and they'd be Rose Bowl bound.

The first win came easily, a 45–3 thrashing of Purdue. That set up an unlikely winner-take-all showdown in East Lansing against Indiana, having its own magical season under Bill Mallory. Behind White's 292 rushing yards on a staggering 56 carries, the Spartans ground down the Hoosiers 27–3. The defense excelled again, limiting the Hoosiers to 33 yards rushing. "The game against Indiana," White said, "I'm talking about that whole week, fans everywhere you go in the store, at the gas station, at the bus stop, leading up until that [game]…that was more exciting than actually the Rose Bowl itself." Fans stormed the field afterward, dreaming of mountains and beaches and Southern California on New Year's Day.

The emotionally spent Spartans still clobbered hapless Wisconsin 30–9 to complete an unbeaten conference season, the school's first since 1966. The defense, which allowed its first touchdown in more than 12 quarters, wrapped up a remarkable season. It held Big Ten opponents to 37.6 rushing and 184.5 total yards per game. The Spartans led the nation in rushing yards allowed per game and finished second in total yards a game. Safety-turned-cornerback Krumm, who made up for a lack of speed with immeasurable heart and instincts, set an MSU record with nine interceptions. Defensive tackle Travis Davis topped the Big Ten in sacks with 12. Five of them came in MSU's strangulation of Ohio State.

The Big Ten had lost 16 of the last 18 Rose Bowls, perhaps a reason why Bill Mallory had entered the Spartans locker room postgame to congratulate MSU and exhort them to "Go win the Rose Bowl."

Perles approached the Rose Bowl with a double mind-set. Win but enjoy the experience, something he learned from Daugherty. The Spartans didn't miss a thing: Disney, Universal Studios, Lawry's Prime Rib, *The Today Show*, a Bob Hope performance, constant pep rallies. Spartans fans seemed to emerge in every wave that washed ashore. Some estimated that more than 50,000 Green and White fans made the trip to Pasadena, California. One pep rally attracted more than 10,000 fans. The hoopla left old timers wondering if a repeat of the 1966 Rose Bowl loomed when the heavily favored Spartans lost in Pasadena to a team they had already beaten.

The oddsmakers, who made MSU a three-point underdog to USC, and others fretting about excessive distractions misread the tea leaves. After falling behind 3–0, the Spartans scored twice in the first half to take a 14–3 lead into the locker room. USC evened the score at 17, but after a helter-skelter pass from McAllister to

Rison for 36 yards, Langeloh nailed a field goal with 4:14 to break the tie. The Spartans iced the game and their third Rose Bowl championship when USC fumbled at the MSU 30-yard line in the closing moments. Percy Snow racked up 17 tackles to earn MVP honors. "The greatest day of my coaching career," Perles said, "one that I wanted to savor and cradle."

17 Izzo's First Final Four

The first of Izzo's Final Fours, in 1999, not only elicited giddiness, but it also provided validation for what appeared to be building in East Lansing especially after the 26–4 regular season. Riding an 18-game winning streak, which at the time was the longest in school history, the Spartans earned a No. 1 seed in the NCAA Tournament.

Only once before (in 1990) had MSU received a No. 1 seed. The entire 1990 tournament had been a nerve-racking experience. The Spartans barely eked out an overtime victory in the first round and endured a painful and controversial loss in the Sweet 16. That history and the long winning streak provided lots of grist for the superstitious minded in 1999. "The pressure started to get to us as far as how many games we'd won," said Tom Izzo in *Green Glory*. In the view of fans, the media, and the Spartans themselves, an early exit in the tournament would have undermined much of their regular season success.

The Spartans faced Mount St. Mary's, surprise winner of the Northeast Conference tournament, in the opener. Izzo's last college game at Northern Michigan was a disappointing loss that came against the Mountaineers and head coach Jim Phelan, and it appeared early in the game that Phelan just might oust Izzo again.

The 15–14 Mountaineers led for a good portion of the first seven minutes. The Spartans eventually gained control, ballooning their lead to 32 before winning 76–53. "We didn't come close to giving a championship effort tonight," Morris Peterson said. Izzo agreed. He had rattled the walls of the locker room at halftime, detonating a blistering critique.

Mississippi, the Spartans' opponent in the next round, pushed them to the bitter end, surprising MSU with its quickness and out-rebounding them in the first half. After Ole Miss' Jason Harrison, a 5'5" guard, hit a three, the Spartans trailed by three with just more than five minutes left in the game. "[Harrison's] three ignited us a little bit," Cleaves said, "because the guys realized that we had to step it up on defense." The Spartans would force a stop, score eight consecutive points, and win 74–66 to advance to the Sweet 16 for the second year in a row. Relieved that they had survived the first weekend, the Spartans geared up for Oklahoma. The Sweet 16 had been MSU's bugaboo ever since 1979. It had advanced three times to the second weekend only to lose in the first game. Moreover, some of Michigan State's most stomach-churning moments had occurred here. Program demons needed to be exorcised.

Coached by Heathcote protégé Kelvin Sampson, Oklahoma could have been MSU's doppelganger. Izzo and Sampson borrowed heavily from the system of the former Spartans coach. They emphasized rebounding and defense. They obsessed about hustle and intensity. The game unfolded as both coaches expected. They traded leads 13 times in the first half, but the Spartans headed to the locker room up 26–25 thanks to A.J. Granger's 10 points. Then at the 9:04 mark, two bodies collided. OU's Eduardo Najera, the 6'8" 235-pound heart-and-soul of the Sooners, set a blind pick on Cleaves. It was as if two armored trucks had slammed into each other head on. Cleaves crumbled to the floor. Najera lost consciousness and a torrent of blood. Play stopped for 10 minutes as the two warriors stumbled to the bench. They both returned a few minutes later—Najera with six stitches and Cleaves with a welt on his forehead. The collision was only the most violent of the game's numerous physical clashes. The Spartans held on for a 54–46 victory, overcoming history and the temporary loss of their leader.

Cleaves shot only 3-of-14, and the Sooners beat the Spartans on the boards. "It was an ugly game," Cleaves said. "It's been an ugly tournament for MSU, to tell you the truth. But the guys are coming through." MSU's defense overwhelmed Oklahoma, and the offense relied on the balanced scoring of Andre Hutson (12), Peterson (11), and Granger (10). "We found a way to win 31 other games that way, so why not the 32nd?" Izzo said.

Basketball royalty stood between the Spartans and MSU's third ever Final Four. The national media, attuned to watching Kentucky—the defending national champs—prevail against arrivistes, expected a Wildcat victory. Izzo, sensing his team might be anxious, mixed in a few changes to the pregame routine, highlighted by a team viewing of *Jerry Springer Unedited* the night before. The Spartans also attended a spontaneous MSU pep rally in their hotel and had a visit from Izzo's boyhood friend, Steve Mariucci, who tried to lighten the mood with humorous stories about his coaching debut.

None of it worked. Michigan State fell behind 17–4. The 30,000 Kentucky fans in attendance went from loud to insufferable. MSU looked dazed and outclassed. Then during a timeout, Antonio Smith upbraided his teammates for playing sloppily and timidly. Granger responded with a three-pointer out of the timeout, and the Spartans settled down. They closed within a point by half and then took the lead for good with 7:30 left after Cleaves grabbed a long rebound, looked up court quickly, and fired a bullet to Hutson for a layup. Peterson paced the Spartans with 19 points and 10 rebounds, earning him the region's Most Outstanding

Player. Magic Johnson watched in person. So did Jud and many other former Spartans. Izzo teared up as Smith cut down part of the net. "I took Antonio to Michigan State. Now he's taking me to the Final Four," Izzo said. Smith held Kentucky's best player and top scorer, Scott Padgett, to 11 points. "A lot of people didn't believe we could [win the game]," Cleaves said. "A lot of people laughed at us."

Duke, MSU's opponent in the Final Four, was no laughing matter. The Spartans knew that as well as anyone. The Blue Devils, who had lost only one game all season, had beaten them convincingly in November. "It will be tough to get ready to play them," Cleaves said. The Spartans owned something Duke did not, however—a 22-game winning streak.

Izzo later admitted that he made some rookie mistakes in preparing his team for the Final Four. The Spartans stayed too far from Tropicana Field, the site of the game. Furthermore Izzo didn't coordinate practice time and media sessions well. But in the end, it probably wouldn't have altered the outcome of the semifinal. Duke opened a 12-point lead that the Blue Devils took into the half. The Spartans shaved it to three points midway through the second half, but they wouldn't get any closer. Ice cold shooting (37 percent from the field) and subpar rebounding doomed them to a 68–62 loss. MSU stayed in the game because of its tenacious defense. "I really felt they were beatable," Peterson said. "We got away from the things that got us here. They played harder than we did in the first half." Coach Mike Krzyzewski flattered the Spartans after the game. "Michigan State is the No. 2 team in the country. They are not a bump in the road. For us to win a game like that, we are ultimately proud," he said. And Michigan State had proven to a skeptical college basketball world that it belonged.

18 Don Coleman

He weighed 175 pounds. He looked up at anyone taller than 6'0". Yet Don Coleman played in the trenches on both the offensive and defensive line. At that weight today, you'd be lucky to see the field—anywhere. But even in Coleman's day, few coaches trusted 175 pounders to hold their own among the big uglies.

Coleman didn't play football in high school until his senior year of 1947. His mother wouldn't allow it. But he made an immediate impression when he finally suited up, dominating more experienced and larger opponents and helping lead his team to a state championship. In his one and only year, he earned All-State honors. To Coleman's great surprise, major colleges noticed. Michigan and many other Big Ten schools came after him with gusto, but he chose MSC when Duffy Daugherty, the Spartans' lead recruiter and line coach, told Coleman that the Spartans didn't just want him—they needed him. That sealed it for Coleman.

After sitting out his first season in accordance with recent NCAA rules changes, Coleman once again made a quick impact. In his first game as a collegian—against rival Michigan, whom MSC hadn't beaten since 1937—he helped stymie the Wolverines running attack and opened just enough holes to keep MSC competitive, though the Spartans fell 7–3.

One play encapsulated his resounding contribution. Following a Spartans fumble, the Wolverines, trailing 3–0, took over deep in Spartans territory. After a couple of rushing plays yielded zilch, the Wolverines opted for a trick play. Michigan quarterback Bill Bartlett handed the ball to halfback Leo Koceski, who darted wide to his left as if he planned to run the ball. Meanwhile Bartlett slipped into the secondary and headed for the end zone. Lined up on the other side of the action, Coleman sensed what was happening and promptly sprinted to the other side of the field to arrive in the corner of the end zone just in time to break up the pass to Bartlett. It was a stunning display of athletic ability and veteran savvy—all from a kid playing his first college game.

Coleman's versatility served as a perfect match for Biggie Munn's new offense, the Michigan State Multiple. "On straight-ahead blocking or downfield blocking he did so many improbable things that we adopted plays never before attempted," Daugherty explained. In future recruiting Munn and Daugherty never stopped searching for tackles cut from the Coleman model, which they called a "Coleman Tackle." They even started, as Duffy noted, "experimenting with light, quick men in other line positions."

Preternaturally quick, deceptively strong, and blessed with superior football instincts, the under-sized Coleman could battle a couple of linemen and then race upfield, find another defender, and erase him from the play. "I didn't have the physical build or the stamina, so I learned to utilize my speed," Coleman said in a 2010 interview. "I could outrun most backs." In one celebrated game against Penn State in 1951, Coleman, who refused to wear the facemask protection made legal that year, recorded every Spartan tackle on kickoffs and punts despite having his nose torn open early in the game.

Coleman was an integral part of the first 15 games of the Spartans' 28-game winning streak, including the 1951 win against Michigan when he was credited with eight key blocks that led to big gainers or scores in the Spartans' 25–0 win. Linemen rarely are singled out for lofty individual awards, but Coleman earned team MVP honors during MSU's shared national championship season of 1951. He also became the Spartans' first unanimous All-American. After watching Coleman win nearly every collision and battle against his defensive line, Michigan head coach Bennie Oosterbaan said, "pound for pound the Big Ten has never seen a better tackle."

Coleman's jersey was retired by Munn shortly after his senior season, and he was elected into the College Football Hall of Fame in 1975. The Chicago Cardinals drafted him into the NFL, but he never played professionally. Coleman became a teacher in the Flint school district and later a principal before joining Daugherty's MSU staff in 1968. He was the first African American assistant at the school, a feat Coleman later acknowledged made him more proud than having his jersey retired. He only coached one year, resigning to take a position within university administration where he held a number of jobs until his retirement.

19 "Jumpin'" Johnny Green

"Jumpin'" Johnny Green came by his nickname honestly. Sure, legends abound about his jumping ability. He could grab a quarter off the top of the backboard. He once dunked the ball 10 times in 15 seconds. Without any warm-up or previous experience, he effortlessly cleared a six-foot hurdle during intramural track and field. Some of these feats were witnessed and recorded. Others were stories that circulated on campus, perhaps apocryphal but nonetheless believable, because Johnny Green, Michigan State's first genuine national basketball star, could elevate like no Spartan before him.

Green ended up at Michigan State serendipitously. In high school he never exceeded six feet and didn't play on the basketball team. It wasn't until he joined the military during the Korean War that he started to grow, eventually reaching 6'5". Stationed in Japan, Green started playing pickup basketball games and drew the attention of Tom Foster, the Atsugi Base basketball coach, who asked Green if he'd like to play on the team. Without hesitation

Green said yes. Raw but with obvious ability, Green also stirred the interest of Dick Evans, the Atsugi Base football coach who had played at MSC under Biggie Munn. In 1955 Green put on a scintillating dunking show for Evans, who promptly wrote Spartans basketball coach Forddy Anderson about the young soldier and the display of uncommon athletic ability he'd witnessed. Later that year Green visited MSC while on leave. Green asked Julius McCoy, a senior star on the Spartans basketball team, to introduce him to Anderson. The Spartans head coach told Green to come and see him when he got out of the service. When Green left the meeting, Anderson immediately moved on to something else, wiping the encounter from his mind.

Green, however, didn't forget the meeting. He showed up at MSU near the end of 1955 with the intention of enrolling at the school and trying out for the basketball team. Anderson tried to talk him out of it, running through a list of things Green needed to accomplish before he could enroll. Every time Anderson mentioned something on the list, Green nodded and said he'd already done it. He had filled out all the necessary forms, registered properly, and purchased all the books he needed. Anderson told him to go work out with the freshmen, "figuring that would be the end of it."

That was when his assistant Bob Stevens interrupted practice, the day after a bitter loss to Illinois no less, to insist that Anderson come immediately to the upper gym where Green was working out. Muttering to himself up the stairs, Anderson stopped as he reached the top and stared in disbelief when he saw Green leap up—as if he were a spinner dolphin entertaining a boatload of gaping tourists—and grab a net on a cable that hung down about 12 feet above the court. "Find out what this boy needs," Anderson barked. "And get it to him no matter what."

Green had to sit out the 1956 season and didn't become eligible until January of 1957. Unpolished and inexperienced the walk-on probably wouldn't have been much help before then.

But as Anderson watched Green improve each month, he became increasingly impatient for the day he could take the court. When Green finally gained eligibility, the Spartans turned a season that appeared to be in trouble into perhaps the greatest season in Spartan basketball history to date.

Green provided an intimidating presence in the post, swiping rebounds and blocking shots at rates never before seen at MSU. He was by no means the focal point of the offense, scoring most of his points on tip-ins and put-backs, though he and guard Jack Quiggle ran an alley-oop play, one of the first in the college game.

The Spartans won the Big Ten during Green's first season. They beat Notre Dame in the first round of the NCAA tournament, and Green had a monster game, scoring a career-high 20 points and grabbing 27 rebounds. MSU then upset Kentucky in the quarterfinals in Lexington, Kentucky. The upset put the Spartans in the semifinals where they faced No. 1 North Carolina. Green and the Spartans took the Tar Heels to three overtimes before losing. "Jumpin'" Johnny averaged 14.6 rebounds and impressed every opponent he faced. "He's 6'5" and jumps like he's 6'10"," said North Carolina's forward and All-American Lennie Rosenbluth in Jack Ebling's *Magic Moments*. "He has the quickest hands I've ever seen."

In his junior year, Green broke his own rebounding record by averaging 17.8 boards a game. He also the led the team in scoring at 18 points a game as he sharpened his post moves and continued to clean up around the boards. Green finished his career in 1959 with another Big Ten title and a career average of 16.4 rebounds. Only Ohio State's three-time All-American Jerry Lucas has a higher career rebounding average (17.2) in Big Ten history. Green also earned first team All-American honors and won the Big Ten MVP in his senior year. "He was worth at least 50 points a game to us," Anderson said.

Green was inducted as part of the first class into the MSU Athletics Hall of Fame and had his number retired. His 1,036 career rebounds still rank No. 3 on the all-time MSU list. Green went on to spend 14 seasons in the NBA. "The guy was beautiful," Boston Celtics guard Bob Cousy said. "What can I say about him? He was remarkable, fantastic, incredible."

Michigan State's First Final Four

The NCAA basketball tournament featured 23 teams in 1957. No one referred to it as "March Madness," and bracketology experts were decades away. The tournament to determine the national champion in college basketball included only conference champions and a small number of accomplished independent schools. Few expected the Spartans to be one of the "Last Four," as *Sports Illustrated* called the final four teams remaining in the 1957 tournament. Coach Forddy Anderson had forged two straight winning seasons at Michigan State, but Julius McCoy, the Spartans' leading scorer and top rebounder, graduated, and no surefire replacement existed on the roster.

The Spartans opened the season 4–3 and then lost four straight games, including a 70–69 gut punch from Michigan, a nonconference defeat at Notre Dame, and a butt-kicking at the hands of Ohio State. On the surface the Spartans looked done, standing 0–3 and three games out of the conference race. In addition to the hole they had dug themselves in the Big Ten, the Spartans struggled with a handful of issues off the court, most notably a tendency among a few players to show up late for practice.

A deeper look, however, would have revealed that things were on the cusp of changing, for the better. On the precipice of stardom, "Jumpin'" Johnny Green gained his eligibility in January.

He started snaring those rebounds that McCoy had pulled down the year before. Moreover, an extremely productive team meeting to address the discipline issues followed the loss at Ohio State. Tangible evidence of the team's changing fortunes arrived in Minneapolis. Playing without their leading scorer, guard Jack Quiggle, who was suspended for breaking team rules, the Spartans upset Minnesota with 25 points by forward Larry Hedden and 15 from Green.

The win galvanized the Spartans, who, along with a now contrite and re-committed Quiggle, stomped their way to nine more straight conference victories. Each game produced a different hero. Ohio State fell at Jenison Field House with Quiggle and Hedden pacing the way. Forward George Ferguson and guard Pat Wilson led all Spartans scorers in MSU's upset of Illinois, which ended the Illini's 21-game home win streak. Quiggle beat Purdue with a 25-footer for a win in West Lafayette, Indiana. And on it went, until the Spartans hosted Indiana with the Big Ten title on the line.

Jenison throbbed that night as an overcapacity crowd of more than 13,000 watched the Spartans confound the Hoosiers with their fast break en route to a 76–61 victory. Hedden and Quiggle led Michigan State in scoring, and Green owned the boards, pulling down 19. The fans swarmed the court as the buzzer sounded, hoisting the Spartans and Anderson on their shoulders and sweeping them toward the exit. "We didn't play our best," said IU coach Branch McCracken. "And that crowd may have had a lot to do with it."

The win put the Spartans into the NCAA Tournament for the first time where they met Notre Dame in Lexington, Kentucky. Sporting a 14–8 record and No. 11 national ranking, the Spartans edged the Irish 85–83. Next up in the quarterfinals: No. 3-ranked Kentucky…in Lexington.

Trailing 47–35 at halftime and with Green hampered by four fouls, MSU staged a stirring comeback, running the Wildcats off the floor. Green's replacement, Chuck Bencie, made sure the drop-off from Green was negligible, playing stellar defense, rebounding opportunistically, and scoring the go-ahead basket at the 10-minute mark with a layup. Munn called the 80–68 comeback win the greatest he'd ever seen in sports. "This team of mine is wonderfully unpredictable," Anderson said.

The 16–8 Spartans faced No.1 and 30–0 North Carolina in the semifinals in Kansas City, Missouri. The press dubbed Michigan State "the Cinderella team" of the event and expected their plucky run to end against the Tar Heels. But Michigan State, pugnacious and confident, matched the Tar Heels basket for basket. "The Spartans played so aggressively," said Carolina guard Bob Cunningham. The lead changed hands 31 times. It required three overtimes to settle. *Sports Illustrated* called it a "hugger-mugger of speed and suspense… that was as tough to follow onstage as Bob Hope."

Quiggle, who sprained his ankle in the opening minutes of the contest, hit a 40-footer at the end of regulation that the officials waved off because the buzzer sounded milliseconds before he released it. The Spartans protested. The officials ignored them. Leading by two with 11 seconds left at the end of the first overtime, Green had a chance to ice the game at the free throw line. But he missed the first shot. Carolina rebounded the ball, scooted down court quickly, and tied the game on a close-in jumper by Pete Brennan. Green tipped in a miss to send the game into a third overtime where David Scott and Hedden missed critical free throws that allowed UNC to finally prevail 74–70. Frank McGuire, Carolina's head coach, felt fortunate to win. Anderson expressed admiration for his team and said he refused to blame injury or missed free throws for the loss, saying the better team won.

MSU lost to San Francisco the next night in the consolation game without Quiggle, who would eventually earn first team

All-American honors, and then watched North Carolina slow down the pace against Wilt Chamberlain and Kansas to win the national championship in another triple-overtime game, concluding one of the greatest Final Fours in NCAA basketball tournament history.

21 Take a Photo With the Sparty Statue

Take a stroll around Michigan State's park-like campus and you will find no shortage of places to pause and admire what surrounds you: classic architecture, color-streaked beds of flowers, and a panoply of trees that shade the campus like a giant umbrella. For Spartans sports fans, however, one campus landmark is a must-see.

For more than seven decades, Sparty the statue stood tall near Demonstration Hall at the intersection of Red Cedar Road, Kalamazoo Street, and Chestnut Road. Hundreds of thousands of Spartans fans have stopped to salute Sparty and have their photo taken to memorialize the visit, making it the second most photographed site on campus. (Beaumont Tower is No. 1.)

A "symbol of the strength, honor, and courageousness that represents the spirit of MSU's students," according to former legendary MSU president John Hannah, Sparty was designed and produced by assistant art professor Leonard Jungwirth and dedicated on June 9, 1945. Made of terra cotta, the statue weighed 6,600 pounds and stretched to almost 10 feet. Years of exposure to the elements—not to mention mischief on the part of University of Michigan students—took its toll on the statue and forced its move to Spartan Stadium. In its place a bronze replica of Sparty was created in 2005 and stationed just north of Demonstration Hall Field.

The Spartan Marching Band has protected Sparty for years against vandalism during Michigan week when Sparty is most vulnerable to defacing attacks by paint or other means.

The Great 1965 Team

By the early to mid-1960s, Duffy Daugherty's Spartans teams had established a pattern of always being competitive but rarely great. Many fans around during the spectacular Munn era found the trend more and more exasperating. Everyone enjoyed Daugherty's dominance of Michigan. From 1956 to 1964 he went 6–1–2 against the Wolverines, a period unmatched by the Spartans in the history of the rivalry. Their unprecedented 7–1 record against Notre Dame during the same period pleased fans as well. But three losing seasons and zero Big Ten titles? That started to nag like a mole hole that keeps defacing your otherwise groomed lawn.

One of those losing seasons occurred in 1964, perhaps the strangest sub-.500 college team in history. How else to describe a losing team ranked at season's end in the top 20 UPI? But in 1964 Daugherty started to unveil the best young talent he had ever recruited. George Webster, Charlie Thornhill, Gene Washington, Clint Jones, Dick Kenney, Jess Phillips, Jeff Richardson, Bubba Smith, and others made their debut. Fans and the pollsters could see the makings of a championship squad. Thus the 1965 season opened with tremendous promise and hope.

A home game against UCLA kicked things off. Two recruits from Hawaii, Bob Apisa and Kenney, accounted for all the Spartans scoring in the 13–3 win against the Bruins. It marked the first of 10 stellar defensive efforts by Michigan State, who shut out two opponents and never allowed more than 13 points in a game.

Behind the efforts of rising juniors Webster, Thornhill, Smith, Phillips and seniors Harold Lucas, Ron Goovert, and Don Japinga, the Spartans crushed offenses. They shut out Penn State, so thoroughly dominating the Nittany Lions that Penn State head coach Rip Engle called the Spartans, "the best football team we ever played." They held Michigan to minus-51 yards rushing and Ohio State to minus-22 yards rushing and routed both. Iowa gained all of one yard of positive yardage while getting pasted 35–0. Notre Dame ran backward for minus-12 yards, threw positively for 24 yards, and finished with 12 precious total yards for the day, falling 12–3. Illinois, Purdue, and Indiana scraped together 35 points total.

Not since 1952 during the meat of Munn's greatest run had the Spartans finished undefeated and untied. Their 10–0 record earned them a trip to the Rose Bowl and a No. 1 ranking in the AP and UPI polls. The final AP poll would be released after the bowl games, however, MSU led the nation in rushing defense and finished among the nation's leaders in total offense, total defense, and points allowed. Quarterback Steve Juday and wide receiver Washington set many Michigan State passing records. Jones and Apisa made up an All-American backfield.

Few could remember such a dominant and intimidating defense with defensive backs the size of linebackers and linemen the height of basketball players. Everywhere on the field the Spartans featured speed, strength, agility, and just the right amount of attitude. "Our practices were very, very hard and very physical," Jones told espn.com. "We used to beat each other up. So when we got in the games, the games were kind of like a holiday. We didn't feel anybody could beat us."

Almost 15,000 fans made the trip to the Rose Bowl to watch what everyone assumed would be a Spartans coronation as undisputed national champion. Unrestrained accounts about the superior talent and massive size of the Spartans graced every paper from Los Angeles to New York. "Looks like a casting call for a remake of *King Kong*," wrote renowned syndicated columnist Jim Murray. The *Los Angeles Times* noted, "They're even bigger than I expected. If they changed uniforms their defensive line could pass for the Green Bay Packers."

Barely anyone paid attention to UCLA, which started to make Daugherty nervous and likely rankled a Bruins team that only lost to the Spartans by 10 in East Lansing. Listless and unfocused Spartans practices fouled Daugherty's mood further. So did an incident the day before the game. A reporter asked Juday a question about leadership. "Oh, this Spartan team didn't need any coaching or leadership," he said half-jokingly.

The Spartans started the game wobbly, turning the ball over twice in the first 20 minutes. The second one—a fumble by Japinga on a fair catch—led to a UCLA touchdown. Then the Bruins surprised Michigan State with an onside kick, which UCLA recovered at the MSU 42. The Rose Bowl shook, the Bruins celebrated, and the Spartans ego suffered a body blow. Daugherty had even tried to warn the kickoff team of the possibility of such a trick. Five plays later the Bruins plunged into the end zone from the 1-yard line, making it 14–0. The Bruins had deployed numerous unusual offensive sets keeping MSU off-balance, including a tackle-eligible play.

The Spartans defense eventually settled in. The Bruins only gained 65 rushing yards on 41 attempts, but MSU never fully recovered from the Bruins' early blitz. The offense managed two scores. A fake point-after try failed after the first touchdown. And following the Spartans' second touchdown late in the fourth quarter, the extra-point attempt failed again when UCLA quickly closed on Apisa, tackling him inches from the goal line. The 14–12 win was the Bruins' first Rose Bowl victory in five tries.

Daugherty called the defeat the most difficult of his career. He refused to subscribe to the popular theory that MSU suffered from overconfidence. Japinga, one of the Spartans co-captains, hedged.

"We let down subconsciously. We kept telling ourselves that UCLA was tough, but everywhere we went people said we would win easy by 30 points," he told a reporter after the game. "Deep inside I think that got to us."

The Streak

On October 7, 1950, the Spartans were upset by Maryland 34–7, a game that forever haunted Munn. But Don Coleman and his fellow junior teammates would not lose again during their Spartans career. Even more remarkably future All-Americans Don McAuliffe and Dick Tamburo and their fellow sophomores would not either. A 33–14 defeat of William & Mary erased the bitter taste of the Maryland "fiasco," as Munn called it, and launched a stretch of rapturous football for the Spartans that did not end until 1953.

Only six winning streaks since 1953 have been longer. During the streak the Spartans outscored their opponents 881–295, pitched seven shutouts, and scored more than 30 or more points 15 times. The streak began when MSC was an independent. It ended when MSC was a member of the Big Ten. It included 28 games. It included three wins against Notre Dame and two against Michigan. It included offensive fireworks and stirring defensive stands. A handful of close calls almost ended it. And two of the most memorable plays in Spartans history extended it.

In the opening game of 1951 against Oregon State, the Spartans had been held scoreless through most of the first half by a Beavers defense that had surrendered 38 to MSC the year before. The Spartans finally moved deep into OSU territory until stalling at the Beavers 1-yard line. Facing fourth down, Munn went for it. He dialed up a play that started in an unusual formation and proceeded in an unplanned way.

The snap bounced off the chest of halfback Dick Panin, who had received the ball directly from the center. But it hung in the air long enough for Al Dorow to step in and grab it. The Beavers had overreacted to the loose ball in the backfield, leaving McAuliffe a wide-open lane to the end zone. Dorow quickly scanned the field, spotted McAuliffe standing back at the 10-yard line, and lateralled the ball to McAuliffe for the score. Eight Spartans fumbles prevented them from adding to the lead, but the defense recorded its fourth straight shutout—thanks to three interceptions by newcomer Jim Ellis. "We have a long way to go," Munn groused after the game.

Two weeks later the Spartans traveled to Ohio State, and the Buckeyes led by first-year coach Woody Hayes threatened to end the streak while it was still growing whiskers. Trailing 20–10 with 10 minutes to go, the Spartans found the end zone on a 1-yard pass, cutting the deficit to three with 5:46 remaining. The Buckeyes attempted to kill the clock by keeping the ball on the ground, but with four minutes left, OSU fumbled. Defensive end Ed Luke fell on it. Munn sent in his small backfield, hoping they could bust a big play.

After one first down, the Spartans drive stalled at the Buckeye 28-yard line, causing Munn to face another fourth-down decision. With the streak hanging in the balance, he once again shunned the conservative choice, opting to go for it. Dorow lined up at quarterback, along with Evan Slonac and Tom Yewcic. The center snap went to Slonac. He immediately made a feint toward the line, drawing in the Buckeyes defense. Slonac then handed the ball to Dorow, whose back was to the Buckeyes. Yewcic, who had lined up to the right of the line of scrimmage, came sweeping by, and Dorow flipped the ball to him. Yewcic kept running toward the edge of the other side of the line. The Buckeyes chased him. Meanwhile, Dorow furtively slipped into the Buckeyes secondary, standing at the 11-yard line mostly uncovered. That's when Yewcic stopped, pivoted, and hurled a missile across the field in the direction of Dorow, who caught the pass, evaded a couple of Buckeye defenders, and scrambled into the end zone for the decisive score of the game.

Yewcic had never thrown a pass in college. A reporter asked him after the game if he had been nervous. "That was no time be nervous, was it?" he said. "We needed that one." The press immediately dubbed it "the Transcontinental Pass," one that has passed into Michigan State folklore. Munn called the whole game one of the greatest of all time.

Sandwiched between the two streak-preserving plays, the 1951 Paul Bunyan's Axe went to MSC in the most lopsided Spartans win to date. MSC held Michigan to negative total yards in the 25–0 whitewash, MSC's fifth straight shutout and second consecutive victory against the Wolverines. Michigan had made fun of MSC in its gameday program with a cartoon showing a coach talking to his players. "Well, you finally won one," the coach says. "Now, would you like to try for two?" But the Spartans enjoyed the last laugh.

The Streak also included the Spartans' first appearance on national television. In 1950 the NCAA *Game of the Week* debuted. Michigan State's tilt against Notre Dame on October 28, 1950 beamed into the 9 percent of households that owned televisions. Offense erupted in droves, providing the viewers with a thrilling back-and-forth contest. Bob Carey kicked a late field goal to give the Spartans a 36–33 victory. Munn declared the game the greatest offensive duel he'd ever seen. The next year the Spartans whipped Notre Dame 35–0. It was Frank Leahy's worst defeat ever at Notre Dame.

The Spartans closed out the 1950 season without losing. Then they went undefeated in 1951. Three poll services named them national champions, a first for MSC, though Tennessee was named national champion by the more respected AP and UPI polls. Munn always considered the 1951 team to be his best even if the general consensus outside of East Lansing differed.

The 1952 Spartans had fewer close calls and succeeded in winning the AP and UPI national championships with another 9–0 record, which ran the streak to 24 games. The streak finally came to an end during 1953, the Spartans' first season in the Big Ten. After reaching 28, Michigan State fell to Purdue 6–0. A clipping penalty that nullified a 95-yard kickoff return for a touchdown and five Purdue interceptions spelled Michigan State's doom.

Munn's First Team All-Americans

Lynn Chandnois (1949)

Recruited by Charlie Bachman, Chandnois was the first Spartans All-American of Biggie Munn's magical reign. Perhaps one of his many nicknames—"60 Minutes"—best describes his greatest quality as a football player. An adept two-way player, Chandnois still holds numerous Spartans records. His 20 interceptions and 410 yards of interception return yardage remain the highest marks in MSU history. He ranks second in school history in yards per carry (6.55). His 90-yard run against Arizona in his final collegiate game is the longest run from scrimmage in Spartans history. Jack Breslin called him "one of Michigan State's all-time great All-Americans...perhaps its greatest." Born in the Upper Peninsula but raised in Flint, Chandnois played seven years in the NFL for the Pittsburgh Steelers. He averaged 29.6 yards on kickoff returns, the second highest average in NFL history.

Donald Mason (1949) and Ed Bagdon (1949)

Members of Duffy's Toughies, Mason and Bagdon formed a dynamic offensive tandem that Fritz Crisler called "the best pair of guards ever to play in Michigan Stadium." Both were slightly undersized for the position, but they played nearly every game and were key components of Munn's Michigan State Multiple offense. Bagdon, who developed a blocking technique that allowed him to wipe out a defender without losing his feet, earned the Outland Trophy as the nation's best interior lineman.

Dorne Dibble (1950)

Both a receiver and a defensive end, Dibble was named by *Look* magazine as a first team All-American on defense. The recognition probably stemmed from the stout effort of the Spartans' 1950 defense led by Dibble, which held opponents to just 97 yards rushing a game. Born in Adrian, Michigan, Dibble also caught 16 passes for 363 yards in his career. He was drafted by the Detroit Lions, who made him a full-time receiver. He set Lions records for rookie touchdowns receptions and receiving yards.

Sonny Grandelius (1950)

Grandelius from Muskegon, Michigan, became just the 17th back in college football history and first ever at Michigan State to reach the 1,000-yard barrier when he rushed for 1,023 yards on 163 carries in 1950. His 184 yards against Oregon State that year set a single-game MSC rushing yards record that stood until 1962, and his 6.1 yards per carry ranks fourth highest in Spartans history. Grandelius was a hard yet fluid runner who could pick up tough critical yards. "He played with a high motor and loved to run over people," teammate Don McAuliffe said. "Sonny was the ultimate team player." Grandelius later became an assistant for Munn and Daugherty, a head coach at University of Colorado, and an assistant in the NFL.

Robert Carey (1951)

Bob Carey did it all for Munn and for a few other coaches at Michigan State. Using his 6'5" frame, Carey caught passes at a record clip and handled field goals and kickoffs. His 65 career receptions, 1,074 career reception yards, and 14 career touchdown receptions were all Michigan State records at the time. A member of the 1945 Charlevoix, Michigan, high school football team that went undefeated and held teams scoreless, Carey earned nine letters at Michigan State—three in football, three in basketball, and three in track and field. He played four seasons in the NFL for the Chicago Bears and Los Angeles Rams.

Albert Dorow (1951)

As a two-year starter at quarterback, Dorow was 17–1. Things occasionally took a strange turn when he lined up behind center, but no one could be upset with the results. Dorow played football as if he were still 10 years old and horsing around with his brothers. He could be daring, occasionally reckless, and always interesting. He was instrumental in two pivotal plays—one against Oregon State and one against Ohio State—that kept the Spartans' 28-game winning streak alive. In 1951 he threw for 842 yards, a school record at the time, and finished his career as the Spartans leader in pass completions (125), attempts (259), yardage (1,875), and touchdown passes (19). Born in Imlay City, Michigan, Dorow spent seven years in pro football, making one Pro Bowl and one AFL All-Star Game appearance. "Al was definitely at his best when the chips were down," Munn said. "He was more than great when the team needed a lift."

James Ellis (1951, 1952)

The first underclassman to earn first team All-American honors and the first to earn the honor in consecutive years, Ellis roared onto the college football scene by intercepting three passes and returning three punts for 87 yards in his first college game, a win against

Oregon State. His exceptional speed and sure-handed tackling ability allowed him to blanket fast receivers as a defensive back, and his elusive running style made him a dangerous return man on punts and kickoffs. The Saginaw, Michigan, native had punt returns for touchdowns of 54 yards, 57 yards, 59 yards, and his longest, 79 yards against Michigan.

Frank Kush (1952)

One of Munn's many hard-nosed recruits from Pennsylvania coal country, Kush embodied the tough-mindedness of the Keystone state. He began his career as an offensive lineman but moved to middle guard on defense two games into the 1952 season. He blossomed there, becoming a disruptive force in the backfield. An integral part of a defense that held every opponent to 14 points or fewer a game in 1952, Kush went on to coach for Arizona State.

Donald McAuliffe (1952)

McAuliffe finished eighth in the Heisman race in 1952 after rushing for 531 yards on 5.4 a carry. Prematurely balding, he didn't run with the ball so much as bounce along feverishly with it—a style that earned him the nickname "Hopalong." Part of Munn's big back brigade, McAuliffe also won the Walter Camp Award, a player of the year award voted on by coaches and sports information directors. A collegiate boxer as well, McAuliffe finished his career with 1,180 yards rushing and 20 touchdowns, the second highest total in MSC history at the time.

Richard Tamburo (1952)

Tamburo added middle linebacker duties after the first two games of the 1952 season when Oregon State and Michigan found multiple soft spots in the Spartans' defense. The move helped the Spartans win the national championship. A punishing blocker and stalwart defender, Tamburo was named MVP of the Spartans that year. Born in New Kensington, Pennsylvania, he played a brief time in the NFL and then became a college athletic director at Arizona State, Texas Tech, and Missouri.

Tom Yewcic (1952)

Yewcic succeeded Dorow as the Spartans starting quarterback in 1952 and immediately led the Spartans to a come-from-behind win in the season opener against Michigan. He threw for 171 yards on seven completions to spark the victory. Yewcic was no stranger to high drama. His first collegiate pass went for a touchdown, rallying the Spartans past Ohio State to preserve an undefeated season and a long winning streak. A Pennsylvania kid, Yewcic threw for 941 yards in 1952, then a school record. He was also a star on the MSC baseball team, earning the MVP of the 1954 College World Series. He signed with the Detroit Tigers and played in one game with the Tigers before eventually settling in with the Boston Patriots for six seasons.

Donald Dohoney (1953)

An Ann Arbor native rescued from the dark side, Dohoney, a defensive end, was captain of the Spartans first team to compete in the Big Ten and led a nasty defense that held five of its nine opponents under 10 points. He had a reputation for being particularly ornery on the field but exceedingly nice off it in the George Webster mold. He even eschewed a facemask. When the Spartans bottled up Minnesota star Paul Giel in their 21–0 victory against the Gophers in 1953, Dohoney, the leader of the defense and an immovable object at end, received much of the credit. His grandson, Eric Gordon, also starred at MSU.

LeRoy Bolden (1953)

A key member of Munn's small back unit called "the Pony Backfield," Bolden rushed for 691 yards in 1953, played defensive back, and returned punts. He had first-class speed and ran with devastating abandon as if dodging cars on a fast-moving highway. Daugherty called him his best all-around player, blocker, and runner. Bolden, a Flint high school football legend, stood No. 2 all time in total touchdowns (26) and points (165) when he finished his Spartans career. He played two years in the NFL.

Captain Kirk

Kirk Cousins finished his career with nearly every Spartans passing record. While he was under center, Michigan State won 27 games, something no other Spartans quarterback had ever accomplished. And he became one of the greatest leaders in MSU sports history.

Cousins, who grew up in a Chicago suburb before moving to Holland, Michigan, for high school, had always wanted to go to Iowa, the school for which his grandfather played. But a scholarship offer never came from the Hawkeyes. Cousins put up pretty good numbers in high school, but a broken ankle in his junior year abraded his performance, and offers from major colleges never flooded in.

The Spartans coaching staff under John L. Smith had Cousins on their radar but always seemed to be searching for someone else. When Keith Nichol, a highly ranked local quarterback, committed to Michigan State, the Spartans' interest in Cousins evaporated. By the end of Cousins' senior year in high school, his best option appeared to be offers from Toledo and Western Michigan of the Mid-American Conference. Then MSU canned John L. Smith, Keith Nichol reneged on his verbal commitment, and Mark Dantonio became the Spartans head coach. Dantonio picked up a commitment from another highly touted quarterback, Nick Foles from Texas, shortly thereafter. Dantonio worried that Cousins lacked Big Ten athletic ability. But Cousins didn't quit, exhibiting a persistence that has served him well throughout his life. He guile-fully managed to get another high school tape in front of Dantonio. Something stirred Dantonio this time, and he offered Cousins a scholarship.

Once on the Michigan State campus, Cousins knocked down every obstacle in his way. He eventually beat out Foles. When Nichol transferred back to MSU, he beat him out for the starter's job as well. "He's consistently been overlooked and underesti-mated," his father, Don Cousins, told *The New York Times*. "He's seldom the biggest, fastest, or strongest, but in the end he's had a lot of success." To motivate himself during the competition with Foles and then Nichol, Cousins posted negative articles written about him on his bulletin board at home. His MSU teammates held few negative opinions of him. In fact before Cousins even won the quarterback battle with Nichol in his sophomore year, his teammates had made him captain. Cousins held that title for two more years, making him the first Spartan in more than 60 years to be a three-time captain. (Bob McCurry is the other.)

After beating out Foles, he served as Brian Hoyer's backup in 2008. Pressed into service against Ohio State when Hoyer suffered an injury, Cousins offered a glimpse of his skills by going 18-of-25 for 161 yards in a loss. In his sophomore year, the Spartans played inconsistently, perhaps hurt by the two-quarterback system Dantonio employed for the first part of the year. Cousins earned the starters job outright over Nichol by mid-season, and the Spartans won five of their last eight. Cousins' best game statistically may have been his biggest heartbreak, a 33–30 defeat to Notre Dame in which he threw for 302 yards. His inter-ception at the Notre Dame goal line on an ill-advised pass in the final seconds of the game ended the Spartans comeback chances and served as additional motivation going forward. Cousins demonstrated Zen-like poise and good judgment at crunch time during the rest of his career.

That ability in the clutch helped the Spartans win 22 of 25 games during his junior and senior seasons. Eight times Cousins led the Spartans to victory with at least one touchdown pass late in a game that broke a tie or overcame a deficit. The most celebrated pass took down undefeated Wisconsin on the game's final play. Another clutch performance occurred in the Outback Bowl when

Kirk Cousins readies to pass during a 2010 victory against Wisconsin, one of 22 games the quarterback won during his junior and senior years.

Cousins moved the Spartans 85 yards in 10 plays with 1:55 remaining and no timeouts on six passes to five different receivers. The drive sent the game against Georgia to overtime, and the Spartans prevailed.

Cousins ended his Spartan career with 723 completions, 9,131 yards, 66 touchdowns, and 26 200-yard passing games—every single one a Spartans career record. "[Cousins] is a very confident young man," Dantonio said. "He's a tremendous leader on the field… Physically I think he's a gifted athlete, he's got a great arm, all those different type of things. But I think playing quarterback a lot of times is more than just throwing the football. It comes down to the ability to lead and being able to get in and out of the right call and the decision-making process."

He will rightfully be remembered for his heroics on the field. What he did off of it, however, deserves as much praise. He excelled in the classroom, earning Academic All-Big Ten honors four times with a 3.68 grade point average. He volunteered for numerous charitable causes throughout the Lansing area. Before the 2012 Big Ten news media luncheon, he memorably enraptured the gathered reporters with a speech about the privilege of being a collegiate athlete, saying forcefully, "privilege should never lead to entitlement."

John Hannah: The Leonidas of Michigan State

"Michigan State is a diamond in the rough; all it needs is a football victory over Michigan—no, two victories—so people will not say it was a fluke, and the college will become a great educational institution," said John Hannah, supposedly, to Spartans head football coach Charlie Bachman in the 1930s. At the time Hannah was the secretary to the board of agriculture of MSC. He lived next door to Bachman and would often share his vision for the school with the coach, who had Notre Dame roots and also believed in the efficacy of sports as a vehicle to promote the overall growth and prestige of a college.

Hannah, a MAC agricultural graduate, gave up studying law at the University of Michigan to return to MSC in the 1930s, succumbing to the entreaties of Michigan State president Robert Shaw. In 1941 Hannah became MSC's president after overseeing an expansion of the school's boundaries and numerous construction projects on campus.

Hannah's four-decade contributions to Michigan State are innumerable and unmatched. He secured higher faculty salaries and pensions for all employees and successfully lobbied the Michigan legislature for a more equitable distribution of higher-education funds. Upon his promotion to the position of president, MSC had 6,000 students and fewer than 50 academic departments. When he retired in 1969, the college had become a university, enrolled more than 40,000 students, and offered 250 disciplines.

Hannah considered the expansion and improvement of the school's athletic programs an essential component of his efforts to build MSC into a nationally respected university. He did not believe a university's academic reputation would be negatively affected by its athletics. Sports, he argued, simply unified the community and helped reinforce loyalty to the institution among students, faculty, and other advocates. It also represented democracy in its purest form.

To this end Hannah worked tirelessly to upgrade Spartan sports, paying particular attention to football, the most popular sport on campus. He devoted considerable resources to football's infrastructure, pouring money into a new stadium and repeated renovations. Hannah attended every game and assisted in recruiting, approaching the task with characteristic vigor. He also secured funding for a new basketball facility (Jenison Field House), a new track field, and a new baseball practice field.

When local businessman and MAC graduate Fred Jenison died and bequeathed a half million dollars to the college in the 1930s, MSC appointed Hannah as administrator of the money. He used it to establish a fund for students who couldn't afford the school's tuition. Some of the money, however, went to athletes, who had to maintain a C average. Hannah believed granting a portion of these funds to athletes brought more openness to the issue of athletes and inducements. He contended that other schools created hidden athletic funds that the schools couldn't control.

The Jenison Fund became an issue when the Spartans petitioned to join the Big Ten. Hannah and athletic director Ralph Young spent years romancing Big Ten officials in an attempt to gain admission to the conference. With the Jenison Fund representing one of the last sticking points, Hannah agreed to disband it. Michigan State gained its hard fought entrance into the Big Ten in 1949, the capstone of Hannah's contributions to Michigan State athletics. "John Hannah dramatically raised the reputation and profile of our university," said then-MSU President Peter McPherson in 2004. "But just as importantly he raised our expectations and aspirations."

The 2001 Final Four

After three consecutive Big Ten titles, two straight Final Four appearances, and one national championship, Michigan State faced the challenge of maintaining elite-level success without its heart and souls—Mateen Cleaves, Morris Peterson, and A.J. Granger.

Before Spartans fans could begin to contemplate how Tom Izzo would replace the departed seniors, they had to endure a threat from an unexpected source: the NBA. The Atlanta Hawks aggressively pursued Izzo for their head coaching position, offering a salary almost triple what he made at MSU. Sorely tempted, Izzo turned down the offer after—among other things—Cleaves counseled him to "listen to what your heart tells you." During a press conference, Izzo announced his intention to remain at MSU. "We have a chance to win more championships here," he said. "I'd like to take a shot at it."

That drama behind them, the Spartans brought in highly ranked recruits Marcus Taylor and Zach Randolph. The 6'3" Taylor played at Lansing Waverly where he flashed a sweet shooting stroke and smooth overall game from the guard position. The solid but awkwardly built 6'9" Randolph from Indiana had a knack for rebounding and sophisticated post moves rarely found in high school seniors. Both came off the bench for most of the year. They joined returning seniors and starters Charlie Bell and Andre Hutson. Sophomore Jason Richardson, a freakozoid athlete who logged hundreds of hours improving his outside shot over the summer, held down the small forward position, and Aloysius Anagonye, a menacing defensive presence, moved into the post. The last spot in the starting lineup went to senior David Thomas, a combo guard/small forward with long arms and a wiry frame. From top to bottom, the roster featured length at every position. The two concerns rested on Bell's ability to run the point and perimeter shooting.

Ranked No. 3 in the preseason AP poll, the Spartans waltzed through the non-conference portion of the schedule 11–0, the best start in MSU history. Michigan State had won 22 games in a row, stretching back to the previous season. November and December included thumpings of sixth-ranked North Carolina, Florida, and Seton Hall and a one-point squeaker at home against Kentucky.

Florida arrived in East Lansing looking to settle a score from the national championship the year before. The Breslin Center pulsed especially because of the return of Teddy Dupay, the Florida guard who had undercut Cleaves in the championship game. "It's time Dupay the price," read one sign in the Izzone.

Izzo fretted about the defensive effort at times. "There is zero comparison defensively between this year and last year's team," said Izzo after a 103–71 victory against Loyola (Illinois). "Don't even put us in the same league." Many fans, however, started to wonder if the 2001 edition of the Spartans had the potential to be better than the previous year's champions. Bell had proven he could run the point adeptly, and Richardson's surprising marksmanship from the perimeter eased concerns about the outside shooting. And they had two McDonald's All-Americans coming off the bench. Everything appeared to be gelling. "It's kind of scary how good we could actually be when we're all on the same page," Thomas said.

Entering Big Ten play, the Spartans held the top ranking in the AP poll for the first time in 22 years. They were threatening a host of Big Ten records, including most overall and conference wins in a four-year period. Reality arrived in Bloomington, Indiana, where the Hoosiers beat the Spartans on a three-point shot at the buzzer by Kirk Haston. Indiana, which MSU had supplanted as the bully of the conference, went bonkers. IU coach Mike Davis dropped to his knees as Haston's shot went through. Hoosiers fans stormed the court. The hysteria surrounding the Spartans served as a testament to MSU's newfound status. Indiana rushing the court after a victory over Michigan State? Ten years ago that idea would have been roundly mocked in every corner of the Midwest.

Just as one would expect from the new king of the Big Ten hardwood, MSU rallied to win a share of the conference crown with a 13–3 record. MSU became only the third Big Ten school to win at least four consecutive titles. Bell and Hutson set a new mark for conference victories by a senior class. "This is definitely the sweetest one," Huston said. "We heard a lot of criticism this year. And this is the one I'll cherish."

At 24–4 the Spartans earned a No. 1 seed in the NCAA Tournament, which they entered attempting to repeat as national champions. The Spartans rolled to the regional finals. They dispatched Alabama State, Fresno State, and mid-major darling Gonzaga to advance to the Elite Eight. "I don't want to like my team too much," said Izzo after MSU beat Jerry Tarkanian's Fresno State Bulldogs. "But I'm damn proud of this team. All the spokes came together today." The Spartans used a 28–6 blitz in the second half against Gonzaga to take the bite out of the Bulldogs, who succumbed to the waves of athletic and physical athletes Izzo kept sending in. Four Spartans scored in double figures (Richardson, Hutson, Bell, and Randolph), MSU owned a rebound margin of 20, and Bell forced All-American guard Dan Dickau into a subpar shooting day.

The No. 2 through 6 seeds had all lost in MSU's South Region, blowing the path to the Final Four wide open. The South hadn't seen such mayhem since General Sherman. Temple benefited from the carnage. John Chaney, the Owls' wizened head coach, was a popular figure in college basketball. He had made Temple into a national force, employing a funky matchup zone defense that had given MSU trouble two years ago. Despite his success, he had never coached the Owls to a Final Four. At 69 years old, he became the sentimental favorite. MSU didn't play along. Thomas lit up the Owls for a career-high 19 points, and the Spartans never trailed. "When the season started, I thought we could be a good team, maybe a very good team," Izzo said, "but I am not going to lie to you and tell you I thought we definitely could be back to the NCAA Final Four."

The Spartans' season ended with a thud in the semifinals of the Final Four. After leading by two at the half, Arizona harassed the Spartans into a torrent of turnovers that led to a 21–3 run and a

80–61 defeat of MSU. "This might be the worst game we've played in four years," said a distressed Izzo. The sting of failing to repeat as national champs soon faded. It was replaced by the pride of what had been achieved over the four years by Bell and Hutson and the sense that Izzo's Spartans would be a force for years to come.

Land of Opportunity

In 1913 college football at big-time schools was almost completely devoid of African Americans. When Gideon Smith, a young black player from Lansing, turned up for a tryout at Michigan Agricultural College, the coaches told him to go home. Undeterred, he kept coming back until Aggies head coach John Macklin finally relented and gave him a chance. He became the school's first black student-athlete and reportedly only the third in all of major college football at that time.

Macklin had no reason to regret his decision. Through perseverance and forbearance, Smith, a 180-pound tackle who endured racial catcalls and slurs from his opponents, eventually earned a spot on the All-Star teams of the *Chicago Daily News* and *Collier's* magazine. After college he played professionally, becoming one of the first black players to earn money at the sport. Harry Graves, a black man from Kansas, joined the Aggies and threw a touchdown pass to lead MAC to a win against Notre Dame in 1918.

Over the next few decades, the Spartans welcomed a handful of other black players. Before 1940 eight African Americans had suited up for the Spartans, a figure better than most other major college football programs. The 1934 Spartans squad, which finished 8–1, relied heavily on fullback Jim McCrary, one of three blacks on the team. No other major college team on record had more than one black at the time.

Jackie Robinson integrated baseball in 1947. Before that he had played football at UCLA. Old prejudices about blacks and major sports started to slowly recede after WWII, though college football remained predominately white. Schools in the South steadfastly refused to allow blacks to play. With the full support of president John Hannah, Biggie Munn started actively recruiting blacks to play at MSC. Looking to gain every advantage, Munn developed a strong recruiting base among blacks in the North and the South.

One of his first big gets was Don Coleman from Flint. "We changed the rules, changed the game, and changed some attitudes," Coleman said. He became MSC's first black All-American. Another black recruit, Willie Thrower, played quarterback at Michigan State and helped the school win its first national championship in 1952. He later went on to play quarterback for the Chicago Bears where he became the first black quarterback in the NFL. Hank Bullough played at MSC from 1952 to 1954. "No school was more receptive to black players at that time than Michigan State," Bullough told the *Detroit Free Press*. "[The other Big Ten teams] probably averaged four or five blacks on the entire team. We'd have five or six starting alone."

Munn dipped his toe in these roiling waters. His successor, Duffy Daugherty, bathed in them. He went beyond just recruiting high school kids to helping black coaches throughout the South sharpen their coaching knowledge and skills. When Daugherty become head coach at Michigan State, black coaches were prohibited from attending national coaching conventions and seminars. In response Daugherty, aided by his winning personality and hoping to build lasting relationships and good will, established coaching clinics run by his assistants for black coaches throughout the South. Occasionally the instruction materials offered at the seminars went beyond football. Some coaches brought home class-room books and supplies, which could be sorely lacking at their underfunded schools.

These community outreach efforts resulted in a pipeline to college football talent nearly unmatched. Future All-American George "Bubba" Smith, who grew up in Beaumont, Texas, came to Michigan State because his father had attended a coaching seminar and left with school supplies. George Webster grew up only 15 miles from Clemson, South Carolina, but he couldn't play there because of his skin color. He went to Michigan State instead. As did dozens of other young man from the South, including Charlie Thornhill, Gene Washington, Jess Phillips, and Jimmy Raye.

By the early 1960s, Daugherty had made Michigan State a top destination for the best black talent in the country. The defense from the feared 1966 Spartans, one of the greatest in college foot-ball history, started six blacks. Four started on offense. Few schools anywhere even had more than a half dozen blacks on the entire roster. As of the mid-1960s, the South still refused to allow blacks to play on their college teams. "All of the states where we were from, they would not take black athletes," Washington told espn. com. "We bonded at Michigan State because we all had similar stories. We could make a contribution. That was very important to us. We didn't talk about that all the time, but we knew we had something to prove, and this is our opportunity."

Creating that pipeline to the South brought MSU many great players. Cynics might say Daugherty acted out of nothing but self-interest. Better players meant more winning. But those who knew Daugherty vehemently disagree. Bullough said that Daugherty "was a very compassionate man who saw something that was wrong. A door was closed to many people, and he helped open it." Two facts support the less cynical view. Daugherty did not allow his white seniors to participate in the Senior Bowl until it allowed blacks to play in the game. He also refused to schedule schools that abided by the segregationist rules in place in the South until 1967.

Through its history Michigan State has tended to be ahead of the rest in its racial integration. Many believe the South eventually integrated in part because of what was happening in East Lansing. Bear Bryant, who had steered a few blacks to Michigan State, and other Southern coaches feared they were falling too far behind by limiting their recruiting to white players only.

29 The Magical New Era

"It's a dream come true," Earvin "Magic" Johnson told TV color man Billy Packer a day before the Spartans played upstart Indiana State for the 1979 NCAA National Championship.

The origins of this fantasy started in April of 1977 when Magic made his commitment to Michigan State. Another commitment a few days earlier barely caused a ripple—relative to Johnson's nationally ballyhooed announcement—but remained just as essential. Jay Vincent, Magic's prep rival from Lansing Eastern High School, agreed to join Greg Kelser, Ron Charles, Terry Donnelly, and Mike Brkovich at Michigan State. They would form the core of the national championship team.

Along with senior guard and outside shooting threat Bob Chapman, they started drawing attention to East Lansing in the winter of 1977. Under second-year head coach Jud Heathcote, the Spartans ran away from the Big Ten in 1978, winning the conference by three games and taking eventual national champion Kentucky to the wire in the Elite Eight. The 25–5 record represented the most wins in school history.

Entering the season, optimism among Spartans fans spread as widely as Johnson's broad smile. Demand for tickets soared, forcing the school to implement a ticket lottery for the students, an unprecedented but necessary decision given the seating constraints of cozy Jenison Field House. Even an exhibition game against the University of Windsor was played before a standing room-only crowd. Despite all the hype, no one knew for sure just how good Magic or the team would be. "When practice began, it was really hard to gauge how good we were going to be and how much fun we were going to have because practice was so darn structured. We didn't get a lot of action up and down the court," wrote Kelser in *Tales from Michigan State Basketball.* "We knew we were going to be a running team—flying through the open court and catching passes from Earvin, but we couldn't tell how effective we would be because Coach was putting in a system."

With everyone but Chapman returning, the Spartans were pegged as one of the preseason favorites to win the national championship in 1979. Magic appeared on the cover of *Sports Illustrated* dressed in a tuxedo. "Super Sophs" was the headline, with the tag, "Michigan State's Classy Earvin Johnson." The magazine put the Spartans at No. 4 in its preseason ranking. "Kelser and Johnson needn't get a whole lot better," stated *Sports Illustrated.* "They were one-two in both scoring and rebounding and a dazzling combo on the fast break. The Spartans' break should be even more effective because of improved rebounding." The magazine's central concern about the Spartans heading into the season: outside shooting, due to the graduation of Chapman.

After defeating Brazil during a preseason trip to South America, a true early-season test of the national plaudits would occur when the Spartans traveled to Chapel Hill, North Carolina, to face No. 13-ranked North Carolina. Magic viewed the trip as an opportunity "for national attention, prestige, and pride." Despite trailing most of the game, Michigan State turned the screws defensively and pulled close late. With 10 seconds remaining, they gained possession of the ball down only a point. At the buzzer Vincent had a clean look from eight feet. He missed. "An eight-footer for Jay is something that he'll hit 60 percent of the time," Heathcote said. "This was one of the 40."

The Spartans didn't overreact to a loss to a powerhouse program. But a lackluster win against Cincinnati in the Pontiac Silverdome aroused a few concerns. MSU trailed at the half before rallying to win by 11. "We just don't have the spirit and enthusiasm we had last season," Johnson lamented. The players started complaining to each other about Heathcote's tight leash, his tendency to take the air out of the ball, and his verbal missiles.

The 4–1 Spartans flew to Portland, Oregon, to compete in the Far West Classic, which they won in comfortable fashion, downing Washington State, Oregon State, and Big Ten brethren Indiana. Despite leading by 11 points at the half against the Hoosiers, Heathcote—unhappy that Indiana's Mike Woodson had 17 points—tore into his team, directing much of his vituperation at Johnson. Magic started to argue back. Heathcote cut him off, unleashing an expletive-filled tirade about nobody being bigger than the program.

When the Spartans finally returned home, they arrived holding something no other Michigan State basketball team had ever grasped: the No. 1 ranking in the AP poll. The teams ranked ahead of Michigan State—Duke, Notre Dame, and UCLA—all lost while the Spartans swept to the Far West Classic championship.

The Spartans began defense of their Big Ten title and No. 1 ranking in an odd state. Heathcote worried privately about the team despite its 7–1 record. "The intensity just wasn't there," wrote Heathcote in *Jud*. "And it wasn't one game. It was that way almost every practice." To compound matters the Big Ten sparkled with supreme talent and highly competitive teams. Excluding Michigan State the league included 11 future NBA first-round picks: Kevin

McHale and Trent Tucker (Minnesota), Ronnie Lester (Iowa), Mike Woodson and Ray Tolbert (Indiana), Joe Barry Carroll (Purdue), Wes Matthews (Wisconsin), Mike McGee and Phil Hubbard (Michigan), and Herb Williams and Kelvin Ransey (Ohio State). Billy Packer suggested the Big Ten in 1979 had been the best conference in the history of college basketball.

Michigan State opened the Big Ten season at home with a rout of Wisconsin. Johnson posted his second consecutive triple double. A sloppy 69–62 home win against Minnesota followed, and then the wheels came off when Eddie Johnson buried a last-second jumper at Illinois to drop MSU off from the top spot in the polls. The 57–55 win moved the Illini to No. 1 in the polls the next week. Two days later Purdue's Arnette Hallman grabbed a loose ball, turned around frantically, and launched a 22-footer at the buzzer that hit nothing but net to give the Boilermakers a 52–50 victory.

An unlikely blowout of Indiana preceded an overtime win against Iowa that the Spartans probably should have lost in regulation. Brkovich hit two foul shots with no time on the clock to extend the game. Iowa coach Lute Olson screamed bloody murder about the foul. Heathcote wasn't sure he saw contact either. He was sure he saw no contact the next week when host Michigan toppled the Spartans 49–48 on two free throws by UM's Keith Smith with no time left. Magic picked up the phantom foul on Smith's drive to the basket.

Reeling MSU tumbled to new depths against Northwestern, who had been winless in the conference. The overarching issue was a casualness that led to mistakes and lack of execution. The Wildcats exploited every weakness plaguing the Spartans. They led by 10 at half, and when the Spartans tried to press in the second half, the Wildcats beat them repeatedly with back door cuts to expand its lead. Northwestern won by 18. "The realization of what other clubs were doing to us and what we weren't doing hit us square in the face," Heathcote said.

Panic set in. Fans grumbled. The media attacked. Then Heathcote called a meeting on the following Monday. Accounts vary on what actually transpired. Most agree that Mike Longaker, a highly respected 4.0 pre-med student and benchwarmer, challenged the team to come together and play up to their abilities. A little while later, Heathcote changed personnel, moving Brkovich into the starting lineup in place of Charles, the laid-back 6'7" center/forward from the Bahamas who did most of his scoring around the basket. Brkovich, "the Golden Arm" as Heathcote dubbed him, would be able to stretch the defense and open lanes for Vincent, Johnson, and Kelser. He would also provide a second outlet along with Donnelly to start the fast break.

With the league-leading Buckeyes coming to town, the Spartans hit the reset button. It almost rejected the input. The Spartans jumped to a nine-point lead, but with 2:23 remaining in the first half, Magic pulled up, clutching his ankle. He limped to the locker room and didn't return after the half. Then Kelser picked up his fourth foul, sending him to the bench. The Buckeyes surged, grabbing the lead by a point on two occasions. Heathcote countered by putting Kelser back in. As Kelser waited to check in with 8:42 left, cheering suddenly erupted in the corner of Jenison. Johnson emerged, telling Heathcote he was good to go. "Some things you remember all your life. If you put headphones over my ears and turned up the heavy metal as high as it would go," Heathcote wrote, "it wouldn't match the unbelievable din and noise when Earvin came back." The game remained close even with Magic and Kelser back. The Buckeyes sent it to overtime on a bizarre four-point play. But with their season on the line, the Spartans scratched out the win in overtime. Heathcote called it the most memorable game of his career.

The Buckeye scare behind them, the Spartans rolled to nine consecutive wins to earn a share of the Big Ten title and the automatic NCAA tournament berth (by virtue of a better head-to-head record against Iowa and Purdue). MSU also impressively humbled nonconference power Kansas 85–61, prompting announcer Al McGuire to wonder how the Spartans could have ever lost five games.

The key stretch during the winning streak was a three-game, eight-day road trip to Iowa, Ohio State, and Indiana. Only Iowa made it close. With Johnson playing along the baseline, Heathcote's matchup zone strangled the opposition. Kelser broke Terry Furlow's MSU career scoring record in the Spartans' 23-point rout of Michigan. Winning at Minnesota wrapped up a share of the conference crown. But Wisconsin denied the Spartans an outright title on the final day of the season when Matthews hit a 55-footer at the buzzer. "If I never see another long shot at the buzzer, it will be too soon," Kelser said. "I've seen enough for a lifetime this season."

30 Reasons to Hate Michigan

The dislike for our in-state rival comes with a reason. The source of the vitriol started from the very beginning of the school's founding. Michigan vehemently opposed the creation of the Agricultural College of the State of Michigan despite repeated failings to establish its own agricultural school, which the state's farmers and legislature deemed essential. Over the objections of Michigan president Henry Tappan and in spite of numerous underhanded moves by state senators likely influenced by Tappan, the Agricultural College of the State of Michigan (Michigan Agricultural College) opened its doors to 63 students in 1857.

MAC was chronically underfunded and cash-strapped until Abraham Lincoln and the U.S. Congress passed the Morrill Act in 1862, which offered grants for prime land to colleges devoted to teaching agriculture, and later mechanical engineering to the state's farmers. Michigan chafed at being left out of the grant money, even though they didn't offer agricultural instruction. To circumvent this, Michigan suggested a merger with MAC whereby all agricultural instruction would be transferred to Ann Arbor, and Michigan would receive the land granted in the Morrill Act. The state legislature said no—primarily because Michigan lacked any of the facilities to teach agriculture. UM then petitioned the state every other year for the next six years for the grant. When that didn't succeed, Michigan attempted to starve MAC out of existence by garnering enough votes in the legislature to deny funds to MAC for building and grounds expansion and maintenance. MAC survived that as well by finding enough outside funding support to build the structures it needed.

Over the years Michigan made additional attempts to undermine MAC. Michigan offered inducements to the president of MAC to merge with it. When that failed UM unsuccessfully tried to cripple MAC by swiping its key individual departments such as forestry and engineering. Michigan Agricultural College's engineering curriculum was expanded from just mechanical to civil and electrical in 1885. When MAC's engineering building burned down in 1916, Michigan, which had lobbied unsuccessfully for control of MAC's engineering department in 1913 and 1915, smelled blood. Local automobile tycoon Ransom Olds saved the day, however, by donating $100,000 to MAC for a new engineering building. "I have great faith in the Michigan Agricultural College and see no reason why it should not become one of the foremost colleges in the United States," Olds told the state board of agriculture at the time of his donation.

MAC changed its name to Michigan State College and Applied Science (MSC) in 1925. By this time MSC had been playing

National Championships: MSU vs. Michigan

Michigan has won 11 football national championships in football (as chosen by at least one NCAA-recognized major selector) and one in basketball. Michigan State has won six football national championships and two in basketball. MSU fans, though, shouldn't despair.

Since Michigan State joined the Big Ten in 1949, which evened the playing field considerably, the Spartans lead UM in football and hoops championships eight to five. The upshot: in the modern era, beginning around 1950, Michigan State has comfortably topped its rival in collecting the most prestigious hardware.

football for 30 years. Most of the games were against regional foes such as Alma, Albion, and Olivet. One exception was Michigan, who had agreed to play MSC starting in 1898, but only under exceedingly favorable terms to the Wolverines. From 1907 to 1931, MSC and Michigan met 24 times, but only four of those were played in East Lansing. Spartans athletic director Ralph Young made a move in 1932 that threatened to make this grossly unfair arrangement permanent. He agreed with Fielding Yost, Michigan's legendary coach and athletic director, to play all future games in the rivalry on the first weekend of the season and in Ann Arbor. Why the sell out? Michigan guaranteed a handsome payout to MSC, money Young needed to balance his athletic budget. Born out of desperation, this decision would serve as another source of discord between the schools in the years to come.

When the University of Chicago dropped out of the Big Ten for good in 1946, John Hannah ramped up his efforts to gain admission to the conference. Michigan's stance on MSC's admission was ambiguous. UM's president Alexander Ruthven wrote to Hannah that he supported MSC's admission, and the head of the UM Alumni Club in Lansing also gave his public support. The real power, however, rested in the hands of the faculty representatives from the Big Ten member schools. And the faculty representative at Michigan, Ralph Aigler, loathed Michigan State.

Aigler's rancor stemmed partly from the fact that Michigan State had given money for years to athletes from a trust called the Jenison Awards, a fund created by Frederick Cowles Jenison, a graduate of State Agricultural College and successful insurance agent. Aigler, the high priest in the Big Ten of the virtues of amateurism, believed Michigan State used the money as inducements for athletes. Such recruiting was forbidden in the Big Ten, which did not offer its athletes scholarships. Michigan State argued that funds from the trust were available to all students based on need not athletic ability. Plus most of the other schools paid athletes under the table and often in more copious amounts.

Ultimately after a thorough vetting of the school and sworn promises from MSC to follow the Big Ten handbook on amateurism and other threats and complaints, the Big Ten admitted Michigan State to the conference on May 20, 1949. The conference stated the vote was unanimous, though a *The Detroit News* writer claimed MSC slipped in with a 5–4 vote and that Aigler was one of the dissenters. (Aigler denied it.) Once Michigan State gained admittance, it could compete in all sports starting in the fall of 1950 except for football. Football would have to wait until 1953, which, according to Aigler, would give MSC time to comply with the Big Ten's rules on amateurism.

The final indignity from Michigan in the formative years of MSC came in 1954. The college wanted to change its name to Michigan State University. All other land grant schools had made the change by the 1950s, and MSC had been functioning as a de facto university for at least two decades. The Michigan board of regents dusted off the old Michigan playbook and cried foul. "Having two major universities in the same state would be confusing," they bleated. "It would be unconstitutional," they warned, in very somber tones. "It would lead to a duplication of programs," they argued. The Michigan legislature approved MSC's name change in a lopsided vote 18 months later, Michigan's unhinged objections notwithstanding.

In the last few decades, the indignities suffered by MSU at the hands of Michigan have been less overt but annoying and damaging nonetheless. In 1968 *The Michigan Daily*, the UM student newspaper, accused Michigan State of football recruiting violations. Always unduly concerned about the feelings of Michigan, the Big Ten dutifully launched an investigation and found no truth to the allegations. Proving its innocence, however, cost the school thousands of dollars and incalculable embarrassment.

The most egregious college recruiting scandal in the state didn't even involve football. While Jud Heathcote attempted to convince the best basketball players in the state of Michigan to play at MSU in the 1980s and 1990s, Michigan under head coach Bill Frieder and then Steve Fisher was the one implicated in a large college basketball cheating scandal that indirectly hurt MSU hoops for years.

On two occasions in football, the Spartans beat the Wolverines head to head and finished with an equal or better record overall but saw Michigan leapfrog them in the bowl selections. In 1999 the two schools finished with identical conference and overall records. In 2011 the Spartans finished with more overall wins and ahead of UM in the conference. Both times, however, Michigan lobbied the conference and college football for superior bowls based on nothing more than their name. Both times Michigan was rewarded for their audacity. "We won head-to-head," Spartans safety Aric Morris said in reference to the 1999 scenario. "[Bowl selection] shouldn't be decided based on politics. They should reward us for our hard work."

Lorenzo White

Lorenzo White loved to run the football. George Perles loved the ground game. That they found each other—despite a gap of 1,500 miles and 50 degrees of temperature—shouldn't surprise anyone. White was a back who could carry the ball whenever and under almost all circumstances playing for a coach who wanted to run the ball whenever and under almost all circumstances.

Recruited by all the heavyweights out of high school, the 1983 Florida Player of the Year strongly considered going to the University of Michigan until he visited East Lansing. Michigan State entranced him instantly. So did the opportunity to stand out and leave a lasting mark. Coach Perles' strong emphasis on running the football and his proclivity for riding one particular back provided the clincher.

Perles brought White along slowly during his freshman year of 1984, but his talent demanded an early look. At the end of the season—one that sparked a renewal of winning football at Michigan State—White made his first start against Minnesota. The next week he rushed for 170 yards at Spartan Stadium against Northwestern. One play augured the type of runner he would be. White knocked down a linebacker trying to tackle him, lost his balance after inadvertently stepping on the defender's chest and facemask, then regained his balance and scooted away for a bigger gain. He finished the year with more than 600 yards rushing on 4.3 yards a carry and left fans drooling over what the future held.

The future turned out even better than expected. Quiet and somewhat unprepossessing off the field, White was impossible to ignore on it. Running the ball a staggering 419 times his sophomore year, he wiggled, cut, and glided his way to 2,066 rushing

Legendary Spartans back Lorenzo White runs through the USC defense during the 1988 Rose Bowl, which the Spartans won 20–17, for a portion of his 113 yards.

yards, the fourth most in college football history at that time and the most ever by a sophomore.

The 5-11, 205-pound back proved sturdier than a 3,000-year-old Sequoia and more elusive than Bigfoot, whose feet couldn't possibly have been any bigger than White's. His size 13 EE helped him maintain balance and make sharp cuts. "Many running backs have excellent peripheral vision, but the great ones have the innate ability to cut and change direction. Lorenzo White's feet give him that ability," Perles said in an interview in 1987. White gained considerable national attention for his prolific season, which included consensus All-American honors and an invitation to the Downtown Coaches Club where he hoped to win the Heisman. The award went to Bo Jackson at Auburn, but White's fourth-place finish represented the highest for a Spartan since Sherman Lewis finished third in 1963.

White entered 1986 as one of the Heisman favorites. "He can hurdle people, he can catch the ball, he can throw the ball, he can cut back against the grain. I don't know how fast he is, but no one catches him," Perles rhapsodized to *Sports Illustrated* before the season. Alas, an injury limited White to only 164 carries and 633 yards in 1986. The Spartans felt his absence, failing to make a bowl game for the first time since 1983.

Healthy and reinvigorated his senior year, White gained 1,572 yards and led the Spartans to their first Rose Bowl since 1966. In two pivotal games, White performed at his best. He rushed for 185 yards in the Spartans' win against Michigan and then in the winner-take-all contest against Indiana—the biggest game of his career—White carried the ball 56 times for 292 yards in helping the Spartans down the Hoosiers to secure the Big Ten and nail down a spot in the Rose Bowl.

In Pasadena, California, he notched another 100-yard rushing game (113) and scored two touchdowns in the Spartans' 20–17 triumph against USC. Individual accolades also came his way. He was a consensus All-American once again and made another trip to New York, where he again finished fourth in the Heisman voting.

White finished his career as the all-time Michigan State leader in rushing yards (4,887), rushing attempts (1,082), rushing touchdowns (43), and 100-yard games (23). He ranks fifth all time in the Big Ten in career rushing yards.

White never ceased to impress his coach—both for his ability on the field and his character off it. "In all my years of coaching," said Perles in 1987, "I've never met a man with that much ability who is that humble. It's hard to imagine a young guy getting that much publicity being that humble." Lorenzo White is arguably the best back in Spartans history. A first-round pick of the Houston Oilers, White made one Pro Bowl and spent eight productive years in the NFL.

1965 and 1966 All-Americans

Bob Apisa (1965 and 1966)

A prolific fullback, Apisa was one of 11 Hawaiians to earn a letter at Michigan State—most of them under Duffy Daugherty. Nicknamed the "Samoan Bull," he had massive hips and a downhill running style that victimized many a defender, who usually needed help to bring him down. In 1965 Apisa amassed 666 yards on the ground—then the most ever for a Spartans fullback—and in 1966 he rushed for 445 yards. In both seasons he battled injuries and missed games. A highlight of his career came against Michigan in 1966 when he punished the Wolverines defense for 140 yards in the Spartans' 20–7 victory. His 1,343 career rushing yards still stand as the most ever for a Spartans fullback. Apisa was drafted in the ninth round by the Green Bay Packers, but the injuries he suffered in college ended his pro career before it ever started. Apisa returned to Hawaii, where he appeared on the hit television show *Hawaii Five-O* a few times. He parlayed that experience into a long career as a highly respected Hollywood stuntman.

Ron Goovert (1965)

A linebacker with exceptional instincts, Goovert teamed with George Webster and Charlie Thornhill to form the best linebacking corps in college football, and Daugherty considered Goovert the best of that bunch in 1965. Undersized at 205 pounds, the Ferndale, Michigan, native had an interception and a key sack in the Spartans' tight win against Purdue in 1965. He also recorded a safety in the Spartans' 32–7 win against Ohio State. Goovert played two seasons with the Detroit Lions.

Clinton Jones (1965 and 1966)

An explosive back with cat-like moves and game-breaking speed, Jones represented a new breed of back emerging in the mid 1960s. They possessed top-line speed and posed a threat to score any time they touched the ball. The dependable Jones averaged 4.9 yards a carry in his career at MSU, gaining 787 yards in 1965 and 784 yards in 1966. His 68 points led the Big Ten in 1965, and he won the conference rushing title in 1966. On a blustery, snowy day against Iowa in 1966, Jones set a then-Big Ten record by rushing for 268 yards. Touchdown runs of 79 and 70 were among his mere 21 carries that day. Jones spent seven solid years in the NFL with the Minnesota Vikings and San Diego Chargers.

Steve Juday (1965)

The Northville, Michigan, native was a dual threat at quarterback from 1963 to 1965. Dangerous as a runner and robotically efficient as a passer (*Sports Illustrated* called him a "gifted" passer), Juday led the Spartans to six come-from-behind wins in his career. He became the first Spartan to throw for more than 1,000 yards when he completed 89 passes on 168 attempts for 1,173 yards in 1965. Named an Academic All-American, Juday's decision-making helped the Spartans average 29 points a game during his senior year, which ranked tops in the conference. He graduated as the all-time leader in passing yardage, pass attempts, completions, and touchdown passes. In 1965 Juday finished sixth in the Heisman race.

Harold Lucas (1965)

At 6'2", 286 pounds, Lucas, a middle guard, helped form an impenetrable wall of beef, brawn, and blast that suffocated opposing running games and flattened more quarterbacks than a rolling pin in a pizza joint. Believed to be the heaviest man to put on a Spartans uniform at that time, Lucas moved as well as someone 30 pounds lighter. The Detroit native and his defensive teammates held opponents to just 34.6 rushing yards a game during Lucas' senior season. Lucas relished the physical nature of football, explaining to a reporter for the *Detroit Free Press* that, "It's sort of fun to get the feel of [his opponent], mess him up, bend him a little." The St. Louis Cardinals drafted him in the second round, but his pro career never developed.

Gene Washington (1965 and 1966)

Washington served as Juday's favorite target in 1964 and 1965 and Jimmy Raye's in 1966. For three straight seasons, he led the Spartans in catches and receiving yards. A Texas native, whom MSU recruited sight unseen on the recommendation of Bubba Smith, Washington stood 6'3", a frame he used expertly to haul in passes over smaller defensive backs. "Gene is a tremendous threat just being in the lineup," Daugherty said. "He has super coordination and speed." An All-American, he piled up numerous Spartans career receiving records (102 catches, 1,857 yards, and

16 touchdown catches) and one that still stands—his average of 25 yards per catch. A first-round draft pick by the Vikings, who also drafted four of his teammates, Washington played eight years in the NFL and made two Pro Bowls before becoming an executive at 3M.

Jerry West (1966)

The bulwark of an offensive line that opened holes for a talented backfield and protected the quarterback when needed, West helped the 1966 Spartans lead the Big Ten in rushing and scoring. The Spartans averaged 223 yards a game on the ground and scored 30 points a game. The offensive line of 1965 and 1966 quietly performed at a high level, allowing the Spartans skill players to set a boatload of school records. Without West winning a majority of collisions in the trenches, the Spartans probably wouldn't have won as often on the scoreboard.

33 The Origin of the Spartans Nickname

Michigan State hasn't been the Spartans forever. In fact it almost ended up with a nickname only a rival could love.

When Michigan State was known as Michigan Agricultural College, it called itself the Aggies, a nod to its status as the first land-grant college. A few early references to MAC also used the nickname "Farmers," an even more direct—albeit drab—tribute to the school's agricultural roots. For a brief period during Chester Brewer's coaching tenure in the aughts, some forestry students kept a brown bear cub, who they had captured in Montana and named

Montie, in a cage on campus. The bear soon became known as "Brewer's Bruin" and served as the football team's mascot. No nicknames relating to bears ever took hold, however, and the bear and its nickname soon vanished from the scene.

To reflect MAC's growth and expanding influence, the state legislature approved a name change for the school in 1925. "Aggies" seemed too small and confining for a school now called Michigan State College of Agriculture and Applied Sciences or Michigan State College for short. Sentiment grew on campus for abandoning Aggies and replacing it with something more robust.

The *Lansing State Journal* stepped in to offer assistance in finding a compelling new nickname. The paper conducted a vote, and the winner was a decidedly non-compelling "Michigan Staters." Future MSU fans can thank *Lansing State Journal* sports editor and MSC advocate George Alderton for saving them from something so utterly clumsy and ridiculously redundant. (Imagine Michigan State University Michigan Staters.) Alderton despised that unoriginal nickname and sifted through the rejected entries for a better alternative. One entry in particular, whose source remains unknown, intrigued Alderton: Spartans. But he waited for the right opportunity to introduce his choice, which arrived in the spring of 1926.

Perry Fremont, a catcher on the MSC baseball team, provided written accounts of the team's Southern trip that spring to Alderton, who rewrote them for publication in the paper. The sports editor gradually sprinkled in the name "Spartans" in the articles, though he spelled it "Spartons" the first two times before a friend tipped him off on the proper spelling. Alderton then started putting Spartans in the headlines.

No records suggest that Alderton knew of an interesting historical connection Michigan State had with his chosen nickname. In 1858 U.S. Congressman Justin Morrill, the sponsor of the

Morrill Act that created land-grant colleges, mentioned the school in East Lansing and then evoked the spirit of ancient Sparta when arguing for the bill's passage, according to Jack Ebling's book *Heart of a Spartan*. Whether it was fate or pure coincidence, Michigan State eventually adopted Spartans as its nickname. Dale Stafford at the *Capital* (Michigan) *Times* aided the effort, too. He also started using Spartans in his stories after Alderton, who was essentially his rival, called him to urge the writer to refer to MSC athletes as Spartans.

Levi Jackson's Run Against Ohio State

Before November 9, 1974, no one would have imagined, suggested, or otherwise associated Levi Jackson with unforgettable moments and epic games. Jackson was a sophomore fullback best known for his blazing 9.6 speed in the 100 and his casualness with the ball, which seemed to find the ground too often after touching his hands. This ball security issue landed him on the bench for a brief period in the middle of the 1974 season. Slowly, however, he worked his way back onto the field.

The 1974 season was Denny Stolz's second as head coach of the Spartans. The defensive coordinator at MSU in 1971 and 1972, he had succeeded, in a modest upset, the legendary Duffy Daugherty in 1973. "Coach Stolz's is more down to business," said senior All-American Bill Simpson when asked to compare the two coaches. "There's not a lot of joking anymore. It's a serious atmosphere on the practice field."

When Stolz took over, Spartans fans suffered from a general restlessness, a feeling that football was sliding into permanent mediocrity. The rebirth of Michigan under Bo Schembechler intensified these concerns. The Spartans won their first two games in 1974, then got clobbered by UCLA, lost a close one to Notre Dame, and tumbled in a hard fought game to Michigan. Another loss, a tie, and then two straight victories restored a pulse to the season. Indeed, the Spartans now stood 3–1–1 in the Big Ten with an outside chance at winning the conference.

The next game featured No. 1-ranked Ohio State. These were the Archie Griffin-led Buckeyes, one of head coach Woody Hayes' most impressive squads. They were riding a 19-game unbeaten streak, which included a 35–0 drubbing of the Spartans the year before and averaging 45 points. The Spartans defense, which included standouts Tom Hannon and Tommy Graves in the secondary; Terry McClowry and Paul Rudzinski at linebacker; and Greg Schaum, James Taubert, and Otto Smith on the line, had been showing steady, if unspectacular, improvement, holding seven of eight opponents to 21 points or fewer. But the expectation was that OSU would roll.

The game was televised nationally and more than 79,000 fans shoehorned their way into Spartan Stadium. Stolz, before the game, talked tough, snorting, "Don't give me any of that Big Two, Little Eight business. We're going after the Big Ten Championship." The media—and nation—snickered. But after 30 minutes of play, the Spartans and Buckeyes stood tied 3–3 at the half due in great part to a stubborn Spartans defense and three Buckeye turnovers.

Inexplicably, Archie Griffin, the sublime Buckeyes running back and future Heisman winner, carried only eight times in the first half. Part of Stolz's strategy had been to focus on handcuffing Cornelius Greene, OSU's elusive quarterback, while giving Griffin his yards. In the first half, the Spartans had managed to limit Greene's damage without being torched by Griffin. Michigan State expected to see more of Griffin in the second half.

And Griffin received twice as many carries in the second half, helping the Buckeyes take a 13–3 lead with 9:03 left in the game. Needing to score quickly, the Spartans aired it out. Charlie Baggett, the Spartans' dual-threat quarterback, hit a streaking Mike Jones in stride for a 44-yard touchdown. Bucking convention, Stolz went for two. The attempt failed when Jackson, losing track of his position on the field, caught Baggett's pass at the two and tumbled to the ground, thinking he'd crossed the goal line. The score remained 13–9. A determined MSU defense forced Ohio State to punt, giving the Spartans the ball at their own 12 with 3:30 left.

Jackson had been quiet so far, unable to find running room. Hoping to surprise the Buckeyes with a run but wanting to avoid a second-and-long, MSU opted for a play with variable options—Veer 44. Baggett needed to read the defensive end and either keep the ball himself or give it to Jackson. Baggett took the snap, moved a step to his right, and then handed the ball to Jackson.

The OSU line reacted in the direction of Baggett, tilting slightly to the right. That left a small crease for Jackson over the guard. He raced through the hole, saw the safety closing quickly, hesitated slightly, and then burst to the outside. The OSU safety, Tim Fox, lunged at Jackson, who was already two steps past him and putting his deceptive speed on display along the Spartans sideline. No other Buckeye defender was within 10 yards. The Spartans on the bench erupted; the crowd sprang up, sensing the unimaginable. Jackson had 80 more yards to cover, and only one Buckeye stood any hope of stopping him. At the Ohio State 40-yard line, Jackson pulverized that idea, stepping just outside the grasp of a diving defender to settle the issue. He ran untouched into the end zone where his teammates, cheerleaders, and fans spilling down from the stands engulfed him. "I gave [Fox] the inside and cut to the sidelines," Jackson said. "He was the only one I saw, and it was a footrace from then on. I knew I had to take it to the end zone…after I missed that extra point." Daugherty, calling the game on national television with Chris Schenkel, could barely contain himself, gushing about the run and the quality of the game.

Behind 16–13 the Buckeyes started at their own 29 with 3:17 left. They quickly entered Spartans territory on a 31-yard Griffin run. A couple of Greene scrambles, a pass, and two more runs moved the Buckeyes to the Spartans 1-yard line. Ohio State had no timeouts, a first down, and 29 seconds left. The Buckeyes hurried to get the next snap off. A dive into the line by the fullback netted nothing. The Spartans slowly disentangled from the pile. The clock continued to run...tick...tick...Greene exhorted his teammates to get set...tick...tick...Then chaos ensued. The Buckeyes snapped the ball, Greene bobbled it, Brian Baschnagel picked it up and fell into the end zone. Touchdown Ohio State. Or was it? Suddenly another official started signaling that the clock had expired and that the final play did not count. The Spartans had won. A fuming Hayes stormed across the field. Spartans fans cascaded down from the stands to celebrate the biggest win in years. But the only definite thing was confusion. After a 25-minute delay, one in which the officials consulted with Big Ten commissioner Wayne Duke, who was at Spartan Stadium that day, the officials announced that the Spartans had won.

Hayes never forgot the loss, insisting that the referees should have called a timeout at the goal line after the pileup. When a reporter approached him after the final decision, he snapped. "Unless you quit bothering me, I'm going to put my fist down your...throat." According to Fox, Hayes continued raging in the locker room, even suggesting that his players storm over to the MSU locker room and start a brawl.

For Michigan State, it was a grand moment in the limelight, a limelight that used to shine on the program regularly but had deserted it recently. "I never saw a finer performance by a Michigan

State football team," Stolz said. He would lead his re-energized team to two more wins that year and a 7–3–1 season, the Spartans' best in eight years. The glow of the Ohio State upset and sense of rebirth, though, ended abruptly in 1975 when an NCAA investigation revealed a series of rules violations that resulted in a stiff three-year probation. MSU cleaned house, firing Stolz and his coaching staff.

35 Jud Heathcote

"When I started at Montana, they had a press conference for me. He and I got along just fine," cracked Jud Heathcote, the new Michigan State basketball coach, in front of the 50 reporters on hand that day in 1976 to cover his introduction as the head man of Spartans basketball. "He's the funniest guy I've ever known," said Lynn Henning, a longtime media adversary in *When March Went Mad*.

The jokes never stopped coming in Heathcote's 19 seasons at Michigan State. He could warm up a room with the best of 'em. But playing for Jud was no joking matter. The rest of the Big Ten didn't spend a lot of time laughing either especially in the 1970s, 1980s, and early 1990s. During that tenure he won 340 games.

The North Dakota-born Jud Heathcote was raised in Washingon State and served as a bench player for the Cougars in the late 1940s. He began his coaching career at a nearby high school, became an assistant to Marv Harshman at Washington State, and then headed a few hours east to Missoula, Montana, for his first college head-coaching gig. He guided Montana to the NCAA tournament in 1975 and came within a whisker of knocking off John Wooden and UCLA. Michigan State fired Gus Ganakas that same year. MSU athletic director Joe Kearney, who had West Coast roots, wanted to hire Harshman, now at the University of Washington, but the Huskies head coach expressed no interest, recommending Heathcote instead.

After an interview in East Lansing, Heathcote returned home to Missoula, received an offer from Kearney that night, and then slept on the decision. He accepted the job the next day despite his reservations about the program's facilities—especially creaky, old Jenison Field House. When he first saw Jenison, he said, "Joe [Kearney], we had a better place than this at Montana."

Though many viewed the hire skeptically at first, Heathcote would change the direction of the program in 1977 when he and assistant coach Vernon Payne persuaded local high school legend Earvin Johnson to commit to Michigan State. Tense moments outnumbered calm ones during his recruitment, which Ganakas' firing the year before had complicated. Eventually Johnson shunned Michigan and other big-name schools to sign with MSU. Jay Vincent, Johnson's crosstown high school rival and less celebrated blue chipper, did the same.

During the 1976–'77 season, talented Ganakas recruits Greg Kelser and Bob Chapman struggled to adjust to Heathcote's system, and Michigan State finished below .500 for the first time since 1970–'71. Heathcote's demanding, uncompromising style, which appealed to MSU administrators still smarting from a player walkout two years earlier, contrasted sharply with Ganakas'. Bitingly sarcastic at times, Heathcote screamed and berated in coarse and colorful terms. He imposed a rigid structure from top to bottom. Everyone knew who was in charge. "I may not have liked the way he said things, or went about getting things done, or motivated us, but I always respected him," wrote Kelser in *Tales from Michigan State Basketball*. "His game prep was outstanding, and we knew everything we could expect from the other team. We never lost a game because we were caught by surprise by something. We may not have played well, shot well, or defended well, but it wasn't because we weren't prepared."

Heathcote's playbook was thicker than the Bible but no less sacred, including a variety of options off of a multitude of plays. He had a keen understanding of shooting. "I don't think people realize that Jud is a great, great shooting coach," said one of his best shooters, Shawn Respert. On the defensive front, he preferred a match-up zone, which employed the tenets of both man-to-man and zone principles.

With Kelser, Chapman, Johnson, and Vincent in the fold the next season, Heathcote, teaching and thundering, steered the divine talent at his disposal to one of the finest seasons in Spartans basketball history. A Big Ten title, earned with 15 wins and secured with an 8–1 final kick, sent the Spartans to the NCAA tournament for only the third time in their history. The Spartans sailed to the conference crown behind Kelser's 17.7 points a game, Johnson's 17, and Chapman's 12.3. Johnson also dished out a staggering 222 assists.

His relationship with Johnson required finding the proper calibration between freedom and discipline—between treating Magic as the special talent he was and still holding him to the same standards as the rest of the team. "I don't think Coach compromised himself to coach Earvin at all," said Kelser in *When March Went Mad*. "But I will say this—I think he was smart enough to understand various temperaments that guys had." Jay Vincent added: "Coach picked his fights with Magic." All in all, Heathcote managed Johnson adroitly, giving him a longer leash than anyone else and pulling it in at strategic times.

After beating Providence and Western Kentucky, Michigan State faced No. 1-ranked Kentucky in the Mideast Regional Final. Johnson picked up his fourth foul with 10 minutes remaining in the game and only scored six points. The Spartans lost by three. "If we'd made more adjustments and Earvin hadn't gotten his fourth foul... we'd have won that game. We were up by five at halftime and scored off the tip to start the second half. But we couldn't quite hang on. It wasn't our time yet," wrote Heathcote in his autobiography, *Jud*.

Their time came the next year when Heathcote and his Spartans went on to win the Big Ten again and beat Indiana State to become national champions. Then Magic departed and Kelser graduated, and one of Heathcote's bugaboos emerged to complicate matters going forward. Jud did not play games on the recruiting trail. He refused to excessively flatter recruits and refrained from making promises he couldn't keep. In general Heathcote had a strong distaste for recruiting. "I'd rather worry about what I have than what I don't have," he'd often say.

As a result, the remainder of Heathcote's tenure ran hot and cold. The upswings included a Sweet 16 run in the mid '80s; a Big Ten championship and deep Tournament run in 1990; and a Big Ten title near-miss in 1995. Heathcote retired after that 1995 season, putting in mothballs forever the garish, bright green blazer he wore for every game and the histrionics he displayed on the bench for most. Each school in the Big Ten feted him with sincere tributes and smile-inducing gifts. Heathcote coached a year longer than he had planned after learning of an official university memo urging the MSU president to force him to retire. A public relations disaster ensued, ending with Heathcote promising to coach just one more year before turning the reins over to his assistant, Tom Izzo.

Heathcote never rid himself of his epic impatience (on one occasion two airport security guards carted him away after he hopped on a luggage conveyor belt in search of his tardy bags)

131

nor did he stop cajoling, pleading, and yelling at his players or the officials. Sometimes that got him in trouble as well. After catching a loose basketball while in a fit of rage during a game at Illinois, he slammed the ball down on the court only to have it bounce up and dent his chin.

In the end, though, despite his blunt criticisms, Heathcote won over most of the student-athletes under his charge. "Jud Heathcote was a great basketball coach," wrote Magic in the foreword to *Jud*. "But he's a better person. You couldn't find anyone more honest if you looked for another 19 years…He had a tough exterior like a drill sergeant. Underneath he truly cared about his players' well-being."

1957: What Might Have Been

Blown calls, freakish hostile bounces, gusts of wind at inopportune times. Any of these circumstances and dozens of others can flatten national championship hopes or derail undefeated seasons. The 1957 Spartans, a splendid football team, can attest to that—especially the former issue.

Without a few ill-timed injuries in 1956, the 7–2 Spartans, who lost two games by eight points, might have gone undefeated. Most of the key contributors from that team returned in 1957, including 20 seniors, bolstering hopes that MSU could finish the job one year later. Veterans Dave Kaiser, Jim Ninowski, Dan Currie, and Walt Kowalczyk headlined the list of returnees. That made Duffy even more bullish than usual. Two games into the 1957 season everyone started to see why.

The Spartans smashed Indiana 54–0 and California 19–0 heading into a big third week tilt against Michigan. The defense, which ended up leading the Big Ten and finished third nationally in yards allowed, flowed quickly to the ball and tackled exceptionally well especially Currie. On offense Daugherty employed his ample depth to keep opponents off balance and wear them down. Twenty-one different Spartans carried the ball against Indiana, and three different receivers caught touchdown passes against Cal.

The Spartans traveled to Ann Arbor for the annual showdown, the last year of the lopsided road arrangement. (Starting in 1958 the series would alternate between Ann Arbor and East Lansing.) Behind Kowalczyk, who ran for 113 yards, and two touchdown passes by Ninowski, the Spartans defanged the Wolverines 35–6, Michigan State's largest margin of victory against Michigan in its history.

Having outscored their first three opponents 108–6, the Spartans, clicking, confident, and ranked number one, returned home to play Purdue, a perennial burr in their saddle. In front of a loud, energetic crowd, which filled the newly added upper decks, the Spartans edged out to a 7–0 lead. Michigan State then drove deep into Purdue territory and scored on a Kowalczyk 1-yard plunge. After the whistle blew, a Spartans lineman continued his block, drawing a dead-ball flag. Everyone assumed the touchdown would stand. But for some reason, the officials went against the rulebook and assessed the penalty on the touchdown instead of the kickoff, wiping out Kowalczyk's dive. With the ball moved back 15 yards, the Spartans failed to score at all.

The bad call cast a pall on the rest of the game as Purdue, buttressed by the non-touchdown gift, scored late in the first half to even the game and eventually won 20–13. Erasing that Kowalczyk touchdown shifted momentum, changed the complexion of the game, and left the Spartans steaming mad afterward. An official came to their locker room at the half to apologize. The Big Ten offices followed up this informal apology with an official one the next week that admitted the mistake.

Michigan State, shaking off the Purdue loss, ran the table to finish 8–1. Only Illinois, which the Spartans played immediately after Purdue, managed to stay within two touchdowns. The Spartans even destroyed Notre Dame 34–6. MSU finished behind Ohio State for the Big Ten title and third in the final AP poll. Three lesser polls actually named the Spartans their national champion, the fourth time in the school's history they had earned the honor from at least one poll. "I think what stands out most about that team is that we could do almost anything," guard Ellison Kelly told writer Jack Ebling. "We could outscore you or we could shut you out. I can't think of any weak spots we had."

The Spartans had played at a national champion caliber for much of the year. Daugherty called the 1957 squad—not the more celebrated 1965 and 1966 monster teams—the best he ever coached. Six Spartans were named All-Big Ten—Kowalczyk, Ninowski, Currie, Pat Burke, Ellison Kelly, and Sam Williams. Kowalczyk and Currie were named All-Americans. Did an official's call singlehandedly ruin a Big Ten title and unanimous national championship? Daugherty thinks so. "I'm persuaded that call cost us the Big Ten championship and the national title," he wrote in his autobiography.

George Perles

By 1983 Spartans fans thirsted for a return to the big time. Sixteen years had passed since MSU had been part of the national college football conversation. When Coach Muddy Waters, a lineman under

Biggie Munn, finished 10–23 from 1980 to 1982, Spartan Nation became restive and cynical. "Roses don't grow in Muddy Waters," read a popular bumper sticker near the end of Water's tenure.

A Munn protégé had proved a failure, so the Spartans turned to a man Duffy had recruited, coached, and mentored. George Perles came to MSU in 1956 from a hard-edged, working-class, immigrant neighborhood in Detroit. He arrived in East Lansing via college stops in Tennessee and Florida and then a stint in the military where Daugherty reconnected with him during a seminar. Cut short by a serious knee injury in 1958, Perles' playing career ended prematurely. Duffy offered him a graduate assistant position, helped him get two high school coaching positions, and then hired him away from University of Dayton as an assistant in 1967.

Perles' big break came in 1972 when the Pittsburgh Steelers hired him as their defensive line coach. He crafted a defense called the 4–3 Stunt, designed to take advantage of the physical strengths of his best defenders—tackles "Mean" Joe Greene and Ernie Holmes and linebacker Jack Lambert. The aptly named "Steel Curtain" defense of the Steelers, which blundered offenses throughout the decade, helped Pittsburgh win four Super Bowls in the 1970s and made Perles a hot name in coaching circles.

Michigan State had considered Perles after head coach Darryl Rogers took his wide-open offense to Arizona State in 1979. Perles pursued the job, but the administration hesitated to pull the trigger on him, hiring Waters instead. The rejection surprised and hurt Perles. Down but not out, he moved on, searching for a head coaching opportunity to strengthen his resume. He eventually found one with the Philadelphia Stars of the upstart USFL pro league. But sooner than anyone thought, the Michigan State job reopened in the winter of 1982. MSU again reached out to Perles.

A few messy details needed to be ironed out before Perles could leave his job in Philadelphia. But like a salmon swimming furiously to the place of his birth, his instinct and will took over, and nothing was going to stop him from reaching his desired destination. Michigan State eventually agreed to a buyout settlement with Philadelphia, clearing the path for Perles to be named the 19th head coach in Michigan State history.

In the press conference, Perles came out swinging; warning rival Michigan that MSU would "knock their socks off" in recruiting; challenging UM, Notre Dame, and others that they better "buckle up;" and promoting a single mission: getting to the Rose Bowl. It had been years since an MSU head coach had talked so forcefully about taking on Michigan and returning to Pasadena, California. Perles easily seduced Spartans fans with the intoxicating talk and interest in the program soared.

He swiftly tapped into his vast NFL and college network to hire top assistant coaches. Perles hit the recruiting trail hard, using his NFL success to gain entry into recruits' living rooms and then selling them and their parents with his straight-shooter approach and earnest passion for the school.

Waters had left talent behind—especially linebacker Carl Banks and wide receiver Daryl Turner—but the entire operation sorely needed to be retooled from attitude on down. During his first meeting with the team, Perles noticed someone slumped down, seemingly disinterested, wearing a baseball cap, and sipping a can of Coke. Perles bellowed in the direction of the offending party, "Gentlemen don't wear hats when they go in a building. Not very respectful appearance—and not very smart either when you're trying to make an impression on the new coach." He told the player to get out. Each straightened up in his chair, put down anything in his hands, took off his hat, and leaned in to listen. Perles also ratcheted up the intensity of practices. "From the time coach blew the whistle," Banks told a reporter in Philadelphia, "it was nonstop. You woke up dreading it, but then you remembered how bad it felt to lose and you realized this was one way to turn it around."

Perles wanted to run the ball, control the line of scrimmage, and win with defense and field position. He implemented his 4–3 Stunt defense. He preached toughness and discipline. He despised complainers, phonies, and those not fully committed to the mission. After three years of loose and sloppy play by the Spartans, Michigan State fans eagerly embraced Perles' no frills, almost plodding approach to the game. They even accepted his propensity for malapropisms and clichés, which made him an easy target for the press and rivals. But MSU fans found it endearing.

Perles put the dismal results of the previous three years in permanent storage. In his first year, the Spartans beat Notre Dame, but the season ended 4–6–1, including a humbling 42–0 defeat to Michigan that reminded fans there would be no miracles or quick fixes.

A mini-miracle seized the Spartans the next year when MSU ambushed Michigan 19–7. Bobby Morse, who was supposed to come to MSU as a walk-on but instead received the last scholarship available in Perles' first recruiting class, sparked the win. He returned a punt 87 yards and the Spartans defense, employing the 4–3 Stunt, crossed up the timing and rhythm of Michigan's offense. The "knock your socks off" comment from Perles' first press conference seemed more than just bravado. The Spartans won five more times that year to finish 6–5, the first winning season since 1978, and earned a spot in the Cherry Bowl, which they lost.

Progress continued into 1985 when Perles guided the Spartans to seven wins and a warm weather bowl, the All-American Bowl, though they lost 17–14 to Georgia Tech. Running back Lorenzo White rushed for 2,066 yards, which smashed numerous records.

Everyone expected 1986 to be another step forward. Instead the Spartans stalled, finishing 6–5 and out of the bowl picture. Senior quarterback Dave Yarema set countless MSU passing records as the Spartans went to the air to compensate for White's injury-induced absences. But Michigan State lost four games by 12 points. Morse lamented to reporters after the final game that, "another 24 yards, and we would have been 10–1."

1987 was his watershed year. The Spartans returned to the Rose Bowl for the first time in 21 years and defeated Southern California to earn a spot in the Top Ten. Perles became the toast of East Lansing, edging closer to Biggie and Duffy status. He had made MSU relevant again and fans dreamed of more Rose Bowls and victory parades over Michigan and Notre Dame. More victories followed, including a monumental upset of Michigan in 1990, a Sun Bowl triumph over USC in 1990, and more bowl appearances. But the sheer chest-thumping exhilaration of 1987 never returned. Rose Bowl appearances and lofty national rankings always seemed just out of reach, undone by a missed field goal or some other cruel act of misfortune or bad karma.

Or maybe it was the call Perles received mere days after the 1987 Rose Bowl. The Green Bay Packers—desperate for their own return to glory—took notice of what was happening in East Lansing and offered their vacant head-coaching job to Perles. He said no—but not immediately. Then it happened again at the end of the 1988 season. The New York Jets offered Perles the job, and this time he almost hit the send key. Only an MSU offer of the athletic director job from the board of trustees kept him. The backdoor deal to give Perles the MSU AD job led to a contentious political battle, pitting Perles against university president John DiBiaggio. MSU divided into Perles and DiBaggio camps. The feud lasted for years and served as a stubborn distraction for the remainder of Perles' time as head coach.

MSU fired Perles at the end of a 5–6 season in 1994. In addition to his clash with the president over the AD position, which he ultimately had to relinquish, Perles had also been hounded by an NCAA investigation into grade tampering that concluded with the

Spartans on probation at the end of 1994. His time to move on had come. In 12 turbulent seasons, Perles posted a decidedly mediocre 73–62–4 record. (Five victories from 1994 were forfeited, making the official record 68–67–4.) However, his Rose Bowl triumph and other glory years are remembered favorably, and in 2006 he was elected to the MSU board of trustees, a position he continues to serve for the school he loves.

38 Greg Kelser

He committed to one coach he never met and finished his career with another he would have never selected as a high school senior. During his first two seasons, the Spartans won 24 games combined. In his final season, they won 26 and something even more special. When Greg "Special K" Kelser first put on his Spartans uniform, Michigan State basketball had the feel of a small, yet passionate club. When Kelser stepped off the court as a Spartan for the last time, MSU basketball had gone mainstream and changed forever.

Before attending Detroit Henry Ford High School, Kelser grew up a military brat. The Spartans discovered Kelser by accident. Vernon Payne, Gus Ganakas' top assistant, spotted "Special K" while scouting Alan Hardy, who ended up at Michigan, in a holiday tournament game against Henry Ford. Payne developed a strong relationship with Kelser and his father. So after seriously considering Arizona State, Kelser chose the Spartans. Throughout the entire recruiting process, he had never met his future head coach or even set foot on Michigan State's campus. "What I knew about my prospective teammates was based on what I read in the paper or saw on TV. I signed completely based on my confidence in coach Ganakas and Vernon. They calmed whatever apprehension I had about anything," Kelser wrote in *Tales from Michigan State Basketball.*

His freshman year turned out to be Ganakas' last. The Spartans stumbled to a 14–13 overall record and a fourth-place finish in the conference. It, though, had been a productive freshman year for Kelser, who moved into the starting lineup as a 6'7" center a few games into the season and averaged 11.7 points and 9.5 rebounds per game. His first start came against Northern Michigan. Starting at guard for the Division II school from the Upper Peninsula was a short, pugnacious kid named Tom Izzo. Coming off the heels of a season blemished by a player walkout, missing out on the NIT offered the administration an excuse to fire Ganakas. The firing shook Kelser. "I thought Gus got a raw deal," Kelser said.

Ganakas and his successor, Jud Heathcote, were night and day. Many of the players chafed at Heathcote's martinet style, including Kelser, who even considered transferring. But his military father helped him understand the method behind Heathcote's overt madness. Kelser also appreciated Heathcote's decision to move him back to forward and build the offense around him and his multiple offensive skills, which included a developing hook shot, post game, and an improving jump shot. "What helped Gregory tremendously was he was a great worker. He worked and worked and made himself into a very good basketball player," wrote Heathcote in *Jud.* His scoring average increased by 10 points to 21.7 a game. At the same time, he continued to produce on the boards, grabbing 10.8 a game. The Spartans took their lumps that year, winning only 10 games (12 if you include two forfeited wins from Minnesota). One rules change in 1976 benefitted Kelser. The NCAA reinstated the dunk—banned since the 1967–'68 season—clearing the path for some of Spartans fans' most vivid memories of Special K.

Retired Jerseys

Basketball	Football
Coach Jud Heathcote	#46: John Hannah
#4: Scott Skiles	#78: Don Coleman
#12: Mateen Cleaves	#90: George Webster
#21: Steve Smith	#95: Charles "Bubba" Smith
#24: Johnny Green	
#24: Shawn Respert	
#31: Jay Vincent	
#32: Greg Kelser	
#33: Earvin "Magic" Johnson	
#42: Morris Peterson	

As talented as Kelser was, he couldn't do it alone. He needed a partner to help lift the Spartans out of the doldrums of Kelser's first two years. Enter Earvin Johnson. Magic Johnson made everyone around him better. No one enjoyed the rewards of Johnson's team-oriented style more than Kelser. They developed a close bond and seemed to communicate telepathically, Kelser intuitively anticipating Johnson's next move. The result often ended in a crowd-pleasing and opponent-morale-crushing alley-oop dunk with Kelser reaching high above the rim to grab Johnson's perfectly timed pass. The play symbolized the breathtaking majesty of the next two years, one with untold high-fives, which Johnson and Kelser popularized. Kelser's scoring and rebounding average dipped a notch, a tradeoff he eagerly accepted in exchange for two Big Ten titles, two long NCAA Tournament runs, and a national championship.

Two games stood out in his career. Early in Kelser's junior year, the Spartans traveled to Detroit to play the University of Detroit in a much-hyped game. Dick Vitale had resurrected the Detroit program in the mid-'70s but retired in 1977 to become the school's athletic director. The Titans, perhaps feeling threatened by the upstarts in East Lansing, geared up for the game, packing Calihan Hall with a sellout crowd that rocked the arena even before tipoff. Then Vitale grabbed the microphone right before the game and starting screaming, "We're going to show the Magic Man that there will be no magic here in Calihan Hall tonight." By the end of the night, however, Calihan Hall could not cast a spell on Magic or the Spartans. Kelser, who had 20 points at half, scalded UD for 36 points and 10 rebounds. Michigan State sprinted away to a 103–74 victory, executing Heathcote's astute game plan with precision. In a game with bigger stakes, Kelser performed even better. After missing his first six shots in the 1979 Mideast Regional Final, Kelser buried 15 of his final 19 attempts to help finish off the Irish, who came in as the favorites, and put the Spartans in the Final Four. His final tally for the game: 34 points and 13 rebounds, a performance, which helped him earn Mideast Regional MVP.

A sharp dresser who painstakingly worried about every detail, including his uniform and how he tied his shoelaces, Kelser excelled in the classroom as well, earning Academic All-American honors. He didn't graduate right away, however, returning in part due to the relentless hounding of Heathcote, to finish his degree in 1981. Michigan State later granted him an honorary doctorate. "Special K was more than another catchy nickname," wrote Heathcote. "It was a description of a truly special student athlete."

Kelser finished his career at MSU as the all-time leader in points and rebounds. His rebounding mark (1,092) stood until 2012 when Draymond Green broke it by pulling down 1,096 boards. With an NCAA championship and All-American honors to his credit, Kelser was drafted No. 4 overall by the Detroit Pistons, who were coached by Vitale. Endless injuries derailed his professional career after six up-and-down years. After his pro career, Kelser built a successful career in basketball broadcasting.

39 Party With Sparty

Why not invite the ultimate MSU team player, the epitome of the heart and soul of Spartan Nation, to your next special event, wedding, birthday party, or family reunion? The Spartans mascot, Sparty, will don a tux (for formal events), boogie to the MSU fight song, and dance the night away with any willing guests—maybe even the bride. Sparty is happy to ham it up. Just don't expect witty repartee or brilliant orations. Talking is not his thing. And don't expect his true identity to be revealed. That's a secret reserved for a handful of folks at the Student Alumni Foundation, which chooses the student who plays Sparty based on an essay, a two-minute skit, and lengthy interviews.

Sparty debuted at Michigan State in 1955 as a papier-mache replica of a Spartan head that stood six feet tall, weighed 60 pounds, and bore a jaunty expression. A member of Theta Chi fraternity wore the head to pep rallies, and it made its first appearance before the Notre Dame game that year. For the 1956 Rose Bowl, Theta Chi did a slight makeover on Sparty, changing the head from papier-mache to fiberglass. That shaved nearly 30 pounds off of the bulky head. Sparty marched with the band before, during, and after football games, though it appears he was more of a curiosity than a permanent tradition.

The MSU student government assumed control of managing Sparty in 1960, but by the early 1980s, Sparty had disappeared from the tableaux of Spartans football. That started changing in 1982 with the reincarnation of Sparty as a more churlish, fierce, and unshaven-looking Spartan designed to appear more life-like from head to toe. The president of the MSU Alumni Association had championed the idea of reviving Sparty when he spotted the

Sparty is not only popular at Michigan State games, but the mascot also can be rented out for parties. (Getty Images)

old Sparty head lying around in storage. He gave the graphic artist at the alumni office a rendition of Bucky Badger, which he had seen at a retreat of university alumni directors. The finished illustration, which earned the nickname "Gruff Sparty," became the model for table tents that the alumni association used at its events during the 1980s. The image of Sparty returned to the consciousness of Spartans fans.

A few years passed before sentiment grew for a revival of Sparty as official mascot. After weeks of a teasing advertising campaign that revealed only the tip of his hands, new Sparty was unveiled to a roaring crowd on September 16, 1989. In the words of the MSU PR department, the new Sparty was "approachable, fierce yet kind, a man for all seasons." And riotously popular. Sparty has won the Universal Cheer Association's mascot competition three times.

Most of the 50 students who have played the Spartans icon over the last 23 years have been men, though at least one was a woman. "Athletes come and go," Darren Rovell, an ESPN reporter and former high school mascot, told *The Detroit News* in 2012. "People cheer for the jersey. That's the value of college athletics. Sparty is the ultimate player. He is always there."

Izzo's First Great Team

After MSU's 1996–1997 team missed out on the NCAA Tournament for the second consecutive year, *The Lansing State Journal* asked its readers whether Tom Izzo could do the job at Michigan State. Concerns intensified—and became more vocal— when the Spartans lost to Detroit to fall to 4–3 at the start of Year Three. Fans expected much better especially because McDonald's

All-American Mateen Cleaves had a year under his belt and the leading scorer in Flint history, Charlie Bell, had now joined him in East Lansing. Moreover, two other celebrated Flint products, Antonio Smith and Morris Peterson, plus Jason Klein and Andre Hutson rounded out a team talented enough to beat UD.

The Spartans headed to Purdue for the conference opener as a huge underdog and irrelevant factor in the Big Ten race. Cleaves bloomed, scoring 25, and Izzo gained his first signature win as Michigan State smashed Purdue 74–57. "Purdue gave me credibility with the fans," he said to the *State Journal* in 2007. Parlaying the Purdue upset into a 12–3 finish to win the Big Ten in another upset, the Spartans never looked back. MSU lacked many aesthetically pleasing wins. Instead they grinded out victories by relying on staples Izzo had been establishing since he started: relentless man-to-man defense, aggressive rebounding, scripted plays, and no-holds-barred effort.

After getting bounced in the first round of the Big Ten Tournament, the Spartans won two games in the NCAA, their first wins in the Big Dance since 1994. The nation awakened to Izzo and his ascendant tourney savvy after MSU beat Princeton in the second round. Among other things that impressed, Izzo prepared his team for Princeton's thorny offense by limiting film and study to 30-minute increments spread out over 48 hours. The Spartans eviscerated the Tigers, regularly snuffing out their back door cuts and moved on to the Sweet 16 where North Carolina pummeled them. "We want to get where Purdue is, in terms of consistency," said Izzo presciently after the season. "And in 25 years, we'd like to be North Carolina in terms of tradition."

Expectations soared heading into 1998–'99. Preseason polls rewarded them with a Top Five ranking, a nod to the previous season and the return of all five starters. MSU didn't disappoint. Relying on a balanced attack (five different Spartans led the team in scoring), the Spartans topped the 30-win threshold for the first time in their history, finishing 33–5. They defended their Big Ten title as well, closing out the regular season on a 15-game win streak, the longest in school history. They added a Big Ten Tournament title to the trophy case as well.

Prior to conference play, however, the Spartans appeared awestruck by the lights and burdened by the weighty expectations. Every early opportunity to prove they belonged among the nation's top teams ended in frustration. They coughed up a nine-point lead with 2:19 left at Temple, got manhandled by Duke, and then watched Connecticut erase a nine-point Spartans lead to win by 14 in Storrs, Connecticut. Izzo liked what he saw against Temple despite the heartbreaking loss. He chalked up Duke as a learning experience. The Husky loss, which dropped MSU to 4–3 and shredded their preseason Top 10 ranking, infuriated him—particularly because Cleaves had been drawn into a scoring duel with UConn's All-American Khalid El-Amin. Smith and Huston also raged, urging the Spartans to toughen up on the road.

The words struck a nerve. MSU won seven straight games—all of them by double digits. Peterson, coming off the bench as the sixth man, led the Spartans in scoring through most of the win streak. Cleaves pitched in with points when necessary. More importantly, he returned to the role the team needed most: offensive facilitator and leader. "[Cleaves] bounced back and realized he didn't have to be a great scorer to be a great player," Izzo said.

During the Big Ten opener, Dick Bennett's cloying Badgers blistered the nets in the final 20 minutes. Peterson led the Spartans with a meager 13 points in the 66–51 defeat at the 24th-ranked Badgers. Cleaves, whom the Wisconsin fans taunted endlessly because of his alcohol-related suspension from the year before, struggled shooting the ball, a troubling season-long trend.

After a pep talk with Magic Johnson, Cleaves sprung to life against Michigan, scoring 25 points, handing out eight assists, and picking up four steals. The Spartans drubbed their rival 81–67 in front of a raucous crowd who feted the 1979 MSU championship team at halftime. "Magic told us before the game that fun leads to wins and wins lead to championships," Klein said.

The Spartans swept through the remainder of the regular and post conference season without a loss. Many of the games remained tight through the first half before the Spartans found that second—and third—gear. That included a tense game in Bloomington, Indiana, where the Spartans held Indiana to 15 straight scoreless possessions before winning 73–59. "I thought last year Michigan State would move up and be really, really good this year," said Indiana coach Bob Knight. "The early schedule they played hurt their record. But in the long run, it will help them."

The most intense Big Ten game happened in Minnesota. Strange things tended to occur in Williams Arena, which featured a raised court that had dashed the elevated hopes of many past Spartans teams. But not this one. The Spartans countered the Gophers' 65 percent shooting by nailing nine threes to take a three-point lead into the locker room. To finish the game, the Gophers tied it with a three of their own, leaving Cleaves eight seconds to dribble through a phalanx of Gophers before hitting a short runner with a second left to clinch the victory. The improbable win established a growing aura of invincibility around the Spartans.

They coasted the rest of the way, winning three of their final four by double digits. Crisler Arena, where MSU dominated Michigan 73-58, turned green, with cheers of "Let's go, State" cascading down from the upper reaches of the building. After squeaking out a win against Northwestern in the first round of the Big Ten Tournament, the Spartans coasted to the title with wins over Wisconsin and surprising Illinois, setting the stage for Izzo's first Final Four appearance.

Five Fantastic QBs

Dave Yarema (1982–1986)

George Perles viewed the forward pass with trepidation. As the 1986 season unfolded and injuries mounted to the running game, Perles was left with little choice but to throw the ball if he wanted to score points. Luckily, Perles had Yarema, aa talented fifth-year senior from the Detroit area. Perles watched Yarema pile up huge passing games, cresting with 352 against Northwestern, a then-MSU record. He threw for 2,581 yards in 1986, a school record as well. For a coach hard-wired to mistrust the forward pass, Perles no doubt appreciated Yarema's care with the ball and his accuracy. Yarema completed 67.3 percent of his passes, a school record that still stands.

Despite his precision, one interception overwhelms memories of Yarema's career—and probably reinforced Perles' cheerless perceptions of the passing game. Trailing 11th ranked Iowa 24–21 in 1986, Yarema, standing at the Hawkeye 5-yard line, threw a head-scratching pick in the end zone that stopped cold the Spartans' late rally. Perles had just called a timeout to implore Yarema to throw the ball away if nothing was open. The loss stung and sent the season off the rails. Yarema is the only MSU quarterback to start and win a game in five different seasons.

Dan Enos (1987–1990)

He didn't throw tight spirals from sideline to sideline. His passes fluttered and wobbled instead of zipped and zoomed. Yet Enos compensated with instincts and leadership. When he threw a pass, the ball usually found its intended receiver as evidenced by his 62.1 career completion percentage—fourth best in school history. The

Dearborn native led Michigan State to bowl victories in the Aloha Bowl and Sun Bowl and a share of the 1990 Big Ten championship. He is the only quarterback in MSU history to win two bowl games. After serving as an assistant coach at MSU, Enos became head coach at Central Michigan in 2010.

Bill Burke (1996–1999)

A southpaw from Ohio, the lightly recruited Burke committed to Nick Saban in 1995. He outlasted the competition to earn the starting job in 1998 and 1999. In his first year as a starter, Burke went back to Ohio and passed for more than 300 yards in one of the Spartans' most memorable upsets, a 28–24 victory against Ohio State. He threw for almost 2,595 yards in 1998, a then MSU record, and 19 touchdown passes for second on the all-time Spartans list. Saban called him a superb game manager. With two NFL-caliber wideouts and a future NFL tight end, Burke, despite occasional bouts of inaccuracy, passed his way into the MSU record book by the end of his senior season, the record-tying 10-win 1999 campaign. Burke set a then-school record with 46 career touchdown passes. His 400 passing yards against Michigan remain the MSU record for a single game. "A lefthander with a soft touch and a tight spiral, Burke also has a calmness that borders on somnolence, which is his way of leading the team and keeping the magnitude of a monster season in perspective," *Sports Illustrated* wrote in 1999.

Jeff Smoker (2000–2003)

The checkered career of Jeff Smoker started with an electric pass, continued with an epic pass, careened off the rails for a season, and then finally resurrected in time to set numerous MSU passing records. The Pennsylvania native stunned everyone when he chose the Spartans over Ohio State, Penn State, and Tennessee in 1999. Before he had even memorized the walk to all of his classes, he was thrust into action against Marshall in the Spartans' first game of 2000, a 24–14 win. Two weeks later Smoker stood calmly in the pocket on fourth down in the waning seconds against Notre Dame and hit Herb Haygood on a slant route. Haygood streaked to the end zone, giving the Spartans a riveting come-from-behind victory.

The next year he threw for 2,579 yards and completed 63.4 percent of his passes. He led the Spartans to a bowl victory and an unforgettable comeback win against Michigan. On the final play of that game, he nimbly avoided the Wolverine rush before lofting a touchdown pass to T.J. Duckett. Expectations for the team spiraled in Smoker's junior year, but it ended with him in a drug rehab center and the Spartans program skidding into chaos. A new coach and fresh commitment to football helped Smoker revive his career for his senior year, which ended with an 8–4 record, a bowl bid, and an MSU single-season passing record of 3,395 yards that still stands. Smoker ended his career at Michigan State as the most prolific quarterback in MSU history, holding career passing records for attempts, completions, yards, and touchdown passes.

Drew Stanton (2003–2006)

Stanton appeared in one bowl game—as a special teams player his freshman year. Near the end of that game, he was injured on a cheap shot. During his three years leading the offense, the Spartans never finished above .500. He was prone to injury and to mistakes. But in terms of pure entertainment and edge-of-seat viewing, Drew Stanton, a heavily decorated recruit from Farmington Hills, Michigan, has few equals in the history of MSU football.

In his quarterback debut in 2004, Stanton surprised Indiana by running for 134 yards on just 12 carries in leading the Spartans to a comeback victory. Stanton could run for big yardage on either a designed or broken play or pass with precision. (His 64.2 career completion percentage is a school record.) "He is tough and fearless and loves to do things that people think he can't do," MSU guard Gordon Niebylski said.

Unfortunately, the Spartans defense gave up points as fast as the offense scored them. This arms race eventually wore down Stanton and the offense, leading each year to mental and physical mistakes that snowballed as the season progressed. Nonetheless, Stanton ended his Spartans career ranked in the Top 10 in every passing category. His five touchdown passes against Illinois in 2005 is the most ever by a Spartans quarterback in a single game.

42 Forddy's Greatest Hits

Forddy Anderson, who replaced Pete Newell as basketball coach in 1954, liked offense. He also loved music. For the first five seasons of his coaching tenure at Michigan State, the Spartans played a brand of basketball as melodious as any performance at Carnegie Hall.

Anderson, who grew up in a musical family in Gary, Indiana, starred at Stanford, eventually earning induction into the Cardinal Hall of Fame. He went into coaching, beginning at the Great Lakes Naval Training Station where he was named Coach of the Year by the Chicago Basketball Writers Association at age 25, then at Drake, and finally at Bradley. At that latter stop, he led the Braves to a 142–56 record and second place finishes in the NIT and NCAA. Ralph Young, the then-athletic director at Michigan State, had approached Anderson about the head coaching position when Ben Van Alsytne resigned. Anderson turned the job down then but accepted it five years later when athletic director Biggie Munn called at the suggestion of outgoing coach Pete Newell.

An innovator on offense, Anderson ran something akin to today's motion offense, emphasizing never-ending cuts and drives that forced action to the middle and resulted in layups. Outside shots were rare. "An average player can become outstanding," Anderson said, "by simply learning ways to get a defender out of position or off balance."

As a motivator Anderson harkened back to his youth when his high school gym teacher had his students move around the floor to the rhythms of music without a basketball. The teacher insisted a relationship existed between sports and music. Anderson became a convert of the idea and wove music into his coaching philosophy. The locker room before a game blared whatever music Anderson deemed most effective, usually building in intensity as the tip-off inched closer. But his motivational tactics were not confined to music. Before meeting Kentucky in 1957 with a trip to the Final Four on the line, Anderson took his team out of town for a fishing trip, hoping to get away from the pregame noise and sooth the nerves of his team, which had no tournament experience.

Newell had left Anderson with two standout performers, Julius McCoy, a chiseled athlete with a knack for scoring and rebounding, and Al Ferrari, described by Newell as an "acrobatic player," who was perfectly suited for Anderson's high-speed offense. McCoy broke every Spartans scoring record, averaging 20.9 points per game from 1954 to 1956. They helped Anderson post winning records overall and in the Big Ten in his first two seasons.

By his third year, Anderson had added recruits who would lead MSU to two conference crowns and deep NCAA runs over the next three seasons. Jack Quiggle, an adept passer and proficient scorer; Horace Walker, a ferocious rebounder; and Johnny Green, one of the school's greatest all-around players, emerged as stars. In 1957 Anderson guided the Spartans to the Final Four, the school's first ever. Stirring victories against Notre Dame and Kentucky put the Spartans in the semifinals where they fell in triple-overtime to North Carolina.

Two years later Anderson won the Big Ten by four games, finishing the year 19–4 overall and 12–2 in the conference, the best Big Ten showing by Michigan State to date. Tom Izzo would have appreciated this team. Green and Walker helped the Spartans punish the opposition on the boards, routinely outrebounding them by 15 to 20 a game. In the Spartans' 92–77 blowout of Ohio State, MSU had a mind-blowing 84 rebounds; Ohio State had 47. The Spartans beat Michigan by scoring a then-school record 103 points and outrebounding the Wolverines by 23 boards. "I've never seen a team with the spring and muscles MSU has on the boards," said Michigan coach Bill Perigo. The Spartans bowed out of the NCAA tournament in the second round in 1959, losing in an upset to Louisville. Anderson thought his Spartans had an excellent chance to win it all that year, but they played "miserable" against the Cardinals.

The loss to Louisville seemed to take the starch out of Anderson and the Spartans program. From 1960 to 1965, the Spartans finished above .500 only once, though they continued to score points at an ABA pace. During the 1963–'64 season, MSU scored 100 points 10 times and averaged 92.1. Too many recruiting failures, too many indifferent defenses, a more competitive Big Ten, and Anderson's weakness for nightlife and drinking eventually took its toll. His relationship with Munn stretched to the breaking point, Anderson was fired after the '65 season. "He had a horrible drinking problem at the end," said his former player and author Pete Gent in *Magic Moments*. "It was a time when everyone drank. And no one ever saw fit to deal with it." Anderson's career record at MSU was 125–124, a mediocre winning percentage that masked the contributions he made to Michigan State and basketball in general.

Paul Bunyan Trophy

No game on the Spartans' schedule is bigger. Plain and simple—Michigan State does not like Michigan. Michigan just wishes MSU would disappear like a bad smell or stubborn itch. The history, the emotion, and the disdain is on display in the annual game, and the Paul Bunyan Trophy has been presented to the winner of the Michigan State-Michigan football game since 1953.

The trophy is a four-foot wooden statue depicting the legendary lumberjack standing cheekily over an axe stuck in a map of the state of Michigan and flags representing MSU and UM. Former Michigan governor G. Mennen Williams donated it to celebrate Michigan State's acceptance into the Big Ten. The trophy may be one of the few things Michigan and Michigan State ever agreed on.

The series between the two schools can be divided into four rough periods. Michigan and Michigan State (then Michigan Agricultural College) first played in 1898, a 39–0 UM victory. UM won the first three games by a combined score of 204–0. The Spartans stunned the Wolverines by tying them 0–0 in 1908, the first time the game was played in East Lansing. Three more losses followed before the Spartans finally broke through with a win in 1913. They won again in 1915. But for the first six decades, Michigan had most of the fun, posting a 33–6–3 record against its nonrival. The Spartans could fall back on one excuse: only four of the games were played in East Lansing, though three of those were losses and the other a tie.

The second period in the rivalry started in 1950 when the Spartans ended a 10-game losing streak by winning 14–7. The victory swung control of the series to Michigan State. Under Biggie Munn and then Duffy Daugherty, the Spartans went 13–4–2 over

Other Notable Michigan-Michigan State Games

1915: Michigan State 24, Michigan 0

The Spartans humbled the Wolverines in Ann Arbor, and Michigan could not make any excuses afterward. Heroes abounded. MAC halfback Jerry DePrato gained 153 yards on the ground and scored 18 points. He and Blake Miller became the school's first All-Americans largely because of their performance in this game. Quarterback "Hub" Huebel, a transfer from Michigan who had played against the Aggies the year before, guided the offense with smarts and precision. And lineman Gideon Smith, the first African American to play for MAC, repeatedly tackled Johnny Maulbetsch, Michigan's renowned back, for limited or no gain. As if things weren't bad enough for Michigan, the MAC band marched through the streets of Ann Arbor mockingly playing the "The Victors," Michigan's fight song. "In music, cheering, fighting, and playing football, the Aggies just naturally outclassed their foeman so badly that the Maize and Blue crowd could find no single straw at which to clutch as it drowned in a sea of tears," wrote the *Detroit Times.*

1924: Michigan 7, Michigan State 0

The Aggies failed to win, but they ended years of serving as Michigan's punching bag. In six of the previous seven meetings between the two schools, MAC fell by least three touchdowns. The lone score came on a 45-yard pass from UM's Freddy Parker, inserted just to make the long throw, to Herb Steger in the last two minutes. Michigan completed only two passes on the day and picked up a mere three first downs. But the Aggies couldn't move the ball themselves, settling instead for the moral victory of a one-score loss. Besides the narrow final margin, the 1924 contest was noteworthy for another reason. It was played in East Lansing for the official dedication ceremony of MAC Field, which had opened the year before. The crowd was the largest in MAC history. The first Michigan State-Michigan game played in East Lansing since 1914 was one of the first college football games broadcast on the radio.

1937: Michigan State 19, Michigan 14

The Spartans, riding an unprecedented three-game win streak against Michigan, came from behind twice to beat the Wolverines in Ann Arbor. Ole Nelson, usually mild-mannered and not easily provoked, had been annoyed earlier in the game when a Wolverine purposely kicked him in the head. Down the stretch of the tight game, he pleaded for the ball and was rewarded with two big pass plays, including a 25-yard touchdown reception that put the Spartans ahead for good. The Spartans' earlier scores included an 89-yard run by Gene Ciolek and a 30-yard pass from Johnny Pingel to Nelson. The victory meant that the senior class at MSC had never suffered a loss to Michigan, the first time any Spartan class could say that.

1953: Michigan State 14, Michigan 6

The first Spartans win against Michigan in East Lansing also earned them a share of the Big Ten title in their first season in the conference. Yards were tougher to pick up than a ticket to the game. The Spartans managed to cobble together two long drives to account for both scores, which came on passes from Earl Morrall. Matched at the time only by the 1934 to 1937 Spartans, the fourth-straight win against Michigan was settled after the Spartans defense stopped Michigan at the Michigan State four-yard line.

1960: Michigan State 24, Michigan 17

The lead changed hands five times before Carl Charon bulled his way into the end zone from the 3-yard-line to put MSU up for good with 2:18 left in the game. The largest crowd in Spartan Stadium history enjoyed one of the most entertaining games in the series. It was highlighted by a 99-yard kick return for a touchdown by Michigan and 258 rushing yards by the Spartans, including 124 on just 14 attempts by Charon. The win extended the Spartans' unbeaten streak over Michigan to five games.

1967: Michigan State 34, Michigan 0

After a 1–2 start to the season, the Spartans routed Michigan in Ann Arbor in MSU's most lopsided win ever against UM. The Spartans rolled up 424 yards of offense led by quarterback Jimmy Raye, who rushed for 56 yards and passed for 130. Al Brenner caught a 65-yard touchdown pass, Bob Apisa ran for 58, and Reggie Cavender ran for 44. The win was the Spartans' 16th straight in the Big Ten, the second longest in conference history at the time.

1989: Michigan 10, Michigan State 7

Two early scores by Michigan, a goal-line stand by the Wolverines in the fourth quarter, a back-breaking offensive face mask penalty, and two MSU field goals gone astray finished off the Spartans in a game separated by an inch here or there. That's why Bo Schembechler's comment after the game that "the better team won" so rankled George Perles, whose team outgained the Wolverines by almost 50 yards.

1993: Michigan State 17, Michigan 7

The Spartans surprised the ninth-ranked Wolverines early by racing out to 17–0 lead and holding on. The UM loss ended its unbeaten streak at 22 games. Doing its best Gang Green impersonation, the Spartans defense held Michigan, which came in averaging 436 yards a game and 32.5 points, to just 245 yards. Jim Miller was exceptionally accurate, completing 18-of-24 passes for 187 yards. Gary Moeller, Michigan's head coach, resisted 90 years of tradition and made no excuses for the loss. "I give Michigan State all the credit," he said. "They did an excellent job."

1995: Michigan State 28, Michigan 25

In Nick Saban's first year as head coach of Michigan State, the Spartans toppled the Wolverines in a frenzied fourth quarter. After coughing up a 14–3 halftime lead, Michigan State trailed 24–20 with 3:38 left in the game. Tony Banks, who would finish 24-of-38 with 318 yards, led the Spartans on a dazzling, heart-thumping drive, one that nearly ended centimeters short on a fourth-down play. Banks passed the Spartans down the field 88 yards in just 2:06 to regain the lead for good. He completed eight passes on the drive, including a 25-yard laser to Nigea Carter in the corner of the end zone.

2004: Michigan 45, Michigan State 37

This tilt saw Michigan State open a large lead behind the arm and leg of Drew Stanton. But then Stanton had to leave the game after a bruising hit by LaMarr Woodley near the end of the half. Still ahead 27–10 with 8:43 left in the fourth quarter, the Spartans collapsed. Michigan blitzed MSU with 17 unanswered points in less than six minutes. A field goal, an onside kick, and two long touchdown passes to UM's Braylon Edwards sent the game to overtime. During the first overtime game in series history, Edwards caught the decisive score. Few losses in the rivalry wounded as sharply as this one.

Michigan State offensive tackle Jared McGaha raises the Paul Bunyan Trophy, awarded to the winner of the annual Michigan-Michigan State football game, after helping the Spartans defeat Michigan 28–14 in 2011.

the next 19 games. During this period starting in 1958, the series finally became a home and home one, ending a 60-year era in which only six games in the rivalry were played in East Lansing.

Michigan controlled the next period, which coincided with UM's hiring of Bo Schembechler. Beginning in 1970 UM went

13–1 against MSU. Most of the games lacked even a hint of drama. Since 1984, a year after MSU hired George Perles, the series moved into its current state, one absent long periods of domination by one side or the other. Through 2012 the Wolverines have won 18 and the Spartans 11.

1999: A Good Year

A quick scan of the practice field during August 1999 would have revealed more talent than at any time since probably 1966. Plaxico Burress was the star on offense and a future NFL first-round pick. Julian Peterson, evoking memories of linebacker George Webster, headlined the defense at linebacker. Peterson was a first-round pick, and others who would play in the NFL included Aric Morris, Lemar Marshall, and Robert Newkirk on defense and Gari Scott, Chris Baker, and Greg Randall on offense. Paul Edinger, the placekicker, also enjoyed a lengthy NFL career. Furthermore, experienced and savvy Bill Burke manned the quarterback position.

During August practices Saban was more intense than usual after the disappointment of the previous year. He attacked the Spartans' manhood. "You know what people have started to say about the Michigan State program?" he asked them. "They say we won't compete hard. They say we're not tough. They say we won't be there in the fourth quarter." Then he went in for the kill: "They say we're soft."

The season opener, a night game on national television, offered the Spartans a first chance for payback. The year before, Oregon had humiliated Michigan State 48–14 in Eugene, Oregon, and popular defensive back Amp Campbell sustained a season-ending neck injury that threatened to end his career. But Campbell persevered through months of rehab and returned to the team for the start of the 1999 season. In a sign that perhaps things were turning around for Campbell—and the Spartans—the defensive back picked up a fumble and returned it 85 yards for a touchdown, the decisive score in the Spartans' 27–20 victory against the Ducks. Campbell was reflective after the game. "I thank God for giving me the strength and health just to walk around," he said. "I remember times in the hospital I couldn't roll over and answer the phone. I couldn't even bathe myself." Saban was emotional as well. "I've never felt lower as a coach than when he got hurt," he said. "I've never felt higher as a coach than when he picked up that football and ran it back for a touchdown."

The Spartans showed further resiliency against Notre Dame. With the score tied in the fourth quarter, Burke caught the Irish in a blitz and lofted a pass to Scott over a Notre Dame defensive back. Careful to stay in bounds, Scott snared the pass, eluded a defender, and hugged the sideline for an 80-yard touchdown to help MSU beat the Irish 23–13.

Two blowout wins later, the 11th-ranked Spartans welcomed No. 3-ranked Michigan, who also stood at 5–0 and had NFL talent up and down its roster. Wolverines linebacker Ian Gold set the tone for the week when he mockingly said there was only one program in the state. In one of the most physical and riveting games in the rivalry's history, the Spartans opened a big lead with a dizzying passing attack punctuated by a few well-timed trick plays. Michigan's two quarterbacks, Drew Henson and Tom Brady, spent most of their time running for their lives or on their backs, contemplating the color of the East Lansing sky. Down 31–17 Michigan managed to rally late in the fourth quarter but came up short to fall 34–31. Burke threw for 400 yards, and Burress caught 10 passes for a massive 255 yards. The muscular 6'6" receiver toyed with the Michigan secondary, tormenting them with big play receptions and erasing them with abusive blocks. "There's nothing like this," Burke said. "Coach has been telling us all week that if you experience something like this, you will remember it for the rest of your life."

The Big Ten was as strong in 1999 as it has ever been. The Spartans discovered that during the next two weeks when Purdue led by Drew Brees and then Wisconsin led by Ron Dayne blasted the Spartans' NFL-laden but injury-riddled defense, which was missing a few key starters due to injury. Such beatings may have had lasting effects on Spartans teams of the recent past, but this group proved its ultimate mettle by whipping Ohio State 23–7, Northwestern 34–0, and Penn State 35–28. Freshman T.J. Duckett blossomed in the win against the Nittany Lions, collecting four touchdowns. Two losses kept the Spartans out of the Rose Bowl, but the nine wins represented the most in the regular season since 1966.

Wins against Notre Dame, Ohio State, Michigan, and Penn State marked the first time all four regional powers had been taken down by MSU in the same season since 1951. The Spartans earned a bid to the Citrus Bowl (now the Capital One Bowl) to play SEC powerhouse Florida on New Year's Day, the program's first appearance on January 1 since the 1989 Gator Bowl. Peterson earned first team All-American honors, and 15 Spartans earned some kind of distinction from the Big Ten, including All-Big Ten first teamers Peterson, Burress, Campbell, and punter Craig Jarrett.

But before the Spartans bowl game, Saban, who had been courted for years by NFL teams, accepted LSU's $6 million king's ransom to become the Tigers' next head coach. Saban had been lobbying MSU president Peter McPherson for a raise all season, intensifying his demands after the last game. McPherson refused to play ball for various reasons, including Saban's winless bowl record.

Saban offered coaching jobs to his assistants at MSU, even sending a plane from Baton Rouge to East Lansing for those interested in a job. The plane returned to LSU empty. Every assistant chose to stay at Michigan State and with interim head coach Bobby Williams. According to Burress, Saban had assured his team the day before he accepted the LSU job that he wasn't going anywhere. That left many of them bitter and disillusioned for a few days. But they quickly regrouped for the Citrus Bowl.

The 2000 Citrus Bowl

The 1999 season had been a great season with nine victories, Top 10 ranking, and an invitation to a New Year's Day Bowl. But soon after the season ended, fireworks erupted in the office of MSU president Peter McPherson. Nick Saban was on the verge of accepting the head coach's job at Louisiana State unless McPherson would engineer a raise. McPherson said no, Saban took the job, and Bobby Williams—on the advice of Saban—became the interim head coach.

Williams stepped in, calming those betrayed and refocusing those distracted. The other assistant coaches remained with MSU. They rallied around Williams, marching one night to McPherson's house to lobby the president to remove the interim label and make Williams the permanent head coach. McPherson responded by naming Williams the school's 21st head coach before the bowl game. The decision made history. Thirty-three years after the groundbreaking Spartans started six blacks on its legendary defense, Williams became the first black head coach in Spartans history and only the second in conference history. "First and foremost our objective was to select the most qualified person for the position,"

McPherson said. "But once it's completed and you step back and see what you've done, it's impossible not to measure the historic aspects of the decision."

A 10-year assistant coach at Michigan State under George Perles and Saban, Williams enjoyed immense popularity and respect among the players. With Williams' status settled, everyone's attention finally turned to the football game against Florida and its wizardly head coach Steve Spurrier. One of college football's marquee programs, the Gators had won a national championship three years earlier but had slipped a notch in 1999. Nevertheless, they still featured speed and athleticism at nearly every position.

On the night before the game on New Year's Eve, the Spartans players were ordered to bed at 10:00, giving them ample time to dream of heroics to come. "We'd be down by four points with a couple of minutes to go," Bill Burke fantasized prophetically the night before. "We'd get the ball back, then drive down the field, and score the winning touchdown."

After a 7–3 first-quarter lead for the Gators, both offenses turbo-charged the second quarter, combining to score 31 points. Plaxico Burress scored on a 37-yard touchdown pass, and linebacker T.J. Turner returned a fumble 24 yards to give Michigan State a 17–7 lead. Behind quarterback Doug Johnson and receiver Travis Taylor, Florida charged back to move in front just before half.

The lead changed hands two times in the third quarter, a period marked by chippy play and rising tempers. Ejections removed three players, including Spartans defensive end Hubert Thompson, a Florida native. By the early fourth quarter, the Gators had grabbed a 34–26 lead despite a banner day so far for Burress. That day got better when Burress hauled in a 30-yard pass for his third touchdown reception of the day. Burke hit Gari Scott for the two-point conversion to tie the game at 34.

The two teams slugged it out until the Spartans gained possession of the ball at their own 45-yard line with time quickly winding down. A short pass to Burress—his career-high 13th reception on the day—and four carries for 28 yards by Lloyd Clemons, a gritty, overachieving senior back, moved the ball to the Gators 18-yard line.

With seconds remaining in the game, Paul Edinger trotted on the field for the biggest field goal attempt of his career. He turned his back to the ball—his usual, yet unorthodox delivery—waited for the snap, then pivoted around, and booted the football calmly through the uprights with no time left. The Spartans were Citrus Bowl champions, marking the program's first bowl win since 1990.

"This was a very big win for Michigan State," Williams said. "We played an entire game for 60 minutes. I am extremely proud of the way our team fought back." Burress picked up 185 receiving yards and left for the NFL after the season. "It means a lot, winning on national TV and picking up a bowl win. [Williams] has made all the right decisions," Burress said. "I wanted to come here and play as hard as I could." The Citrus Bowl victory made it 10 wins for the Spartans on the season—only the second time in school history Michigan State had won that many games.

Williams' coaching career had started like a lion; three years later it ended like a lamb. The highs included a dramatic win against Notre Dame in 2000, a memorable victory against Michigan the next year, and another bowl win against Fresno State in the Silicon Valley Bowl in 2001. Hopes boomed heading into 2002, but the season turned ugly fast. After suffering a 49–3 loss to Michigan in 2002, the Spartans' worst loss in 55 years, a reporter asked Williams if he had lost his team. "I don't know," he responded candidly. On the following Monday, Michigan State athletic director Ron Mason fired Williams.

46 The Whiny, 1990 Michigan Game

"When you've been around football as long as I have, you know that in the old fields, there's a big crown, and that field at Oregon to me looked like an eight to 10-inch crown, and that affects the throws to the sidelines particularly, and I think that affected John [Navarre]. We haven't played on a field with a crown like that. We don't make excuses, but I'm making one for him because I don't think it's an excuse; it's the truth."

—UM head coach Lloyd Carr, describing Autzen Stadium after Michigan lost to Oregon 31–27 in Eugene, Oregon in 2003.

To date the University of Michigan has lost 314 football games. How many were the fault of circumstances beyond the control of the Wolverines is unknown. What is certain is that Michigan would have far fewer losses if they hadn't been forced to play on such antiquities as crowned fields and with referees and officials determined to screw them. At least that is the impression one gets listening to the Men in Blue after many a loss. And rarely are the excuses and injustices greater than when the Wolverines fall to the Spartans. A prominent example is the 1990 rivalry game, one purportedly stolen by Michigan State.

Michigan entered the game ranked No. 1 in the country in Gary Moeller's first year as head coach. Students around the Michigan campus that week sported T-shirts that read: "NO 1 vs NO ONE." The Spartans, trying to recover from an irksome previous year, started 1990 in typically slow fashion: 1–2–1. The record masked a solid team that had lost a couple of close, heartbreaking games (also typical). The Spartans possessed a physical running game featuring two backs with different styles, Tico Duckett, the speed burner, and Hyland Hickson, the masher. Canny quarter-back Dan Enos could also run when necessary. Running back Jon Vaughn, drop-back quarterback Elvis Grbac, and Heisman Trophy hopeful Desmond Howard, a flashy receiver and kick returner, headlined Michigan. ABC broadcast the game to a national television audience with iconic Keith Jackson calling the action.

Michigan took the opening kickoff and marched down for a quick touchdown. Before MSU fans could down a shot of Pepto-Bismol, a 12-play, 76-yard drive capped by Enos' eight-yard touchdown run. The half ended 7–7 but not before MSU gained momentum with a goal-line stand. The action revved up in the second half. The Wolverines scored; the Spartans answered. Mike Iaquaniello picked off Grbac's pass at the Spartans 31-yard line, and eight plays later Hyland Hickson, in his greatest run as a Spartan, shed numerous tackles and high-stepped his way 26 yards into the end zone. MSU went up 21–14.

Apocalyptic Michigan fans breathed a sigh of relief the size of the Big House when Howard took the ensuing kickoff the distance. Tied again. On this day, however, the vaunted Michigan defense had no answer for the two-headed beast that kept battering at them. Hickson and Duckett—with a pass to Hickson mixed in—bulled their way 70 yards down the field to score on Duckett's nine-yard touchdown run. That gave the Spartans the lead and 236 rushing yards in the game. (Hickson and Duckett would finish the year with 1,000 yards each, the only duo in the history of the Big Ten to accomplish that in a single season.)

Down by seven with just 1:59 remaining, Grbac swiftly drove the Wolverines to the 13. With six seconds left he connected with Derrick Alexander on a seven-yard touchdown pass. Moeller, in the era before overtime and wanting to preserve the Wolverines' No. 1 ranking, decided to go for the win.

Howard lined up on the right side of the Spartans defense across from Eddie Brown. On the snap Howard made a quick juke to his left and then broke right. Brown lunged after him, just as Grbac lofted a pass in Howard's direction. Howard stumbled as the ball hit his chest. It then popped out as he fell to the ground. The officials ruled the pass incomplete. "He dropped it...He dropped it," screamed Keith Jackson in the broadcast booth. The Wolverines recovered the onside kick, but Grbac's Hail Mary pass was intercepted by Brown.

"No One" had upset Number 1. "This is a classic for the state of Michigan," crowed Perles. "These two teams showed the country what this state is made of. This is a big victory for us. We've had some big wins—like the Rose Bowl. But this is really a big one."

While the Spartans celebrated, Jackson called it, "one of the great college football games of my lifetime." The Wolverines couldn't have disagreed more. Howard and his teammates stood around forlornly, wondering why no flag had been thrown for what everyone in Ann Arbor thought was an obvious trip by Brown. In the postgame press conference, Moeller snapped at a reporter who asked about the play. "You guys saw it," he growled. "It was ridiculous." Grbac was even more combative and blunt. "Regardless of everything else, the guys thought he caught it," the UM quarterback said. "We didn't think they could stop us and we don't think they did."

Two decades later Michigan has not budged off that position. "They [MSU] cheated," said Howard, hardly letting bygones be bygones. "You can laugh, but it's a fact. They cheated...The wrong team won. The team that won cheated. Michigan State cheated. They got away with it."

Brown, the man accused of cheating, remains coy about what actually happened. He admits to contact, but insists it was a good football play. UM fans, former players, bloggers, and other Maize and Blue sympathizers have spent the past two decades arguing the opposite. In the process, they have further reinforced the notion that for Michigan losing fair and square is not what the other guys do.

47 Mark Dantonio

Changing head coaches as often as college seniors come and go is a recipe for trouble. But that's what happens when a school suffers through six non-winning conference seasons in seven years, the worst stretch in its history. Mark Dantonio, officially named Michigan State football head coach on November 27, 2006, was hired to put an end to the coaching carousel. So far so good.

Dantonio hails from Ohio and played football, basketball, and track in high school. After a one-year stint at West Point, he eventually found his way to South Carolina where he lettered three years as a fifth defensive back and special teams player. Then he embarked on a college coaching career that started slowly and included numerous stops throughout the Midwest: Ohio, Purdue, Butler (Kansas) Community College, Ohio State, Akron, Youngstown State, Kansas, and then MSU under Nick Saban. He stayed at Michigan State through the 2000 season. In the next year, Jim Tressel, who hired Dantonio at Akron, offered him the Ohio State defensive coordinator position, an offer too good to refuse. The Buckeyes won the national championship in 2002 behind a world-beating defense, which captured the attention of Cincinnati, who hired Dantonio as its head coach after the 2003 season.

Cincinnati went to two bowl games, posted an 18–17 record, and played a physical brand of football under Dantonio. The record failed to overwhelm, but keen observers of college football could see what Dantonio was starting to build at Cincinnati. Among those were MSU administrators—especially president Lou Anna Simon and soon-to-be athletic director Mark Hollis, who knew Dantonio and his family from their stay at MSU in the 1990s. Both sides tentatively put out feelers in the late fall of

2006, but Dantonio refused any direct contact with MSU until after the Bearcats regular season ended. MSU complied with Dantonio's no-contact wish, though not without some sweaty palms as the coaching search dragged on.

MSU came calling. Dantonio's family remembered their time in East Lansing fondly. "It was a place that Becky and I believed in," Dantonio said. So he accepted the job and returned to East Lansing six years after saying good-bye for what he figured would be forever. Two days after his initial press conference, Dantonio appeared on a Lansing area radio show with his family. The new coach's two daughters brought the house down with their rendition of the Spartans fight song.

Dantonio didn't bring the press corps to its feet during his press conference. "I believe in toughness," he said. "I believe in establishing a mind-set. Everyone talks about wanting the most talented team, but I want a team that's the toughest mentally and physically. That's the team that will fight to every last ounce of its being. And that's the team that usually wins." The words didn't necessarily stir. But the demeanor did: earnest, determined, combative. Something about it said the days of MSU riding coach were over.

Dantonio scrapped the spread offense run by his predecessor and replaced it with a pro-style, two-back attack. He relentlessly upgraded the defense. Most importantly he took a sledgehammer to the culture of the program. In his first five seasons at MSU, Dantonio won a school-record 44 games. He did it by emulating and tweaking the ideas and philosophies of Tressel and Saban and the countless other coaches he encountered along the way. He did it with a stoic persona that belies a dry sense of humor and proclivity for the wild and occasionally crazy. And he did it by not backing down from any challenge. "Coach keeps things in perspective better than any person I've been around," said Dan Enos, a former Spartan quarterback and assistant under Dantonio. "He doesn't get caught up on a daily basis on his emotions—whether you win or lose. Actually, some of the toughest losses that occurred when he and I were together, that's when he's at his best."

The Ups and Downs of Nick Saban

"Who wouldn't want to play here?" first-year head coach Nick Saban shouted above the pulsing Spartan Stadium crowd to the ABC sideline reporter after his Spartans had beaten Michigan in thrilling come-from-behind fashion in 1995. Swept up in the euphoria of a big win against Michigan, Saban used the opportunity to sell what he was trying to build at MSU. But over the next few years, many Spartans fans started to wonder if he really wanted to be at Michigan State. A few more moments like the 1995 win against Michigan followed but so did an untold number of bizarre and gut-wrenching losses all set against a backdrop of constant rumors that Saban sought an NFL job. It was a dizzying and maddening time that culminated in an abrupt and bitter departure.

Saban, a West Virginia native who played at Kent State, served as George Perles' defensive coordinator for the Gang Green defense of 1987, one of the best defenses in Spartans history. He drove his players relentlessly, harangued them mercilessly, and squeezed out every ounce of talent they had. In 1990 he became head coach of Toledo, turning a 6–5 team into a 9–2 one. The NFL contacted him after the season, and establishing a future pattern, he left after just a single season to become defensive coordinator under Bill Belichick at Cleveland. The Browns defense developed into one of the NFL's best, and Saban's reputation climbed.

Michigan State hired Saban in 1995 to put things back on track after the program had slipped—and been slapped with probation—in the final years of Perles. The decision to hire Saban was almost universally praised. He quickly cleaned up the mess off the field and started improving the product between the white lines as well. His first team finished 6–4–1 and played in a bowl, only Michigan State's second in the last five years. And the stirring 28–25 win against Michigan served as the season's undisputed highlight.

But a Saban tirade showed he had not mellowed since his days as defensive coordinator at MSU. After Michigan State had been whipped by Nebraska in Saban's first game as head coach, the Spartans somberly trekked back to their locker room. Meanwhile Saban delivered a harsh assessment to the press. The players had "quit," he bellowed, a stinging rebuke for a team just getting acquainted with its new coach.

The heat never really lifted even as the results changed for the better. Practices were intense and characterized by severe and nearly uninterrupted criticism. The assistant coaches worked long hours. Saban worked even longer. Smart, abrasive, and expedient, he was single-mindedly devoted to the job of winning football games. Saban didn't care if his players, the boosters, the fans, or anyone liked him. He wooed recruits with a messianic abandon, casting a wide net (that resulted in a few bad apples). The only thing that mattered was football and how well someone played it. He possessed the type of personality that survives only when things are going well. But they didn't always go well.

During the next three seasons, the Spartans continued to straddle the .500 line. Big wins teased but led to nothing but gray skies. The Spartans dominated Wisconsin 30–13 in 1996 and then suffered a drubbing at the hands of Michigan the next week. The Spartans then blew a late lead against the Nittany Lions, which also happened the year before, to drop to 6–5.

Championship Pedigree

Seven national championship head coaches learned their craft at MSU, having coached in some capacity at the school. Frank Kush played and coached there. (*indicates head coach at MSU):

*Harry Kipke (Michigan, 1932, 1933)
Frank Leahy (Notre Dame, 1940, 1943, 1946, 1947, 1949)
Forest Evashevski (Iowa, 1958)
Frank Kush (Arizona State, 1975)
Dob Devaney (Nebraska, 1970, 1971)
Dan Devine (Notre Dame, 1977)
*Nick Saban (LSU, 2003; Alabama, 2009, 2011, 2012)

Michigan State started 1997 by winning their first five games all in blowout fashion, including a 23–7 win against Notre Dame. That moved them to No. 11 in the AP poll and created the possibility of a titanic matchup of two undefeated teams when the Spartans and Wolverines were to meet in two weeks. But a blocked field goal as time expired against Northwestern smothered those hopes. The loss snowballed into four more losses, including the final one to Purdue, a defeat not even Ripley could believe.

The folly in West Lafayette, Indiana, deserves its own wing in not just the Spartans Hall of Shame but all of college football. Leading 21–10 with just under three minutes to play in the game, the Spartans had the ball deep in Boilermakers territory and decided to kick a field goal. Chris Gardner's 43-yard attempt was blocked, which was bad enough, but Roosevelt Colvin of Purdue scooped up the ball and returned it the distance for a touchdown, the worst scenario of all the possible outcomes. Then the home team recovered an onside kick and easily sliced through the tottering Spartans defense to score the go-ahead touchdown with 40 seconds left. MSU still managed to get in field goal range, but Gardner badly missed his 40-plus yard attempt on the game's final play. "This is about as disappointed as I've ever been," said Saban after the game.

Somehow the Spartans picked up the pieces from the Purdue "disappointment" and saved their season with an improbable 49–14 thrashing of Penn State to finish the year 7–4.

No season symbolized better the Jekyll and Hyde nature of the Spartans under Saban than 1998. A dispiriting blowout loss on the road to Oregon was immediately followed by a near-flawless takedown of Notre Dame. An upset of No. 1-ranked Ohio State was offset by a humiliating wipeout by Penn State. The 6–6 season also included an upset loss to Minnesota in which the Spartans couldn't recover an onside kick late, and after the epic Ohio State win, another loss to Purdue was decided by—you guessed it—a Boilermaker recovery of an onside kick.

An inability to recover onside kicks was only surpassed by the futility shown in bowl games under Saban. Getting into the bowls was a needed boost for the program. Losing 45–26, 38–0, and 51–23 was not. Perhaps the players only had so much tolerance for the insanely demanding tactics of their head coach and tuned him out after November. Perhaps Saban proved his true genius just by getting MSU to bowl games where programs with superior talent exposed the overachieving Spartans. Or perhaps the annual rumors that the NFL wanted to hire Saban, and the subsequent flirtations with the Miami Dolphins and New York Giants, created too many distractions.

After leading MSU to a 9–2 season in 1999, Saban resigned before the Citrus Bowl to take the head coaching job at LSU. One year after winning a national title there, he briefly coached the Dolphins before returning to college football at Alabama. With the Crimson Tide, Saban has become one of college football's coaching greats, winning three national championships in a four-year stretch.

Kirk Gibson

Though it did not change the outcome of another blowout win in 1978, it was an unforgettable play by an unforgettable Spartan. Michigan State had moved inside the Minnesota 10-yard line. Wide receiver Kirk Gibson lined up to the left and ran his route to the corner of the left end zone. As Gibson turned around, Spartans quarterback Eddie Smith pitched the ball right to running back Steve Smith. A Gopher defender immediately popped him. The ball squirted in the air and landed in the arms of a Minnesota defensive back. Ninety yards of empty turf stared him in the face. A touchdown seemed certain.

Gibson stood clear on the other side of the play at least 15 yards away. Most players in his situation would have taken a step or two for show and stopped. But Gibson started sprinting in the direction of the ball carrier. Like a horse coming from 10 lengths back on the final post, he kept passing teammates until he improbably caught the Minnesota ball carrier and wrestled him to the ground around midfield. The Spartans bench and the crowd at Spartan Stadium watched in disbelief at the world-class speed, raw desire, and relentless hustle. That was Gibson, a man of uncommon ability and red-hot coil intensity.

Few major colleges recruited Gibson, a star at Waterford Kettering outside Detroit. He nearly ended up at Central Michigan until an MSU assistant under Denny Stolz saw his film while watching potential recruits from another school. He arrived at Michigan State without acclaim or high expectations. That changed in August. Gibson ran much faster than he appeared to on film. Moreover, on the field he growled and snarled and backed down from no one. He loved to hit.

Gibson earned a starting job as a receiver his freshman year. He only caught nine passes in Stolz's run-oriented offense, but four of them went for touchdowns. MSU fired Stolz after the 1975 season and replaced him with Darryl Rogers. The Californian believed in the omnipotence of the forward pass. That meant a larger role for Gibson and a three-year treat for Spartans fans.

Initially, Rogers wanted to move Gibson to linebacker. His size, temperament, and athletic skill would make for a potent defender. But the Spartans lacked speed at wide receiver, so the coach left him at his original position. Three years later Gibson had obliterated Spartans receiving records. Gibson beat defensive backs with sprinter speed, decent hands, and precise routes. He roamed intrepidly over the middle of the field, a place many receivers feared to tread. But Gibson feared little. "Football is an intimidating sport, and you absolutely must be the intimidator," Gibson wrote in his autobiography. "When I looked across the line of scrimmage, I knew I had to own the defender physically and mentally because when you've defeated him both ways you have an edge." The linebacker that Rogers thought Gibson could be never fully deserted him. Neither did his work ethic. Each year he decreased his 40 time, going from 4.6 as a freshman to 4.3 as a senior. He added muscle and weight as well, bulking up from 198 pounds his first year to 227 pounds by his senior year

After missing parts of three games during his junior season due to injury, Gibson decided to play baseball at Michigan State. Rogers suggested that might give him negotiating leverage with the NFL, and that decision changed the path of his life. Gibson hit .390, clubbed 16 home runs, and stole 21 bases for Michigan State. Baseball scouts drooled. The Tigers drafted Gibson in the first round. He signed with them for $200,000 and spent the summer in the minor leagues. Some worried that Gibson's football career at MSU had ended. But he never considered that route. "I would

Kirk Gibson, an All-American wide receiver for Michigan State before going on to a successful Major League Baseball career, catches a pass against Michigan. (Getty Images)

never have walked out on those guys. Never. Not for a million dollars. Not for five million dollars," Gibson wrote.

The Spartans soared in 1978, earning a share of the Big Ten title and finishing 12th in the final AP poll. The offense revved like the engine of a Ferrari with Gibson an integral component of that

Four MSU Athletes Famous for Something Else

James Caan—The actor, who notably starred in *The Godfather*, played football at Michigan State in 1956 before transferring to NYU. He used that football background while playing a football coach in *The Program*.

Peter Gent—The pro football player and author of bestselling *North Dallas Forty* was the leading scorer, an adept passer, and a renowned leaper for Spartans basketball from 1961 to 1964.

Steve Garvey—A 10-time All-Star for the Los Angeles Dodgers and San Diego Padres, Garvey played football for Michigan State in 1967.

Seth Mitchell—The heavyweight boxer, who has fought in more than two dozen fights and has 19 wins by knockout, played football for MSU from 2002 to 2003.

engine. He set Michigan State records at the time for receptions (42) and receiving yards (806) in a season. He had two 100-yard games and caught an 86-yard touchdown pass. He was named first team All-American by UPI among others. Gibson finished as Michigan State's all-time leader in receptions (112) and receiving yards (2,347). His 21-yard-per-catch career average is still the MSU record. NFL scouts salivated over his tools and considered using a draft pick on him, but Gibson remained committed to professional baseball and went on to stardom.

Gibson never performed on television with the Spartans due to MSU's three-year television ban, a result of infractions from school boosters providing athletes lucrative jobs involving little actual work. So few outside of East Lansing remember him as a football player. But Spartans fans can still picture blond locks poking out from under the helmet of a green comet streaking down the middle of the field, calling for the ball and looking to deliver a crunching blow.

50 Sing the Fight Song

After the MAC Aggies upset Michigan in 1913 for its first win against Michigan, the Aggie band—made up of ROTC members—marched triumphantly through the streets of Ann Arbor loudly playing…"The Victors." The Aggies had no fight song of their own, so they played Michigan's fight song.

The next week MAC beat national power Wisconsin in Madison. The Aggie band didn't play "On Wisconsin," but MAC civil engineering student and Yellmaster Francis Irving Lankey, a talented piano player as well, found the song stirring and started noodling over the idea of creating a fight song for his school.

In 1915 Lankey finally set to music the words his friend and fellow MAC student Arthur L. Sayles had written for the Aggie fight song. The two didn't publish the song right away, however, and it stayed in mothballs until a tragic event led to its publication.

After graduation Lankey worked as an instructor for the Army Air Corps. During an air demonstration in the spring of 1919, he was killed while attempting to land his plane. His mourning girlfriend, likely seeking a way to honor his memory, published the song, which the football team initially sold at the 1919 Homecoming pep rally. In fewer than 30 minutes, all 770 copies on hand sold. The positive reaction to the song and brisk sales settled the matter. MAC had found its fight song. The band began playing the song at home football games the next year, and it has been played—with only slight variations—ever since.

The words are below:

On the banks of the Red Cedar
There's a school that's known to all
Its specialty is winning
And those Spartans play good ball
Spartan teams are never beaten
All through the game they'll fight
Fight for the only colors
Green and White
Go right through for MSU
Watch the points keep growing
Spartan teams are bound to win
They're fighting with a vim
Rah! Rah! Rah!
See their team is weakening
We're going to win this game
Fight! Fight! Rah! Team, Fight!
Victory for MSU

Double 11s

During the 2010 to 2011 seasons, the Spartans won 22 football games—11 each year behind a savvy quarterback, experienced receivers, two running backs with complementary styles, and their best defense since 1999. That win total exceeded by three the most in any two-year period in Michigan State history. In fact the Spartans had never even won 11 games in a season—let alone two straight.

The 2010 season shared many similarities with past successful MSU seasons: a hard-bitten team returning key parts—especially a strong defense and experienced quarterback—that previously had suffered through a surfeit of close losses. MSU lost just one game in the regular season (Iowa). They carried an undefeated record and No. 5 ranking into Iowa City in late October.

Three quarters into the season, they had the nation talking about a possible (gasp) national championship. Aaron Bates, the punter, threw a game-deciding touchdown pass in overtime! Clutch quarterback Kirk Cousins led comebacks against Illinois, Northwestern, and Purdue. Edwin Baker mixed up a concoction of runs for 1,201 yards on 5.8 yards a carry. The Spartans beat Wisconsin at its own game, snuffed out any hopes of Wolverine redemption in the Big House, and left the denizens of Happy Valley unhappy. They also overcame a scary moment when Mark Dantonio suffered a mild heart attack following the Spartans' heart-thumping victory against Notre Dame, which sidelined him for a couple games.

It all added up to an 11–1 season and a Big Ten title shared with Wisconsin and Ohio State. Because of various arcane rule changes, the Spartans ended up playing in the Capital One Bowl instead of the Rose Bowl. Healthy for the first time all season, the Crimson Tide rolled the Spartans in the bowl game, but the year proved an unadulterated success for Michigan State. A third straight win against Michigan, a thrilling overtime victory against Notre Dame, and the most wins in school history made sure of that. Greg Jones earned All-American honors again, and 11 Spartans made first or second team All-Big Ten.

With a bullish outlook based on the return of the previous season's core, expectations, often the Spartans' boogey man, reached as high as an Aaron Bates punt heading into 2011. Cousins, the two-pronged backfield of Baker and Le'Veon Bell, most of the deep defense, and dynamic receivers B.J. Cunningham and Keshawn Martin were all back for an encore. But few dreamed of another 11-win season.

The defense performed better than expected. Sacks, turnovers, and general mayhem became its calling card. Jerel Worthy, William Golston, Max Bullough, Johnny Adams, and Trenton Robinson all took turns making plays. One memorable individual effort represented the defense's ferocity. Spartans linebacker Denicos Allen pole vaulted over a Buckeye blocker to sack a wide-eyed Ohio State quarterback. All at once it drained the life out of the Buckeyes offense and Ohio Stadium. The most inspiring performance occurred again UM when Michigan's Denard Robinson spent more time staring at the Spartan Stadium turf than he did looking downfield.

On offense Cousins often hooked up with Cunningham or Martin to pull the Spartans out of the fire—or deliver the final blow. When something else was needed, there was a Hail Mary against Wisconsin and a fake punt against Iowa. And when the only thing needed was a tough yard or two, Bell found a way to churn it out.

The alchemy put the Spartans in the inaugural Big Ten Championship Game against Wisconsin. It went down to the final seconds before a roughing the punter penalty ended the Spartans' hopes of returning to the Rose Bowl.

52 The 2012 Outback Bowl

Here we go again.

Burned by five consecutive bowl losses and nine of the last 11, Michigan State fans may have been thinking this after Georgia took a 16–0 lead in the first half of the Outback Bowl. But before the pessimistic outlook could become a reality, the Spartans started clawing back.

The Spartans had spent 2011 dreaming about playing on New Year's Day. They accomplished that much. Tampa, Florida, the site of the Outback Bowl, however, was 2,000 miles away from where they wanted to be. Hopes of appearing in the school's first Rose Bowl in 25 years sank along with the yellow flag thrown for roughing the punter in the final seconds of the Big Ten Championship Game against Wisconsin. The loss dropped the Spartans from the cusp of the Rose Bowl to the Outback Bowl, the fourth bowl in the Big Ten pecking order.

Eventually the Spartans buried the disappointment from the loss and whatever residual bitterness existed from the bowl drop and started preparing for a talented Georgia team, who had lost in the SEC championship to LSU. "All week, all month really, there was a sense of urgency in our preparation because the fact that for me as a senior this was the last shot," said Kirk Cousins leading up to the game.

With Michigan State playing for the first time in the Outback Bowl and in Tampa, the defenses controlled the first 20 minutes. Georgia scored first when Keshawn Martin was tackled in his own end zone after a catching a screen pass. The Spartans offense continued to sputter, falling well short of 100 total first half yards. The only real offense in the first half for either side erupted midway through the second quarter: an 80-yard touchdown catch by Tavarres King and an electric 92-yard punt return for a touchdown by Brandon Boykin. That put the Spartans in a 16–0 hole heading into the locker room. "At halftime we had our doubts," Cousins said.

Those doubts dissipated quickly. The Spartans seized control of the third quarter, scoring on their second possession of the second half, converting a two-point conversion and then scoring again on Georgia native Darqueze Dennard's 38-yard interception return.

The two-point conversion failed, leaving the Spartans behind 16–14. A Georgia field goal, a Spartans drive ending in a 7-yard touchdown pass to Keith Nichol, and a Georgia drive of their own left Georgia leading 27–20 with six minutes and change remaining.

After a Georgia punt, Cousins walked to the huddle with fewer than two minutes remaining, staring at perhaps the final possession of his collegiate career. "I kept thinking: *It can't end with a loss. It can't. We're not going to allow it,*" he said. In 10 plays and without any timeouts, Cousins drove the Spartans 85 yards in 1:36. Six pass completions to Nichol, B.J. Cunningham, Le'Veon Bell, and Martin—with a 20-yard scramble by Cousins mixed in—put the ball at the 1-yard line with fewer than 20 seconds remaining. Mark Dantonio called for a run, a high-risk decision, considering he had no timeouts. Bell churned and churned until finally he crossed the goal line, sending the game into overtime.

Overtime felt like payback against history. It started in typical Spartans fashion. Cousins threw an interception on MSU's first possession of overtime. Georgia only needed a field goal to win. Instead of sending the Spartans to defeat, Blair Walsh, one of the best kickers in college, drifted his attempt wide right from 42 yards. It was a startling break for a program not accustomed to them. After both sides kicked field goals in the second overtime, the Spartans' Bret Conway kicked a 28-yarder in the third overtime. MSU's defense then stiffened, bringing on Walsh for a 47-yarder. The hold and snap were good, but Anthony Rashad White, a Spartans reserve lineman, reached up his heavily bandaged arm and grazed the ball with his fingertips. It flopped to the ground, giving Michigan State the 33–30 victory. "We've been waiting for one of these bowl trophies for five years," Dantonio said. "It just points to us becoming an elite program…We've beaten every football team in the Big Ten the last four years…Two 11-win seasons—there's not many football teams in the country that are saying that right now."

John Macklin
and the Early Years

Michigan Agricultural College kicked off football in 1896, a couple of decades after a few schools on the East Coast starting fielding teams and 17 years after the University of Michigan's first season. Variously referred to as the Aggies and Farmers at the time, MAC knocked off East Lansing High School 10–0 in its first game. Until 1905 the Aggies competed in the MIAA conference, which featured small, local colleges such as Alma, Olivet, and Calvin. In 1906 MAC dropped out of the MIAA and became independent, adding a few intersectional games, including a tilt against still-emerging Notre Dame.

The first game played on campus occurred in 1902 at Old College Field just south of the Red Cedar River. MAC squared off for the first time against Michigan in 1898. The result was one to forget: 39–0. But the true nadir of the formative years—in which the Aggies went 19–23–4—occurred in 1902 when Michigan and coaching luminary Fielding Yost beat the Aggies 119–0. The humiliating defeat forced MAC's president to make a decision: get serious about competing in the sport or abandon it. A former athlete himself, John Snyder chose the former, hiring Chester Brewer from Albion, Michigan, to take over as head coach in 1903.

Brewer, the son of an Owosso, Michigan, farmer, fit in seamlessly at a school devoted to agriculture. He rallied support among the faculty and the community and started regularly beating the small schools on the schedule. Brewer upgraded the competition to include larger regional colleges. In 1907 the Wolverines returned to the schedule, and in 1908 the Aggies drew a prick of blood, tying UM 0–0 in the first rivalry game played in East Lansing. Delirious

MAC fans carried the players across the Red Cedar River bridge and celebrated all night.

Brewer never beat Michigan in his eight seasons, but in 1910 he put another scare in Yost's Wolverines before falling 6–3, a game plagued by the first of the rivalry's many controversial calls. A holding call wiped out Leon Hill's 70-yard punt return for an Aggie touchdown. No flag appeared until after the play when Yost confronted the officials to plead for the call. The officials capitulated, even though the hold took place on the other side of the play, according to the alleged Wolverine victim. Another controversy marred the second half when the Wolverines were rewarded the decisive touchdown after the Michigan ball carrier appeared to be stopped at the 2-yard line.

Brewer's 58–23–7 record helped establish football as a winning proposition in East Lansing. His signature win came in 1910 when the Aggies shut out Notre Dame 17–0 in front of 4,000 raucous fans in East Lansing. The Fighting Irish coach, Shorty Longman, saluted MAC by calling it "vastly underrated." The immensely popular Brewer left for the head coaching job at Missouri in 1911.

Brewer's replacement, John Macklin, grew up on the East Coast and played football at the University of Pennsylvania. He was a commanding figure, standing at 6'5" and weighing 230 pounds, which made him larger than most of his players and helped reinforce his authority, something that could have been easily compromised because of his personable nature.

Macklin drilled his charges relentlessly on proper blocking and tackling techniques. He even employed a tackling dummy, which every player had to attack over and over again in his long and demanding practices. He would develop a reputation for having some of the best lines in college football. The players liked Macklin, who unlike many of his peers, eschewed indiscriminate tirades and other terror tactics. When he did launch a verbal assault, it was calculated and without malice. Macklin's first two teams went 12–2. The only two losses were to Michigan, including a deflating 55–7 defeat. The Aggies, though, enjoyed one cachet victory against Ohio State, who was just beginning its ascent to college football elite.

MAC fans still desperately wanted a win against Michigan, an established power in the sport. If MAC could beat its in-state rival, it would bring newfound credibility to the football program and the college. Macklin knew how much a victory over Michigan would mean. He also sensed his team moving closer to pulling it off. *The MAC Record*, the student newspaper, expressed a similar sanguine view about the Aggies' prospects in 1913: "This year's football season promises to be a most important one in the football history of MAC, and if we can judge by indications of the present, it will be the most successful one that we have ever had."

After opening the 1913 season with two shutout, blowout wins, Macklin ordered extra practice before the upcoming Michigan game. He had electric lights installed so the team could practice at night. He even made a tactical change, moving Blake Miller, the team's star end, to halfback. The campus brimmed with hope as evidenced by the almost 1,500 students (out of 1,634 total) who turned out for a rally the night before the game. The buildup, which included both sides trading pregame barbs, eclipsed in intensity anything before it.

Macklin's intense preparations paid off. In what *The Detroit News* columnist Eddie Batchelor years later called "one of the biggest upsets in all of college football history," the Aggies knocked off Michigan 12–7. George Gauthier surprised the Wolverines with seven pass completions on 19 attempts for 100 yards, a staggering aerial display for the period. The performance earned Gauthier the nickname "Wolverine Killer." Macklin—ahead of his time in his belief that the best way to combat passing was to apply pressure to the quarterback—credited his line for giving Gauthier ample time to throw and took a swipe at Yost in the process. "If a man is allowed to take his own time, he will be very likely to make a good heave and land the ball where he wants," Macklin said. "That is why our forward passes worked so well against Michigan. The Wolverines gave my men so much time to size things up that they were able to make very accurate tosses."

Star halfback Blake Miller suffered an injury midway through the game, a brutally violent and heated affair. Miller's brother, Hewitt, replaced him and scored the decisive touchdown when he recovered a fumble and returned it 46 yards for a score. The Lansing area responded as if Macklin's team had written everyone a $100 check. The students set a bonfire in front of the capitol building and local theatres made admission free for the weekend. MAC even canceled classes on Monday.

Rechanneling its emotions, MAC impressively toppled a very strong Wisconsin squad the next week in Madison. MAC kept right on winning after that, finishing the season 7–0, the first unbeaten and untied year in the school's history. National attention for the first sustained period rained down on East Lansing.

Macklin only coached two more seasons, and neither year matched the heights of 1913. However, a win against eastern power Penn State, MAC's first win against an intersectional power, and one more victory against Michigan in 1915, a 24–0 no-doubter, gave fans plenty to holler about in Macklin's final two seasons. Macklin stepped down after the 1915 season. In his five seasons, he finished 29–5, the second highest winning percentage of any Michigan State coach.

Rocket

Under the lights in Spartan Stadium, the 2011 Wisconsin-Michigan State game lived up to its billing as the two best teams in the Big Ten alternated leads and momentum. The Spartans trailed early by 14 points and then rallied to take a 14-point lead. The Badgers rallied back themselves to tie the score at 31–31 with just more than a minute to play in the game. Overtime looked likely, a bad omen for the Spartans, who appeared to be tiring.

Michigan State moved the ball to the Badgers 44-yard line with only four seconds left in regulation. A field goal from this distance was out of the question. So the Spartans called a Hail Mary play they practice every week for situations such as this: Rocket. Rocket had numerous variations. Head coach Mark Dantonio first called for the one in which quarterback Kirk Cousins rolls left. But after a Wisconsin timeout, Dantonio changed the play so that Cousins would roll out to his right.

Keith Nichol lined up farthest to the right with two other receivers on the same side. Nichol came to Michigan State as a quarterback but not before decommitting from the Spartans as a senior in high school, playing a year at Oklahoma, then returning to Michigan State as sophomore. A prep legend at a school only a few miles from Michigan State, he arrived at MSU as the heir apparent to senior quarterback Brian Hoyer before changing positions to wide receiver.

Nichol took off on the snap, but his defender drove him out of bounds. He would be late by a shallow breath to the end zone. Cousins' primary receiver was B.J. Cunningham, who was greeted in the end zone by three Badgers, including Wisconsin wide receiver turned temporary defensive back Jared Abbrederis. Cousins rolled right, stopped, planted, and then unloaded a 50-yard pass toward the scrum waiting for the ball three yards deep in the end zone.

Meanwhile Nichol had shed his block and arrived just as the ball began its drop into the pile of green and red. Abbrederis jumped prematurely. The ball floated over his head where it hit the facemask of Cunningham and ricocheted about a half yard out of the end zone. Standing there was Nichol. He reached up for the ball, secured it, and then lunged toward the end zone. Badgers Mike Taylor and Antonio Fenelus pulled him back. "I thought I was going to catch it and roll in," Nichol said. "I didn't really see anybody when I caught the ball." He continued to fight forward, managing to twist his body ahead one last time before being wrestled to the ground just short of the goal line. "My stomach almost dropped," he said. "Not like this. You can't lose like this."

The officials marked the ball at about the half-yard line. Spartan Stadium groaned, then fell into silence. To no one's surprise, the officials announced that the play was being reviewed. The crowd cheered. On the big screen, the play was showed again. It appeared as though Nichol had indeed crossed the goal line on his last desperate swing. Watching from a seat right at the goal line, Nichol's father worried that his son may not have had full possession of the ball. Over and over again the controversial action was replayed. Finally, the head official walked to the area near the action, activated his microphone, and said, "After further review, the runner did cross the line."

Whatever else he said was drowned out by the biggest roar heard in Spartan Stadium since...well...since who knows when. The Spartans raced onto the field. Dantonio did a little leap. And Nichol, a man who failed to win the starting quarterback job he desperately wanted but agreed—for the good of the team—to play wide receiver, was mobbed by his teammates. "You've just made history," his brother Kyle, a walk-on, told him in the mad celebration.

The catch sealed the Spartans 37–31 win and—as Kyle predicted—made history. "As much as my career has been up and down, all the adversity," said Keith Nichol, recounting what Dantonio told him. "I'm going to be remembered for a play like that for a long time."

Steve Smith

His name was as vanilla as a sundae without the fudge. But by the end of his college career, Smith's name would sit first among all the Joneses and Smiths and everyone else who played at Michigan State.

After growing from a 5'8" freshman to a 6'5" junior, Smith would average 26 points, 12 rebounds, and 10 assists as a senior at Pershing High School in Detroit. Jud Heathcote had to battle more than 20 major colleges for Smith. But Smith's loyalties always leaned green ever since he discovered Magic Johnson in the 1970s, and he committed to Michigan State over Missouri in 1987. He nearly quit basketball, however, after an altercation with his coach at Pershing during his sophomore year. He wanted to transfer, but his mother refused to allow him, telling Smith he could leave the team but not the school—because he was at Pershing as a student not a basketball player. Smith rejoined the team, chastened and more mature.

By the time he enrolled at MSU, Smith stood 6'7". Heathcote predicted that Smith would be MSU's next great guard. After Heathcote pointed him out to MSU athletic director Doug Weaver before Smith's first practice, Weaver remarked, "That skinny kid down there? You're kidding me." Smith began slowly as the freshman learned how to cope with Heathcote's volley of sharp-edged critiques. His coach taunted him with calls of "wimp" because of his skinny frame and lack of strength.

A two-time All-American, the 6'7" Steve Smith—like Magic Johnson—had the size of a forward but the playmaking skills of a guard. (Getty Images)

Smith also had to deal with Jesse Hall, a more celebrated Spartans recruit and freshman from southern Illinois who possessed boundless athleticism. Smith and Hall jousted for playing time, developing a rivalry, which Smith ultimately dominated, and Hall transferred soon after. Smith started flashing his potential in games as well. He scored 18 and had seven assists in an upset overtime win against Indiana. He sank two free throws to beat Ohio State with no time on the clock. The Spartans stumbled to a 10–18 record, however, keeping Smith a local story.

During the offseason Smith worked strenuously to add weight and strength. With the help of a top-ranked recruiting class, he guided the Spartans to an eight-game improvement for the 1988-'89 season and a spot in the NIT semifinals where Michigan State lost to St. Louis. Smith scored 34 points against Villanova in the quarterfinals. "We saw nine films on him," said Wildcats coach Rollie Massimino. "We knew what he could do. He just did what he had to do and made every shot."

What Smith could do, as Heathcote wrote in his autobiography, was "get a shot for himself." And he became an exceptional guard as well due to his "size, ball skills, and shooting range." Some compared elements of Smith's game to his hero, Magic, because of his height advantage and ball handling skills. Smith, however, enjoyed a better shooting touch and could push his range out farther. "I don't compare anyone to Magic," Heathcote said. "But I can see why the tendency to compare them is there. They are both tremendously versatile and multidimensional."

The Spartans hadn't contended for a Big Ten title since 1986. They hadn't won a conference title since 1979. Smith's junior year ended those droughts. Michigan State, 28–6 overall, finished in first place in the conference and advanced to the Sweet 16 in the NCAA Tournament. Smith raised his scoring average to 20.2 and his rebounds to seven a game. He scored 25 second half points against Michigan on his way to 36 for the game. "I'm still dazzled

Four Better Pros Than Collegians

Kevin Willis (1981 to 1984): He never played on an NCAA tournament team nor made All-Big Ten, but in the NBA, the seven-footer became an All-Star, appeared in 11 postseasons, and won an NBA championship

Herb Adderley (1958 to 1960): A fine college player, Adderley failed to win more than six games in a season as a Spartan. He was named All-Big Ten but never earned All-American honors. He went on to star in the NFL, playing in four of the first six Super Bowls and five Pro Bowls. Adderley earned induction into the Pro Football Hall of Fame in 1980. He's one of only two Spartans in there.

Derrick Mason (1993 to 1996): A great kickoff returner whose 2,575 career return yards set a Big Ten mark, Mason was a middling receiver who caught eight touchdown passes in his MSU career. But in the NFL, he was named to two Pro Bowls as a receiver, caught 943 passes over 15 years, and holds the Baltimore Ravens' record for career receiving yards.

Muhsin Muhammad (1992 to 1995): The footprints he left at MSU washed away almost immediately. But in the NFL, he became a two-time Pro Bowl receiver and caught 860 passes in a 14-year career, which also included a Super Bowl record 85-yard touchdown reception for the Carolina Panthers.

and dizzy over what he did," said Michigan head coach Steve Fisher. After the game Smith grabbed the Spartans flag and waved it around over his head at midcourt. Two days later he scorched Minnesota for 39. The outburst sparked Minnesota coach Clem Haskins to openly plead for Smith to head to the NBA after his junior year. Heathcote called them the two best back-to-back games any player of his ever had.

At home and off the court, Smith was orderly and quiet. Rowdy to Smith meant turning up the volume of his stereo. On the court, however, Smith was a maestro with words, the kind designed to vex and disrupt opponents. "His game, like Magic's, is full of flourishes from the no-look passes to the odd way he drags his gangly 6'7", 200 pound body," wrote *Sports Illustrated* in 1990. "There's also a touch of arrogance about him...Smith has been known to taunt opponents...and [teammate Mark] Montgomery calls him, 'the only guy I know who can strut while he's backpedaling.'" Heathcote grudgingly tolerated Smith's propensity to trash talk, something Smith developed while playing pickup basketball on the streets of Detroit. "The way I learned to play, you had to show that you just weren't going to be intimidated. And to do that you had to be the one doing the intimidating," Smith said.

Smith finished his Spartans career with 2,263 points (most in MSU history at that time) and as the fifth leading scorer in Big Ten history. He was named Spartan MVP three times, Big Ten MVP twice, and All-American twice. The Spartans failed to repeat as Big Ten champs and fell in the second round of the NCAA tournament during his senior year, but Smith hit a game-winning three-point shot at the buzzer against Wisconsin-Green Bay to avoid the opening round upset. He also raised his scoring average by five points to 25. Smith spent 14 seasons in the NBA, earning All-Star honors in 1998 and also won an Olympic gold medal in 2000.

In 1998 he gave MSU $2.5 million to help build the Clara Bell Smith Student-Athlete Academic Center, named after his mother. Smith also earned three sportsmanship awards during his time in the NBA. "It's important that we all remember where we are from, where we are, and who helped us get there. Steve Smith has done that. He remembered his family...and he's remembered Michigan State University," said Heathcote upon Smith's retirement from basketball. "I'm proud to have been Steve Smith's coach, but I'm more proud to call him my friend."

56 Daugherty's First Team All-Americans

Dan Currie (1957)

The oh-so-close Spartans of 1957, who lost one game in controversial fashion, whipped the opposition in the trenches. They led the Big Ten in rushing and total yards allowed and paced the league in total yards and scoring. A linchpin of both units, Currie excelled as a linebacker and center. Earlier in his career at MSU, he played guard and filled in at all the other positions on the line.

Called "the finest linebacker in the school's history" by his coaches, Currie was named the MVP of the 1957 Spartans and was drafted in the first round by the Green Bay Packers. He starred at linebacker and earned All-Pro honors in 1961, the year he appeared on the cover of *Sports Illustrated*.

Walt Kowalczyk (1957)

"Bringing this guy down is trying to bring down a blacksmith," said UCLA coach Red Saunders after his Bruins had spent the 1956 Rose Bowl being punished by Spartans running back Walt Kowalczyk, who played the game with a broken nose after the first quarter and later a fractured rib. "The Sprinting Blacksmith," as he then became known, had a mean stiff-arm, almost unnatural toughness, and surprising speed. He started the day he became eligible as a sophomore in 1955.

Born and raised in Massachusetts, Kowalczyk scored touchdowns in eight of Michigan State's nine games in 1957, rushing for 545 yards in helping the Spartans come within a whisker of winning another Big Ten title and a unanimous national championship. Pivotal in the Spartans' historic rout of Michigan that same year, he rushed for 113 yards in the 35–6 triumph. Heisman

Trophy voters put him third in the balloting, which remains the best showing—along with Sherman Lewis seven years later—of any Spartans player. The Philadelphia Eagles drafted him in the first round, and Kowalcyzk played four years in the league.

Dean Look (1959)

Look, one of three local Lansing kids to earn first team All-American honors for the Spartans, began his career as a halfback and punt returner. His electrifying 92-yard punt return for a touchdown against Michigan in 1958 helped erase a 12-point deficit in a game that ended 12–12. The tie extended a Spartans unbeaten streak against UM that ultimately reached eight games. Before the 1959 season, Daugherty switched Look to quarterback. He struggled early primarily due to a shoulder injury, but eventually Look settled in. "He's just what the doctor ordered for the squad," Duffy Daugherty told the AP. "He has good poise, excellent judgment, and has been an inspiration."

He certainly inspired against Northwestern. Look led the Spartans to a 15–10 victory against the first-place Wildcats while completing all seven passes that he attempted, a conference record for completion percentage. Look finished the season, an up-and-down one for the Spartans, completing 50 percent of his passes for 785 yards and nine touchdowns, sterling numbers for the era. Drafted by the Denver Broncos, Look opted to play professional baseball for the Chicago White Sox instead. After his brief baseball career, he became an NFL referee, officiating in three Super Bowls over his 29-year career. It was Look who signaled touchdown for "The Catch," Dwight Clark's famous grab to capture the 1981 NFC championship for the San Francisco 49ers.

Norm Masters (1955)

With a nose that appeared to have been rearranged by a blender and a sense of humor matched only by his head coach, Masters humorously whipped opposing linemen. The Detroit native played both ways, a key part of a versatile offensive line that helped MSC set school passing records and a stout defensive line that held opponents to just 7.7 points a game, still fourth best in school history. Nicknamed "Stormin' Norman" for his vicious hits, Masters thrived on contact. Drafted by the Chicago Cardinals, he eventually ended up in Green Bay where he played offensive tackle from 1957 to 1964.

Earl Morrall (1955)

Morrall, who suffered through an inconsistent junior season, lost his starting quarterback job briefly before 1955 season. He quickly regained it, passing his way into history, and leading the Spartans to the Rose Bowl. When he dropped back to pass, he didn't piddle with the small stuff. His 9.1 yards a completion led the nation. As accurate as a calculator, the Muskegon, Michigan, native completed 42 of his 68 attempts for 941 yards, which tied the school record. In the final game of the 1955 season, Morrall riddled the Marquette secondary for 274 yards, another school record that stood for 14 years.

Multidimensional, Morrall handled the punting with distinction as well. His 42.9 average was second in the nation. For his career he threw for a then-record 2,015 yards and accounted for 7.4 total offense yards per attempt, a school record that still stands. An infielder on the 1954 MSC baseball team, he helped the Spartans earn a trip to the College World Series.

Morrall spent 21 years in the NFL, developing a reputation as the consummate backup quarterback under Johnny Unitas in Baltimore and then under Bob Griese in Miami. He stepped in seamlessly for both quarterbacks at critical junctures, leading the Colts and the Dolphins, the last NFL team to go undefeated, to Super Bowl wins.

Carl Nystrom (1955)

Relentless and fiery, Nystrom, nicknamed "Buck," played with a perpetually skinned nose, a result of the violent collisions he craved. Daugherty considered the MVP of the 1955 Spartans the greatest guard he ever coached. In the Spartans' memorable 21–7 upset of Notre Dame, Nystrom played all 60 minutes against an unbeaten Fighting Irish team that had never been scored upon. "I was unbelievably tired," he bluntly recalled years later. He also earned a spot on the first team of the Academic All-American squad, the first Spartan to earn both All-Amercian honors in the same year.

Nystrom stayed in the college game for decades after, serving as offensive line coach at Northern Michigan, North Dakota State, Oklahoma, Colorado, and for one year at Michigan State. "He's the greatest line coach who ever coached in high school or college football without question or exception. He's just so special," said Chuck Fairbanks, his boss at Colorado. "There's no one better in his ability to teach young players how to play. He's the unqualified best. He never lost his passion to coach kids."

Gerald Planutis (1955)

In Spartans football lore, Planutis may be as famous for what he didn't do as for what he did. For a while after the 1956 Rose Bowl, many thought Planutis, a Pennsylvania native, had actually kicked the game-winning field goal in the final seconds to beat UCLA. The hard-nosed fullback and regular field goal kicker, however, was lined up as a blocker after Daugherty opted for backup Dave Kaiser. Planutis didn't collect those points, but he scored enough throughout the 1955 season to lead the Spartans with 52 points while rushing for 385 yards, a then-school record for fullbacks, while kicking field goals and extra points. Always fighting the unsung hero scourge throughout his career, Planutis starred in the

Spartans' 1955 upset of Notre Dame when he carried the ball for 91 yards and recovered a fumble at the Fighting Irish 9-yard line that led to Michigan State's final score. Drafted by the Washington Redskins, Planutis only played in three NFL games before calling it quits.

Sam Williams (1958)

A Navy veteran who played on the Naval football squad before he ever put on his Spartans jersey, Williams, from nearby Danville, Michigan, saw plenty of action in 1958, averaging almost 50 minutes a game. He led the Spartans in receptions with 15, but defense was his calling card, helping him defy odds by earning consensus All-American honors on a losing team. Williams made 13 solo tackles against Michigan to help the Spartans forge a tie at home. Opponents showed Williams the ultimate respect by avoiding plays to his side. The Los Angeles Rams actually drafted Williams before he even played a minute at MSU. He eventually settled into a long career with the Detroit Lions, helping form the Fearsome Foursome, which included Alex Karras and stuffed the champion Packers on Thanksgiving Day in 1962.

57 Spartan Bob and the Clock Game

In the eyes of many Michigan fans, the most scurrilous Spartans villain never wore a Spartans jersey or roamed the Green and White sidelines with a whistle. That honor instead belongs to Bob Stehlin, the Spartan Stadium timekeeper who stopped the clock with one second remaining in the 2001 Michigan-Michigan State game.

The Spartans, still trying to find their sea legs under Bobby Williams, jumped out to a promising 4–2 start in 2001. The Spartan offense had wheezed and wobbled through a 5–6 campaign the year before, but its two best players, Jeff Smoker and T.J. Duckett, returned. They joined blue-chip wide receiver Charles Rogers to form a dangerous triple threat. The No. 6-ranked Wolverines countered with a defense especially stingy against the run.

Heavy underdogs, the Spartans stayed close, trailing only 17–14 at the half. MSU pulled even in the third quarter and then took the lead on a Dave Rayner 26-yard field goal with 7:33 left in the game. Both defenses had been tough. The Wolverines sacked Smoker 12 times. The Spartans stopped Michigan on seven straight possessions, forcing five punts and two interceptions. But when Smoker fumbled at the Spartans 39, the Wolverines responded, scoring a touchdown to take the lead 24–20 with 4:44 left.

After an exchange of punts, the Spartans gained possession of the ball at the UM 45. They picked up a first down on a Michigan face-mask penalty, which came on fourth down. Then Smoker hit Herb Haygood for a 17-yard completion to the Michigan 18. Another Michigan penalty for 12 men on the field moved the ball to the 11-yard line with 34 seconds left. Smoker flipped a pass to Duckett for eight yards, moving Michigan State down to the 3-yard-line.

With fewer than 15 seconds remaining and no timeouts, Smoker dropped back. Michigan blanketed his receivers. On instinct he headed for the end zone. But UM stopped him two yards shy. The clock continued running, threatening to expire before the next play. Smoker herded his team, frantically lined them up, and took the snap. He spiked the ball in the turf. Everyone's eyes shot to the clock. *Game over*, thought Michigan. Smoker figured he still had two seconds. The clock split the difference, showing one second. MSU had escaped the Reaper. On the final snap, Smoker, flushed from the pocket, drifted to his right, then lofted a pass narrowly out of reach of two Wolverines that landed in the hands of Duckett, giving Michigan State the 26–24 win. "The Michigan defender jumped high, and I pretty much thought he had it," Duckett said. "It seemed like the ball just climbed up, getting higher. It just came to me, and I caught it."

Frank Beckmann, doing the radio play-by-play for Michigan, lost it on air. "Criminal," he called the game, specifically referring to how the clock had stopped with one second—a tick that seemed like "an eternity." He stated the name of each official and complained bitterly about the injustice of it all. Larry Foote, Michigan's star linebacker, threw his helmet at the officials. Lloyd Carr, frothing in the locker room, said his team "deserved better." Upstairs in the press box, Beckmann prattled on, fomenting further rage among his dejected audience by promising them that the Big Ten offices would be sending an apology to Michigan on Monday.

That apology never came. The man who operated the clock, known around East Lansing as Spartan Bob, acted properly, according to Big Ten coordinator of officials Dave Parry. "We could find nothing that suggested there had been a mistake made," he said. To this day many Michigan fans disagree—some in comical fashion. One particularly disgruntled Michigan fan sent Stehlin a letter, suggesting he pray for forgiveness, according to an interview with Stehlin in the *Lansing State Journal*. Others have expressed their unhappiness in darker terms. In that same interview, Stehlin admits that he has received anonymous threats to his safety. When Michigan went on to win the next six games in the rivalry, Stehlin said Michigan fans inundated him with calls rubbing in it and letting him know how cheaters never prosper. Stehlin insists no monkey business occurred with the clock. He told Duckett, "if college football clocks had tenths of a second back then, there would've been three-tenths left."

Scott Skiles

The state of Indiana worships in two places: church and the basketball courts. Until 1997 the state basketball tournament included every high school competing for one title. Nothing captivated Indiana more than a deep run by a postage-stamp-sized school from a rural area. In 1954, 161-student Milan became the smallest school to ever win the single-class tournament. A permanent part of Indiana folklore, the team was the basis for the movie *Hoosiers*. The second smallest school on the list is Plymouth. They won the 1982 state championship in double-overtime. The star of that team, Scott Skiles, scored 39 points in the finals after scoring 30 in the semifinals, which had been played earlier in the day. His 25-footer at the buzzer sent the championship game into overtime and further cemented his status as an Indiana high school legend.

With skin as pale as his home jersey, Skiles didn't even touch 6'2". He lacked elite athleticism, but he possessed a handful of qualities that drew interest from college recruiters. He could shoot from anywhere, handle the ball adeptly, and burn his opponents with cunning passes. Moreover, he owned a take-charge personality well-suited to playing guard.

Neither Indiana nor Purdue, his boyhood favorite, gave him even a sniff. Fresno State was the only major school to court him seriously. A Michigan State fan sent Jud Heathcote a letter trumpeting Skiles. The Spartans coach, who received hundreds of similar letters over the years, decided to investigate nevertheless. After watching Skiles score 54 points on grainy film, Heathcote remained dubious. But 54 points is 54 points, so he sent his assistant, Bill Norton, to see Skiles live. "Not a great athlete," Norton said. But he was Heathcote's kind of guard. That prompted the coach to make a trip down to Plymouth. Skiles played dreadfully in front of the Spartans coach, but he had displayed just enough intriguing qualities that Heathcote decided to stick around for the afternoon game. "Scott didn't play super the second game either," wrote Heathcote in *Jud*. "But he played very, very well—much better than his morning performance. So I said we were going to go after him."

Heathcote inserted Skiles into the starting lineup four games into his freshman year. Playing along Sam Vincent in the backcourt, Skiles helped lead the Spartans to a 17–13 record, their first winning season in three years. He busted out against Ohio State, scoring 35 in a triple-overtime victory that jump-started a five-game conference win streak. During Skiles' sophomore year, the injury-plagued Spartans finished 16–12. But Skiles continued his ascent, averaging 14.5 a game and handing out 4.6 assists. In one memorable afternoon at Jenison, he connected on 11-of-13 shots—many from beyond what would today be the three-point line—for 24 points in the Spartans' upset of eventual Pac-10 winner Oregon State. "He's out there killing people, and he looks like he should be playing for Acme Hardware in a summer league," said the late North Carolina State coach Jim Valvano.

Skiles' manner on the court thrilled Spartans fans but irritated the opposition. He barked orders to his teammates. He threw dazzling no-look and behind-the-back passes. He buried beautiful, long distance jumpers. He played with a poise that belied his years. And his intensity was off the charts. He pumped his fist and pounded his chest. He woofed and hollered. "Scott was kind of arrogant on the floor. If he made a basket, it was, 'Hey, you can't check me,'" Heathcote said. These antics, of course, did not play well on the road. Fans booed and harangued him. "My style lends itself to people not liking me," Skiles said.

Hostile fans would have another reason to taunt Skiles. On three separate occasions, he had run-ins with the law while at

The Disappointing 1984 Team

The 1983–'84 Spartans included four future NBA players: Skiles, Kevin Willis, Sam Vincent, and Ken Johnson. Ben Tower filled out the starting lineup. Darryl Johnson, a scoring machine at guard who would average 18 a game his last two years, and Larry Polec came off the bench. *Sports Illustrated* ranked the Spartans eighth in its preseason poll. Heathcote thought it was the best team top to bottom he ever had. But Willis played on a bad wheel the entire season, Vincent missed seven conference games with an ankle injury, and Johnson, a transfer, didn't gain eligibility until January. The Spartans stumbled to a 16–12 record.

MSU—one for possession of marijuana and the next two for impaired driving. Heathcote suspended Skiles for the final violation. Many had clamored for the coach to take action before that. Sentiment grew locally and nationally for Michigan State to kick Skiles off the team. But Heathcote refused to succumb to the pressure. He considered Skiles a good person who made a few bad decisions. "People always say I stuck by him. Maybe to you he'd done something wrong. But to me it was nothing like that," wrote Heathcote. "But when Bobby Knight came out and said, 'A guy like that couldn't play in our program,' he didn't know the particulars. All he did was read the Indiana papers where the guy was portrayed as an alcoholic drug addict." For his part Skiles would have understood if Heathcote had booted him. "If I was coach, I would have kicked [me] off the team—no questions asked," he said.

Michigan State reinstated Skiles for the beginning of his senior year. The critics screamed. And opposing fans went from loud and obnoxious to cruel and vicious. The hatred only served as a stimulant for Skiles, who silenced the catcalls and jeers with innumerable in-your-face jumpers and big plays. The Spartans had their best year since 1979, going 23–8, finishing third in the Big Ten, and playing in the Sweet 16. Without the benefit of the three point shot, Skiles averaged 27.4 points a game. "He just blocks everything out and concentrates on the game," said his teammate Larry Polec.

The Spartans twice defeated Michigan, who won the Big Ten. Before the first meeting in East Lansing, the Wolverines talked more smack than Ali. Antoine Joubert, Michigan's ballyhooed point guard, clucked that he was better than Skiles and was going to kill him. Instead Skiles and his teammates did the killing, winning by 12. Skiles scored 40 points, burning Joubert's ear the whole time. When Joubert fouled out and hollered, "We'll get you in Ann Arbor," Skiles skewered him further. "Not unless you lose 20 pounds, fat boy," he said, loud enough that the crowd could hear him. After a score later, he circled back to the UM bench. "How'd you like that one, fat boy?" Skiles sneered. Everyone assumed Michigan would exact its revenge in Ann Arbor. But the Spartans won even more handily 74–59. Skiles insisted MSU eased up on the throttle and should have beaten the Wolverines by 30.

Skiles played all 40 minutes 13 times as a senior. He won the Big Ten MVP for a third-place team, earned first team All-American honors, and was named the national Player of the Year by *Basketball Times* and by Billy Packer. "The mark of a great player is not only how well he plays but how he affects other around him," said Georgetown coach John Thompson after Skiles' Spartans upset the Hoyas in the second round of the 1986 NCAA tournament. "Skiles is contagious." Skiles finished his Spartans career as the all-time leader in points (2,145), assists (645), and steals (175). He played 10 years in the NBA, defying more odds along the way. Skiles also served as head coach for the Phoenix Suns, Chicago Bulls, and Milwaukee Bucks.

Sweet 16
Clock Issues: Part I

When Magic Johnson departed for the NBA after winning a national championship during his 1979 sophomore season, Spartans basketball recovered slowly. MSU failed to make the NCAA tournament for the next five seasons, sliding into national irrelevancy despite a handful of talented players, including two-time Big Ten scoring leader Jay Vincent and future NBA All-Star Kevin Willis. The Spartans ended the NCAA tournament dry spell in 1985 after a fifth place finish in the highly competitive Big Ten. They played one game and went home after a narrow defeat to Alabama-Birmingham.

In 1986 the NCAA tournament expanded to 64 teams, and the Spartans once again made the field after Scott Skiles led MSU to a shocking third-place finish in the Big Ten. "None of us—not me, not my staff, not anybody—thought we could do what we've done," said Heathcote during the NCAA Tournament. "We hoped we could squeeze out eight victories in the preseason and maybe six, seven, eight in the Big Ten and get a bid to the NIT." Instead MSU went 21–7 overall and 12–6 in the Big Ten. And on this trip to the NCAA Tournament they hung around for awhile.

Opening against the University of Washington, the Spartans scraped their way to a two-point win. Skiles scored 31 points, impressing Washington's coach. "He just guts it out for 40 minutes," Andy Russo said. "It's almost impossible to take your eyes off Skiles. He demands attention. He's arrogant, relentless, and driven." It was the Spartans' first NCAA tournament win in seven years.

Two days later MSU throttled perennial 1980s power Georgetown 80–68 to advance to the Sweet 16. Skiles continued his tear, scoring 24 points and cockily chirping at Georgetown coach John Thompson to put someone in who could guard him. His wraparound pass to teammate Larry Polec for a fast break layup pushed the crowd into delirium. Up next for the little engine that could: Kansas.

The No. 1-seeded Jayhawks were led by Ron Kellogg, Greg Dreiling, and star Danny Manning. And with the game played in Kansas City, a 45-minute drive from Kansas' campus, Michigan State entered as the prohibitive underdog. They had no one to match up with the 6'9" Manning, they would be playing in front of mostly hostile fans, and they had little experience in games of this magnitude. If the Spartans were a band they would have been Skiles and the Four Unknowns.

MSU turned the pregame narrative on its head. The Spartans hung tough, eventually pulling ahead late by four. With the Spartans nursing that lead, the clock stopped with two minutes and 21 seconds. The whistle had not blown. The ball had not been knocked out of play. There was no reason for the clock to stop. No one—including coaches, players, and officials—noticed it at first. Finally, Tom Izzo, the lowly assistant charged by Jud Heathcote to pay attention to such things, motioned to Heathcote that the clock had stopped. "When it wasn't moving—and I told Jud—he more or less told me where to go," Izzo said. Soon enough, however, Heathcote noticed the same thing. "I pounded the scorer's table," Heathcote recalled years later. The officials finally called timeout.

What happened next depends on your rooting interest. Heathcote and Spartans fans insist 19 seconds should have been subtracted from the clock. Jayhawks fans insist only 11 seconds. In any event the NCAA did not allow instant replay in 1986, and all disputes were left in the hands of the officials—no questions asked. Play resumed without any time adjustments. The Spartans scored two quick baskets. Kansas coach Larry Brown then picked up a technical for complaining that Heathcote had left the coaches box to alert the officials about the clock stoppage. It appeared the

Spartans would shake off the cosmic gift to the Jayhawks and win nonetheless. Then the best free throw shooting team in the country started missing from the charity stripe. Senior Larry Polec missed a front end of a one-and-one with 29 seconds left. Freshman Mark Brown did the same with only 10 seconds remaining. With just nine seconds left in regulation, the Jayhawks' Archie Marshall tipped in a miss to tie the game. The Spartans did nothing with the remaining nine seconds and the game went to overtime where the Jayhawks wore down the gassed Spartans to win 96–86.

In the aftermath the Spartans seethed about those extra 19 seconds, noting that the tying basket came after the game should have concluded. Many Spartans fans feel the clock malfunction cost Michigan State the game. Ed Steitz, official interpreter of NCAA rules, later said the officials "blew it." But one cannot dismiss another culprit—missed free throws, likely a result of tired legs and nerves. "We missed some key free throws down the stretch," said Heathcote. "We led the nation in free throw shooting all year. Maybe it finally caught up with us."

Sweet 16
Clock Issues: Part II

Three years of wandering around in the outback of college basketball ended in 1990 when the Spartans stormed to the Big Ten conference title. A major reason for the turnaround: recruiting. The Spartans had reeled in one of the best classes in the conference in 1989, a class headlined by brawny big man Mike Peplowski, versatile athletic wing Matt Steigenga, and clever if pencil-thin point guard Mark Montgomery. They joined guard Steve Smith, the lone bright spot from 1988.

Jud Heathcote loved recruiting about as much as he loved sloppy ball-handling. But a significant upgrade made the tedious practice less daunting. In 1990 the Spartans were moving from beloved but antiquated Jenison Field House into a brand new arena, the Jack Breslin Student Events Center. The talent haul didn't generate much discussion outside of East Lansing especially because rival Michigan had just won the national championship and siphoned away most media attention.

MSU's season, though, started with a bang as the Spartans won the Great Alaska Shootout. Then two bad losses to University of Illinois-Chicago and Bowling Green tempered expectations before the Spartans won five of their first eight conference games. But on February 3, MSU took a giant step, knocking off league-leading Purdue 64–53 in West Lafayette, Indiana. "Everybody's back in the race," lamented Gene Keady, Purdue's head coach. "If someone wants to hand us the league title, boy, we'd sure take it," cracked Heathcote. No one needed to hand MSU the title. The Spartans took it—with a mighty flourish, closing out the conference season on a stunning 10-game streak.

The final day of the season against second-place Purdue in East Lansing settled the championship. MSU made a furious come-back in the last four minutes. With 20 seconds left, Ken Redfield knocked the ball loose from a Boilermaker. Dwayne Stephens, a freshman, swooped it up, looked to pass, and then noticed he had an unimpeded path to the basket. His layup gave the Spartans a 72–70 lead—and the championship. Stephens called his basket "a dream come true," an apt description for the entire Spartans season. With a Big Ten championship in hand and a 26–5 overall mark, MSU earned its first ever No. 1 seed, heady stuff for an inconsistent program making only its third appearance in the tournament since 1979.

Being the hunted presented hidden perils. Since the NCAA had expanded the tournament to 64 teams in 1985, no No. 1 seed had lost its opening game. The Spartans almost became the first. Murray State, a plucky team from the Ohio Valley Conference, featured future NBA player Popeye Jones, a 6'8" mismatch power forward. He bedeviled the Spartans from start to finish, pouring in 37 points and helping keep the Racers within an eyelash of the lead the whole game. MSU avoided infamy by eventually pulling out a 75–71 overtime win. Steve Smith led with 22 points, and Kirk Manns hit a reverse layup in overtime to lift the Spartans. They gutted out a 62–58 win against University of California-Santa Barbara in the next round to advance to the Sweet 16 to meet Georgia Tech. It was the Spartans' 12th win in a row.

The Sweet 16 is where the Spartans' last tournament appearance had ended in horrific and bitter fashion. Leading Kansas in the closing minutes, MSU coughed up a lead down the stretch in a game marked by a controversial clock malfunction. Though Heathcote suffered through it personally, mercifully no one on the current roster had. Georgia Tech entered the tournament led by Kenny Anderson, a dazzling freshman guard from Brooklyn, New York.

From the opening tip, it was a closely contested game played at a brisk and entertaining pace. Anderson captivated with his speed and ability to penetrate and finish. Smith, steady as always, ran the offense efficiently, running clock and then hitting big shots. It came down to the final seconds. Anderson scored with six seconds left to draw the Yellow Jackets within two. The Spartans inbounded the ball to Smith, who was fouled. One second ticked off, a strange disconnect from reality because it seemed as if three or four had elapsed.

As in 1986 when the clock stopped for around 20 seconds in the Spartans' loss to Kansas, the rules did not allow for instant replay or review, so one second off it would be. Smith headed to the line to shoot one-and-one with five seconds remaining. Heathcote was livid but resigned, saying, "We were all incredulous. I think we almost got Kansas Citied again."

Smith had a chance to put the game away for good, but he missed the first free throw. Georgia Tech rebounded the ball and put it in the hands of Anderson with about four seconds left. He streaked down the court and pulled up in the shadow of the three-point line to launch a desperate shot. The buzzer sounded simultaneously as the ball swished through. An official raised his arms to indicate a three. Georgia Tech's bench exploded, thinking Anderson's shot had won the game.

The Spartans huddled on their own bench, thinking just the opposite—that the clock had expired before Anderson's shot. The officials conferred for three minutes, three minutes that felt like sitting in a Los Angeles traffic jam. Finally they ruled that Anderson's shot was a two-pointer, but that it occurred before the buzzer. Overtime. The stunned Spartans rallied to take a brief lead, but they eventually ran out of steam and lost 81–80.

Replays later showed that Anderson's shot had come just after the buzzer sounded. But MSU already knew that. "I asked the official if he could look at the replay, and he said you can't replay it," Heathcote said. "There is a lot at stake here for both schools, and there should not be a mistake by officials on whether a shot did or did not beat the buzzer."

Two Sweet 16s, two clock issues, two soul-crushing defeats. Both could have been avoided if the Spartans had hit key free throws. Smith, adopting the high road, said in the locker room after the game: "You've got to count that shot; it was a great shot."

Shortly after the Spartans' second clock fiasco, the NCAA changed the rules to allow for instant replay on last-second shots. The "Jud Heathcote Rule," as it's known colloquially in East Lansing, meant no NCAA tournament game would ever again be decided by a mistake that technology could rectify.

Mark Dantonio vs. Mike Hart

After Appalachian State toppled Michigan in a monumental 2007 upset, a reporter asked Mark Dantonio what he thought about that shocking result. He responded facetiously, saying that he was going to observe "a moment of silence" for woebegone Michigan. That comment bristled the UM fanbase.

So after Mike Hart, Michigan's crafty running back, and his Wolverines had beaten the Spartans for the sixth straight time in a come-from-behind win at Spartan Stadium in 2007, Hart was feeling frisky. First the diminutive back led Michigan in holding a moment of silence at midfield in response to Dantonio's comment. After Michigan's 28–24 victory, Hart then mocked his in-state rival. "Sometimes you get your little brother excited when you're playing basketball and stuff, let them get the lead, then you just come back and take it back," Hart said, laughing.

For Michigan State the loss was no laughing matter. It was painful—a double-digit lead eviscerated by blown assignments and just enough bad luck to underscore the demoralizing possibility that the losses to Michigan would continue seemingly forever. With just under 10 minutes remaining in the game and leading by 10 points, the Spartans sacked UM quarterback Chad Henne on third-and-long. Henne lost the ball, which hit the turf and then bounced providentially in the direction of Hart. The UM back snapped it up and ran 15 yards for a first down. The possession ended in a score because of a long pass thrown into heavy coverage in the corner of the end zone. UM would score the go-ahead touchdown on its next possession with an almost identical pass to the other side of the end zone, leaving the Spartans without enough time to respond.

During the postgame press conference, someone asked Dantonio about Michigan's moment of silence. He paused, started to speak, and then stopped. Dantonio, born and raised in Ohio, was never deferential toward the Wolverines. "I find a lot of things they do amusing," he said. Expecting the usual coach speak, the press grew suddenly more attentive. "They need to check themselves sometimes. Let's just remember: pride comes before the fall. They wanna mock us? I'm telling them—it's not over. They can print all that crap all they want all over their locker room. It's not over. It will never be over here," he snapped, paused again, and then said, "It's just started."

A few moments later, someone asked him about Hart's "little brother" comments. "Does Hart have a little brother?" Dantonio asked tartly. The press snickered. He then made a quick gesture with his hand, palm down, placing it about four feet from the floor, an obvious reference to Hart's 5'6" height. "Or is he the little brother?" More laughter. The press salivated over a juicy story and headlines for the next day. Spartans fans found a new coach they could adore. Dantonio's stature among Spartans fans rose as high as Beaumont Tower that day.

The comments were less warmly received in Ann Arbor. UM head coach Lloyd Carr, who was nearing retirement, never responded with much gusto, but Michigan football fans and bloggers uncovered a new enemy. It was a brazen thing for Dantonio to say: forecasting UM's decline when your own school had yet to really rise. But it stirred in Spartans fans a sense of renewal—a sense that the football program was finally in the hands of someone who really understood. Plus things really were just getting started. The Spartans made six straight bowl appearances, had two 11-win seasons, and won in fairly convincing fashion four games in a row against Michigan. The Wolverines, who suffered through some of its worst seasons ever over the next four years, did indeed fall just as the oracle of Spartans football had warned.

The First Big Ten Season

In 1949 the dream of gaining admittance to the Big Ten finally became a reality. But for a variety of reasons—some practical and some political—it wasn't until 1953 that the Spartans could compete in football. By the time they did, one thing became clear to the rest of the league: a major Rose Bowl contender had just been added.

The Spartans came roaring into the league with a 24-game win streak, a freshly earned national championship, and more swagger than a 1950s-era General Motors executive at a shareholders meeting. As soon as the 1952 season ended, prognosticators started naming them the favorite for the 1954 Rose Bowl.

The schedule included six teams from the Big Ten: Iowa, Minnesota, Indiana, Purdue, Ohio State, and Michigan. New membership in a conference was not the only significant change for the Spartans in 1953. The NCAA had ended free substitutions. Players could be substituted only once a quarter, which severely hampered Biggie Munn's two-platoon system. The graduation of the big "elephant" backs—Don McAuliffe, Vince Pisano, Wayne Benson, and Dick Panin—made the end of free substitutions even more challenging for Munn. His light "pony" backs—quarterback Tom Yewcic, LeRoy Bolden, Billy Wells, and Evan Slonac, who came to be called the "Light Brigade"—would need to play both ways. How would these smaller men fare on defense? Munn shrugged it off, saying the rule would affect all teams equally.

The Spartans played as if didn't matter one iota in their first four games, knocking off Iowa, Minnesota, Texas Christian, and Indiana by a combined score of 115–44. Led by Don Dohoney and Ellis Duckett, the defense allowed only 11 points a game and held Minnesota All-American Paul Giel to 20 yards rushing, a career low. Tied 0–0 after 30 minutes in Minneapolis, the Spartans turned to Light Brigade and lightning quick back Bolden, who ripped off three scoring runs, one a 69-yarder. Munn, a former All-American at Minnesota making his first trip home as a head coach, relished the win, though the homecoming started in a vexing way. A security guard, who didn't recognize the coach of the reigning national champs, refused to allow Munn to enter the stadium because he lacked a ticket. He finally persuaded the overzealous gatekeeper that he was indeed Biggie Munn and gained access to the stadium without a ticket and without much compassion for the guard.

Munn probably wished he'd been denied admission to most of the Texas Christian game the following week. The Spartans played sloppily for three quarters, trailing 19–7 entering the last 15 minutes of play. Three unanswered touchdowns later put the Spartans ahead for good. Indiana then caved in a blowout. The winning streak climbed to 28 games before ending in West Lafayette, Indiana, a traditional house of horrors for Michigan State.

Purdue, who had taken the starch out of MSC's offense the year before, did it again despite suffering through a down year. The Spartans couldn't muster anything, getting shut out 6–0 for the first time since 1947. Purdue's lone score came on a fourth-quarter touchdown dive by Danny Pobojewski, a transfer from Michigan State who left because of dismal playing prospects. Five interceptions killed drive after drive for MSC. "There's no use to be downcast," Munn said. "We'll forget about our setback for a while and get back to work on a few football fundamentals."

Few coaches of the era responded better to a loss or uninspiring effort. But recovering from something not a single active player on the roster had experienced would test Munn's coaching skills like never before. Munn fine-tuned the offense and re-emphasized fundamentals, and MSC trounced Oregon State 34–6 the following week. The winning continued over the next three weeks as well. Bolden almost single-handedly beat Ohio State by rushing for 128 yards and scoring three touchdowns in the Spartans' 28–13 win. "We knew what he [Bolden] could do. He did it to us two years ago, and we were ready for him this time. But he did it to us again," grumbled Ohio State head coach Woody Hayes. In their final Big Ten game, the Spartans defense limited their rivals, the Wolverines, to 81 yards on the ground and six points, making the 14 points the offense spit out just enough. "How I love to win that game," Munn said gleefully.

The win left the Spartans 5–1 in conference play, one behind undefeated Illinois, who needed a win against a strong Wisconsin team to clinch the Big Ten outright. As the Spartans were beating the Wolverines, the Badgers bludgeoned Illinois 34–7, forcing a tie between MSC and Illinois and a vote among the conference athletic directors to determine the Rose Bowl bid. Unlike Illinois the Spartans still had another game, and the vote wasn't scheduled until after Munn's team had played Marquette. No one knew if the outcome of the game would influence the voters or whether the Spartans status as newcomers would help or hurt them. Another wild card: MSU was on probation for questionable infractions from before the Spartans had joined the Big Ten. Would that be held against them?

With the vote still in the balance, the Spartans sleepwalked through an uninspiring 21–15 victory over the outmanned Hilltoppers, falling well short of the kind of emphatic win they hoped might persuade a voter or two. Marquette assistant coach, Carl Schuette, whose team had played both MSC and Illinois, stated emphatically that the Spartans deserved it. "Michigan State is much better. [They] are loaded with talent. Illinois has been pretty lucky. They have been up and down."

For the official vote, the athletic directors from across the conference wired their preference to the Big Ten offices in Chicago.

The first vote ended in a tie. So the athletic directors were called to Chicago to meet in person, and after six hours of debating, arguing, grandstanding, and cajoling, one school—Indiana—switched its vote to the Spartans. Michigan State packed it bags for Pasadena, California, and East Lansing celebrated as if it were VJ Day.

Four Stud Running Backs of the Modern Era

Blake Ezor (1986–1989)

Coach George Perles called the 5'9", 190-pound tailback from Nevada "pound for pound the toughest player I've ever known." Ezor, who replaced Spartans great Lorenzo White at running back, delivered as many hits as defenders and ensured that the drop-off from White would be negligible. He also possessed surprising breakaway speed, which helped him blitz Northwestern for six touchdowns, a then-Big Ten record, in the Spartans' 76–14 annihilation of the Wildcats in 1989. The year before, Ezor eviscerated Indiana's defense for 250 yards, seventh most in Spartans history. Ezor finished his career with 3,749 yards, which places him fourth on the all-time MSU list.

Sedrick Irvin (1996–1998)

Irvin, a high school blue chipper, surprised many in his native Florida when he said yes to Nick Saban and MSU in 1996, making him one of State's best recruits of the 1990s. Nicknamed the "Miami Mouth" because he never stopped talking, Irvin, a cousin of equally mouthy Hall of Fame wide receiver Michael Irvin, brought bravado and color to a shiftless MSU program. "It's

A Tough Trio of All-American Offensive Linemen

Bob Kula moved to tackle for his senior year to replace NFL first-round draft pick Tony Mandarich. He anchored a line that helped MSU score 37 rushing touchdowns and finish 21st in rushing offense in 1989. Kula started 36 straight games. Flozell Adams and Scott Shaw formed a dynamic duo that helped MSU finish 24th in the country in rushing yards. Teammates called Adams "Hotel" because of his 6'7", 330-pound frame. He allowed only two sacks in 1997. Shaw did him one better. After a slow start to his career, Adams, according to Saban, "developed into a tremendous football player." The Cowboys drafted him in the second round in 1998, and he went on to play in five Pro Bowls. Shaw was drafted in the fifth round by the Miami Dolphins and appeared in two games with the Cincinnati Bengals.

refreshing to have a guy with such an upbeat personality," Nick Saban said. "Sedrick's never a clown when it's time to play." Irvin's collegiate debut was as explosive as his personality. He danced, juked, and galloped his way to four touchdowns in the Spartans' 52–14 drubbing of Purdue in 1996. Many more explosions followed. Despite lacking top-line speed, Irvin became the only back in Spartans history to rush for 1,000 yards in his first three seasons and only the second Spartan ever to eclipse that mark three times in a career. Despite leaving after his junior year, Irvin ranks fifth on MSU's all-time rushing list with 3,504 yards. The Detroit Lions drafted Irvin in the fourth round, but injuries ended his career after two seasons.

Javon Ringer (2005–2008)

A heist out of Ohio, Ringer, a *SuperPrep* All-American, committed to MSU during the dark days of John L. Smith. He blossomed, however, under Mark Dantonio, who built his offense around Ringer's durability and game-breaking ability. He muscled his way up the all-time MSU rushing list by carrying the ball 843 times—second only to White. "You can hit him and hit him and hit him, and he just keeps on coming," said Notre Dame coach Charlie Weis. "I learned a long time ago that one attribute that great players have is stamina, and he obviously has great stamina."

The Spartans leaned heavily on that stamina because they had few other options. "Michigan State already has one of the coolest mascots in college football, but if Sparty ever needs a day off, Javon Ringer could do the job," cracked Bruce Hooley of FOXSports.com. "After all, he already does just about everything else for MSU." In 2008 Ringer became the first offensive player in Big Ten history to earn Big Ten Player of the Week for three consecutive weeks when he gained 135 yards against Eastern Michigan, 282 (fourth most in MSU history) against Florida Atlantic, and 201 against Notre Dame. Ringer finished his career with 4,398 yards—second only to White on MSU's all-time list. He also became the first Spartans running back to be named first team All-American since White. The Tennessee Titans drafted him in the fifth round.

Le'Veon Bell (2010–2012)

One of the most anemic MSU offenses of the modern era would have been even more offensive without Bell, a one-man wrecking crew and a beacon of light for the 2012 Spartans offense. Without the threat of the pass to keep defenses from keying on him, Bell rushed for 1,793 yards as a junior, the second most in MSU history. He delivered as many blows as he received, routinely bulling over defenders for an extra few yards after initial contact—or simply jumping over them. In MSU's 2012 finale against Minnesota, Bell rushed for a career-high 266 yards, sixth best in school history. He finished his career at MSU with 3,346 yards, ranking seventh on the all-time Spartans list. Bell was named the MVP of the Buffalo Wild Wings Bowl in 2012. The Pittsburgh Steelers drafted Bell in the second round of the 2013 Draft.

Javon Ringer, who ranks second on the all-time Spartans rushing list, runs for some of his 185 yards during a 2007 overtime loss to Northwestern.

64 Attend the Drum Off and the Walk

A rousing way to start a gameday on Michigan State's campus is to show up at Adams Field about two to three hours before kickoff. Bring blankets, lawn chairs, and other favorite picnic supplies and plant yourself along the edge of the field. Why? Around 90 to 120 minutes before kickoff, Adams Field will be awash with marching and music and just plain good ol'-fashioned fun.

The MSU Marching Band begins to assemble at Adams Field slowly, showing up individually and mixing with the crowd of friends, relatives, and band enthusiasts. Later the sousaphone section can be heard in the distance, which signals to the other band members that it is time to assemble. When the sousaphone section arrives, the band performs a jaunty 10-minute concert that always ends with the MSU Fight Song. With its juices flowing and crowd cheering, the band then begins to march, forming into its parade block and crossing the river onto Red Cedar Road and toward Spartan Stadium through the maw of fans milling about.

If you crave more music and pageantry, you can catch the Spartan Marching Band after games. An added delight, assuming the visiting team brought its band, is the Drum Off. The percussion sections of both bands play together for the benefit of each other and the fans. It's a stirring sight. Two hours before kickoff, the MSU Spartan Drumline performs along the median of Grand River Avenue and in front of the SBS Bookstore.

Finally, another pregame ritual every Spartans fan should consider is the Walk, which dates to the Duffy Daugherty era. The MSU football players spend the evening together before every home game at Kellogg Center Hotel located on Harrison Road.

About two hours before kickoff the next morning, the team walks to Spartan Stadium along Kalamazoo Street and past the Sparty Statue. Each member of the team then rubs Sparty's foot and leaves a penny behind at the base for good luck. Fans line the street, cheering and chanting "Let's Go State," and the MSU band salutes the team by playing the MSU Fight Song. The Spartans also pay homage to Sparty before road trips. The bus carrying the team swings by the statue, and each player performs the same ritual as above. Then they re-board the bus and head to their destination.

The 2005 Final Four

The 2005 Spartans stand alone as the only MSU squad to ever advance to the Final Four and not win at least a share of the Big Ten title. That the Spartans landed in the Final Four astounded many.

MSU lacked marquee preconference wins, losing to Duke in Durham, North Carolina, and getting thumped by George Washington. Subsequent double-digit wins against unranked Stanford and UCLA failed to move the respect needle much, and the Spartans remained at the margins of the AP poll.

MSU entered Big Ten play 8–2, lacking sexy wins. And the college basketball establishment viewed the Big Ten—with the exception of Illinois—suspiciously in 2005. The gap between the Illini and the rest of the Big Ten was considered greater than the distance between Champaign, Illinois, and the ESPN studios in Bristol, Connecticut. MSU's sole quality win came late in February against Wisconsin. The win against the Badgers ended an MSU six-game losing streak to Wisconsin. Early in the year in Madison, MSU had damaged its wan reputation by surrendering an eight-point lead with 2:49 left, abetted by two front-end free throw misses.

Despite finishing alone in second place at 13–3 in the conference and 22–5 overall—an accomplishment that in past years would have meant a high seed and respect—MSU closed out the regular season on a low note, losing to Iowa in the first round of the Big Ten Tournament. Two missed free throws in the closing seconds opened the door for the Hawkeyes to upset the Spartans 71–69.

Coach Tom Izzo took the film of the final Iowa game and with the furor of Moses at Mount Sinai smashed the tape with a sledgehammer in front of his stunned team. "Get it out of your heads right now because it's over," he ordered them. He also destroyed all the tapes from the end of the regular season.

But if one had broken down video of most of the season, one would have seen that the 2005 Spartans were one of the most talented and accomplished teams that year. Perhaps one of Izzo's deepest squads ever, MSU had an 11-man rotation with 10 Spartans averaging at least nine minutes. Six players averaged at least 8.8 points a game. It had senior leadership in Alan Anderson, Chris Hill, and Kelvin Torbert, though they had failed to win a Big Ten title. It had junior experience and savvy in Maurice Ager, a high-flying wing with a sound perimeter game, and Paul Davis, a 6'11" dual threat who could hit the 15-foot jumper and led the Spartans in rebounding. Sophomore Shannon Brown provided speed and athleticism and dangerous perimeter shooting at the off guard position. Matt Trannon, a wide receiver on the football team, offered tenacious defense and eager rebounding off the bench, and freshman guard Drew Neitzel featured press-breaking ball handling skills.

Digging deeper revealed that MSU had handled most of its opponents with ease as 12 of its 13 conference wins were by at least double digits. The Spartans suffered because the Big Ten suffered. One could have argued that the lack of quality wins was due more to a lack of quality analysis than to any inherent flaws in the Spartans.

The 22–6 Spartans received a No. 5 seed in the NCAA tournament. Inspired by Izzo's tape smashing, MSU survived a first round tussle with scrappy Old Dominion and then defeated sentimental favorite Vermont, who had upset No. 4 seed Syracuse. "I'm glad it's over," said a relieved Izzo. "I thought with the entire state [of Massachusetts, the site of the game] and nation pulling for them, it would be tough to overcome."

Waiting for the Spartans in Austin, Texas, was No.1 seed Duke. Izzo had never beaten Duke and already lost to the Blue Devils in November. Few gave the Spartans much chance of reversing the trend. The Blue Devils featured two dangerous shooters, three-point bomber J.J. Redick and Daniel Ewing. But the Spartans forced 22 Blue Devil turnovers and by virtue of a tugging and harassing defense held Redick to 4-of-14 from the field and coasted to a 78–68 victory. "I didn't give them a Knute Rockne speech," Izzo said. "I just told them to give me 40 minutes of intense minutes."

Tied at halftime due to cold outside shooting, the Spartans heated up at the start of the second half when Anderson nailed MSU's first three of the game. That sparked a 16–3 run. Anderson scored 17 points, including three of the Spartans' five threes. Davis paced MSU with 20 points and 12 rebounds. The signature play of the game belonged to Ager, who posterized Redick with a soaring fast break dunk for two of his 14 points. "This is real special," said Anderson. "I mean really special because we beat Duke. We've been preparing for this for a long time."

Anderson, and his two fellow seniors, Hill and Torbert, who came to MSU on the heels of the Spartans' memorable four-year run, now had a chance to leave their own special legacy.

No. 2-seeded Kentucky led by Rajon Rondo stood in the way. Featuring more twists and turns than an Agatha Christie novel, the game took double-overtime to decide. The Spartans led by eight with 5:25 left in regulation. But the Wildcats stormed back. After Kentucky missed a pair of threes in the closing seconds, Patrick Sparks snatched the loose ball after the second miss and launched a shot, straddling the three-point line. As the buzzer sounded, the ball hit the rim and then yo-yoed up and down four times before falling through. The officials reviewed the play for five minutes to ensure Sparks had beaten the clock and had his foot behind the line.

Izzo didn't wait around for the decision. Figuring the shot would count, he grabbed his clipboard and started planning. MSU fell behind in the first overtime and then tied it with 1:03 left. Kentucky had the ball the rest of the first overtime but failed to score, getting off only one shot—a bad one. In the second overtime, Torbert hit a free throw. Then the Spartans made 10 more consecutive foul shots to put away the Wildcats for good 94–88. "It will go down in history as a great college basketball game," said Kentucky head coach Tubby Smith. Brown led MSU with 24 points on 8-of-10 shooting, including five three pointers. Ager had 21, and Davis had 15 and 11 rebounds. "We had plenty of potholes and valleys—even black holes—during this journey," Hill said. We been through it all, but here at the end of the day we are still standing."

Having punched their ticket into MSU immortality, the Spartans and the three seniors, whose collegiate career seemed vindicated by the Final Four appearance, prepared to face North Carolina. Anderson had suffered an unpublicized injury during the week. It limited his mobility, hurting the 26–7 Spartans' hopes of upsetting North Carolina, the eventual national champs. The Spartans led by five at the half but went into a deep freeze in the final 20 minutes, and North Carolina rolled to an 87–71 win. Anderson, who ran the point and threatened defenses with an improved three-point shot, played only 20 minutes and went scoreless. Ager scored 24 points. "This is the worst half of basketball we played all year," said Torbert on the Spartans' second half performance. Despite the disappointing end, a much-maligned senior class took its place among the all-time great ones at MSU.

Darryl Rogers' High-Scoring 1978 Team

A scandal can shake an institution out of rigid, established thinking. Perhaps that NCAA probation explains why Michigan State administrators replaced fired MSU coach Denny Stolz in 1976 with Darryl Rogers, a California native without even a wisp of a connection to the Midwest. As far back as anyone could remember, Michigan State had hired coaches familiar with either the school or the Big Ten region. Not since 1921 when MAC hired Pennsylvania native Albert Barron had the school reached beyond the Midwest to find a coach. Rogers represented a sharp departure from this tradition.

He also represented a break in tradition in another more substantive sense. Rogers arrived with a fresh outlook on offense, one bolstered by years of playing and coaching in a region that favored a more wide-open approach. In the Big Ten, the three-yards-and-a-cloud-of-dust of conference powers Michigan and Ohio State still reigned supreme.

Rogers' tenure started in bumpy fashion. Banned from television and Rose Bowl appearances for three years, Michigan State finished 4–6–1 in 1976. But some offensive potential emerged. Rescued from fourth string, Eddie Smith, a 6'0" thinly framed quarterback from Pennsylvania who beat out Joe Montana for All-State honors, became the starter. Strong-armed and accurate with a high, quick release, Smith zinged passes to a trio of nascent stars. Tight end Mark Brammer and wide receivers Eugene Byrd and Kirk Gibson caught a combined 94 passes in Rogers' air-it-out offense, which included throwing to backs, lining up with five receivers, and employing picks to free up receivers.

The next year the offense edged closer to what Rogers had in mind. The Spartans started threatening the hegemony of the Big Two. They finished a half game out of first in the conference and averaged 36 points over their last four games—all conference wins. The defense showed improvement as well, allowing the third fewest points in the conference. Just about everyone returned in 1978, including Gibson, who had been drafted by the Detroit Tigers and spent the summer playing minor league baseball.

What happened in 1978 had never happened in the Big Ten. The Spartans, deploying an uber-sophisticated passing attack, averaged 523 yards and 41 points a game in Big Ten play. Defensive coordinators had no answer for a passing offense run by savvy veterans with NFL talent designed to outsmart you. The 523 yards was a conference record, which stood until 2002 as did the 41 points a game, which stood until 1994. The Spartans finished 7–1 in the Big Ten tied for first with Michigan. Michigan State owned the tiebreaker by virtue of their first victory against the Wolverines since 1969, but MSU remained on probation and thus ineligible to play in the Rose Bowl—or any bowl.

Smith, who passed for 2,226 yards, suffered an injury in the Spartans' first game of the year. After a touchdown pass that gave MSU a 14–0 lead, Smith broke his hand and left the game for good. Purdue rallied to win 21–14. Smith missed the next two games, which included a loss to USC. He returned against Notre Dame, leading a furious rally in the second half that fell short by four points. The season's turning point occurred the next week.

MSU beat No. 5 Michigan, 24–15. After the 1978 season, Rogers would further inflame passions in Ann Arbor by suggesting UM folks were "arrogant asses." During the Spartans' 1978 win, the Wolverines acted more like mules helpless to stop MSU from blowing past them for 496 total yards of offense. Invigorated by a rare win against their rival, the Spartans closed out the season in virtuoso fashion, posting six lopsided victories, an 8–3 overall record, and a No. 14 ranking. The scores read more like early September sacrificial lamb slaughters than midseason conference tilts: 49–14, 55–2, 59–19, 33–9, 52–3, 42–7.

"We just gelled," Eddie Smith told the *Lansing State Journal* 30 years later. Gibson, in his autobiography, offered a more exact view: "All of us were able to read defenses and react to them. Smith was calling audibles at the line, and the receivers were changing routes on the fly…[Smith] had an amazing ability to deliver the ball before a defender could close." This explains Smith's impressive 58 percent completion rate. Mark Brammer caught 33 passes for 360 yards, which earned him first team All-American honors. Gibson, who caught 42 passes for 806 yards, also became a first team All-American. Smith, who outdueled Michigan's Rick Leach in Ann Arbor, finished second behind Leach for first team All-Big Ten honors, a snub that still stings in East Lansing. The defense, which once again finished third in points allowed in the conference, was led by first team All-Big Ten standouts Melvin Land and Thomas Graves and second teamer Dan Bass.

Two years later Rogers left MSU for Arizona State. Spartans fans felt jilted. The events of the 1978 season are preserved exclusively in the memories of the people who saw them in person, listened to them on the radio, or have relived them in print. That has bestowed the season with a distant feel as if it took place in the leather helmet era. As a result 1978 tends to fall through the cracks, often forgotten or overlooked—a shame for one of the most entertaining teams and Spartans seasons in history.

The Flintstones

The shape of the Spartans' of 1997–2001 dynasty starting taking form in 1995 when two school boys from struggling Flint, Michigan, committed to a struggling MSU basketball program. A year later another Flint All-State high schooler followed his city brethren to MSU. The three welcomed the fourth All-Stater from Flint the very next year.

Antonio Smith and Morris Peterson were the first of the quartet to swear their allegiance to Tom Izzo in 1995. Flint Northern's Smith finished as the runner-up in Michigan's Mr. Basketball voting after ending his prep career as the No. 3 scorer in Flint's rich basketball history. Flint Northwestern's Peterson flew under the radar. But the 6'7" Peterson, who grew 13 inches from his freshman year, offered intriguing potential.

Mateen Cleaves played with Smith at Flint Northern. Pursued aggressively by Izzo, Cleaves, a McDonald's All-American, was recruited from every corner of the country. He eventually committed to MSU in no small part because of Smith. "Having 'Tone there sure made the decision a lot easier," said Cleaves in *Green Glory.*

The last of the quartet, Charlie Bell, played at Flint Southwestern Academy where he shattered all Flint scoring records previously set by Flint high school legend Glen Rice. Bell admired Cleaves immensely and clicked with Izzo. That was enough for Bell to sign with the Spartans in November of 1996.

Smith, Cleaves, Peterson, and Bell had been friends since childhood—sometimes competing in sports as teammates, sometimes as adversaries. When Bell joined the trio in East Lansing, their friendships resumed unabated. They roomed together. They socialized together. All four ended up having the word "Flint" tattooed on their shoulders. Then during the 1997–1998 season, a few students starting dressing as Fred Flintstone and Barney Rubble, which gave birth to the nickname "Flintstones" and a whimsical takeoff on the theme song of the popular animated show from the 1960s. Flint, whose allegiances had for years veered Maize and Blue, turned sharply green. Smith, Cleaves, Peterson, and Bell were treated like the Fab Four in their hometown, causing a stir whenever they showed up at a local event. Flint even held a parade for the Flintstones after the 1999 Final Four.

MSU basketball would not have reached the summit if not for the Flintstones. Smith set the tone, agreeing to play for a coach and program in the doldrums. Cleaves brought instant credibility and cachet. Peterson, more reticent than Cleaves, and Bell added essential mortar to the foundation.

Peterson's rise from curiosity to superstar couldn't have been more important. In high school, Peterson proved he had the ability to score, leading the competitive Saginaw Valley Conference in three-point shooting. Other elements of his game needed upgrades, starting with his attitude. Izzo got to work on that right away. In his freshman year, Peterson did not make the trip to the 1995 Maui Invitational after he missed too many classes. Assistant coach Tom Crean once slapped an image of Peterson on a milk carton and put it in his locker. Peterson had seemingly gone missing, appearing in only four games that year before breaking his thumb and taking a redshirt. By the middle of Peterson's sophomore year, he had yet to establish himself. His defense—never a strength in high school—muddled along, which vexed his defense-minded coach. "Morris is still going dorm-to-dorm, trying to find the first guy he can guard," grumbled Izzo at the time.

At the end of 1997, Peterson broke his right wrist against Gonzaga. That seemed to be the turning point. When he returned to the lineup he had to wear a cast, which everyone started calling "the Club." Because the Club made shooting difficult, Peterson focused on another part of his game. "That was when I finally decided I had to play defense," he said. "I tried to make myself into the person and the player I knew I could be."

Peterson never looked back. Coming off the bench as the sixth man in both his sophomore and junior years, he provided an instant scoring lift. Everyone expected that he would start his junior year. But Izzo preferred bringing him off the bench. As a credit to his increasing maturity, Peterson accepted Izzo's role for him without complaint. Peterson averaged 13.8 points his junior year, scoring a school-record 448 points off the bench. He also proved invaluable as a defensive stopper, shutting down wings and even point guards when necessary.

Izzo moved Peterson into the starting lineup for his senior year. He seized the opportunity zestfully, averaging 16.8 points and earning Big Ten co-MVP honors and first team All-American. "It was incredible," said Izzo. "He rose up to the occasion. For me he had one of the great senior years anybody ever had." By the time the Toronto Raptors of the NBA drafted him at 21, Peterson had made himself into an all-around great player. He could score off the dribble and behind the arc. He shot close to 80 percent from the line. He averaged almost six rebounds his last two years.

Charlie Bell, inserted into the starting lineup immediately as a freshman, became a glue guy, a dependable source of relentless defense, rebounding, and effort. He never missed a game in his four years. When Cleaves graduated, Bell moved seamlessly into the point guard position after spending his first three years as the off guard. (He also filled Cleaves' shoes during Cleaves' injury absence in 1998.) If the Spartans needed a defensive stop, Izzo often turned to Bell. If they needed a three from the corner, Bell often delivered. And probably no guard rebounded with as much vigor and effectiveness. "He's a great athlete," said then-MSU assistant Brian Gregory in *Green Glory*. "But he's more of a basketball player. He doesn't do many things flashy. He just gets the job done." No longer playing in the shadow of his older Flintstone teammates by his senior year, Bell led the Spartans to their fourth consecutive Big Ten title and third consecutive trip to the Final Four.

Bedrocks—pun intended—on the Spartans' 1997 to 2001 run also came from outside of Flint. The 6'9" A.J. Granger ascended slowly, enduring the barbs of MSU fans during his first few years. As a junior Granger started knocking down the three-point shot and developed enough moxie to mix it up in the post. "He has done a phenomenal job of changing my perception of him just being an outside shooter," said Izzo in 2000. "His rebounding has been a key, and he is defending better." He blistered the nets during the Spartans 1999 NCAA Tournament run, averaging 12 points in MSU's wins, including 7-of-8 on threes. Then in the national championship game in 2000, Granger tied his career high with 19 points and hauled down nine boards. Andre Hutson, a Buckeye like Granger who was lured north by Izzo, played in 138 of his team's 140 games over his four-year career. "There aren't many players in the nation like Andre Hutson," said Izzo in *Green Glory*. "He's the ultimate warrior. He's one of the most underrated players around. A lot of what he does doesn't show up in the box score."

68 Charlie Bachman

Having enjoyed a rebirth under one coach with Notre Dame pedigree, MSC turned to another man with Fighting Irish ties to replace him. An All-American at Notre Dame, Charlie Bachman was a friend and frequent collaborator with Notre Dame legend

Knute Rockne, and he turned around moribund programs at then-coaching graveyards Kansas State and Florida.

Bachman assumed control of Michigan State in 1933. The Chicago native took a stronger interest in offense than defense in contrast to his predecessor, Joe Crowley, who nevertheless had left Bachman some talent in that regard, including backs Ed Klewicki and Bernard McNutt. Bachman also greeted three key newcomers in 1933, sophomores Sid Wagner, Jim McCrary—one of the few African Americans in the sport—and Kurt Warmbein.

Tall, broad-shouldered, and balding, Bachman had a two-fold mission: win as many games as possible and put an end to Michigan's dominance against the Spartans. The Wolverines, coming off a national championship, had trounced the Spartans the year before 26–0 and hadn't lost to Michigan State in 18 years. Bachman's strategy to break the Wolverines' stranglehold? Treat the annual holy war against Michigan as just another game.

Bachman's first tilt against Michigan resembled the previous 18 in-state jousts. One difference, however, provided the slightest of silver linings. No MSC team had scored a touchdown against the Wolverines since 1918. Bachman's team put an end to that humiliating streak. Warmbein caught a short pass and went where no Spartan had gone before…at least in almost two decades. The touchdown in a 20–6 loss would have to suffice as progress. Bachman finished 4–2–2 in his first year.

Outgoing and personable, Bachman enjoyed the public relations dimension of his job and understood marketing. He changed the Spartans football uniform colors in 1934 from their traditional green and white to black and gold—the gold intended to evoke Notre Dame. He also added a wing-like graphic to the helmet, a handsome design element that would soon be co-opted by that other school in Michigan. Decked in new duds, the Spartans shined as brightly as the gold in their uniforms, winning 28 of their next 36 games. They capped that run with the school's first bowl game.

Downplaying the Michigan game worked brilliantly as well. The Spartans ripped off four straight wins against the Wolverines. Never had they even won back-to-back games against their rival. The first one surprised. Coming off of consecutive national championships, Michigan stood as the favorite, even though they had lost a number of key performers from the year before. Linebacker and center Gerald Ford returned. But he didn't have much help. This time Warmbein scored not one but two touchdowns, overwhelming the Wolverines by also completing long passes for gains of 18, 10, and 20 yards and picking off a pass. The defense held Michigan to 94 total yards in the Spartans' 16–0 shutout.

The agile-minded Bachman searched for any edge. One amusing—but effective—ploy came against Temple, who was riding a 15-game win streak when the Spartans traveled to Philadelphia. Coached by the legendary Pop Warner, Temple shunned jersey numbers as did many teams at that time. Unlike his peers, however, Warner used this to gain a significant advantage. With their heads down and jerseys bereft of numbers, Temple's linemen and backs would shift into different formations that blurred the distinction between back and lineman and caused great confusion for defenses.

Bachman gave his two guards and two tackles chalk and told them to mark the backfield players with an *X* on the first play. Frank Gaines, an end on the Spartans, recalled with delight: "I can still see Sid Wagner walking up to one of their backs and turning him around and with this black chalk making a big black *X* on his shirt with the man standing in complete amazement." Bachman then surprised the Owls by playing his second team for the entire third quarter.

MSC gained control in the fourth quarter and won 12–7. Art Brandstatter, a member of Bachman's "Mighty Mites," a fleet of quick backs that included Warmbein and Steve Sebo, scored one touchdown when he reversed his field and then knifed through the Owls secondary for 59 yards. He set up the second Spartans score on a 15-yard run, breaking six tackles and dragging a host of Owls. John Hannah called it the greatest Spartans performance he had ever seen.

Bachman, who authored numerous books on football, also created the Flying Z, the term he used for an offense he developed in the mid 1940s. The Flying Z employed the threat of the fullback on almost every play. The offense now is called the play-action pass, a staple of most NFL offenses.

Wagner, a lithe, agile guard, and Brandstatter earned All-American honors under Bachman. Johnny Pingel added more hardware later. They all helped the Spartans win a bushel of games under Bachman from 1933 to 1937. But each year at least one bad loss against an underdog kept the Spartans out of the national championship conversation. One of those losses came against Marquette in 1935 when Lou Zarza picked up a Marquette fumble in the last minute of play, rumbled a few exhausting yards, then lateraled the ball to Bandstatter, who dropped it. Marquette recovered for a 13–7 upset.

After the 1938 Orange Bowl, which the Spartans lost 6–0 to Auburn, Bachman misplaced the recipe to his grand success. His teams still won more than they lost, but the 38–26–6 record during his last eight years, which included no wins against Michigan, seemed full of too many empty calories. On a couple of occasions in the subsequent years, the Spartans took down a heavyweight. Employing the Flying Z, Bachmann's 1945 Spartans shocked three-touchdown favorite Pittsburgh 12–7 and clobbered 12th-ranked Penn State 33–0. Jack Breslin starred in both games, running the Flying Z to perfection. "Breslin is the best college back I've seen in five years," said Pitt coach Clark Shaughnessy after his Panthers lost to Michigan State.

Bachman retired in 1946, ending his career at Michigan State with a 70–34–1 record. He felt another coach could better mold the promising talent he had recently accumulated (George Guerre, Bob

McCurry, Frank Waters, and Lynn Chandois would star for the next coach.) Collecting more wins than any of his Michigan State predecessors, Bachman was elected into the College Football Hall of Fame in 1978. He died in 1985.

Brad Van Pelt

Brad Van Pelt wasn't everybody's All-American; he was every sport's All-American. A three-sport star at Owosso High School, a few stone throws away from East Lansing, he played quarterback and also played on defense. He set a single-game Michigan high school rebounding record in basketball that still ranks third today. In 1968 to 1969, he made first team All-League in baseball, basketball, and on both offense and defense in football—the only athlete in conference history to accomplish that. To top things off, he made first team All-State at quarterback.

At 6'5", 220 pounds, Van Pelt had the frame of a linebacker or defensive end, but he was also fleet of foot. Duffy Daugherty, who practically decamped to Owosso to ensure Van Pelt's commitment, put him at strong safety at the urging of defensive coordinator Hank Bullough. The decision was a boon for the defense where Van Pelt ranged from one end of the field to the other, seemingly pulled by magnetic force to wherever the ball appeared. "When he hit people, you could hear it throughout the stands," said his teammate Mark Niesen to the *Lansing State Journal* more than 25 years later. During his junior and senior years in 1971 to 1972, Van Pelt was the cornerstone of the second best defense in the conference. An inconsistent offense, however, doomed Van Pelt's teams to mediocre records. One of his teammates thinks he knows why the

Lyman's Letters

Only one Spartans athlete in history has earned 10 letters. Lyman Frimodig, a neighbor of Notre Dame's famed George Gipp while growing up in the Upper Peninsula, played football, basketball, and baseball at MAC until he graduated in 1917. Frimodig returned to East Lansing after serving in World War I to coach the MAC freshman football team. He never left, spending 41 years as assistant athletic director and business manager.

offense struggled. "Brad played the wrong position in college," said Van Pelt's teammate, offensive lineman Joe DeLamielleure, many years later. "He could have been our starting quarterback because he could throw the ball a mile. He also had an offensive player's personality. We spent my entire college career searching for a quarterback. If Brad had played quarterback, we would have won a lot more games."

That strong arm referred to by DeLamielleure helped Van Pelt star on the baseball diamond where he pitched for two seasons, striking out 94 batters in just 64.1 innings and posting a 2.10 ERA in his career. He earned second team All-Big Ten honors in 1972 and pitched eight innings on the 1971 MSU Big Ten Championship team. During the winter he suited up for the Spartans basketball team. Known for his stellar defense, he once shut down the Big Ten's leading scorer and rebounder, Indiana's George McGinnis. "Van Pelt helped define the position of power forward," said basketball coach Gus Ganakas.

Whether making a big hit on the football field, stopping one on the baseball diamond, or handcuffing someone on the basketball court, Van Pelt possessed an ineffable quality that drew people to him and created a murmur of excitement wherever he went. Even though he owned BMOC status, he never strutted around campus like a peacock flaring its colors. "Brad had a good heart," said Ganakas. "Despite all of his success…he was simply a nice guy."

A nice guy who could do some amazing things—at least according to Spartans lore. His fastball reportedly topped 100 miles an hour. He could hit a golf ball 300 yards or more and could have played goalie on the Spartans soccer team. He never trained for any sport, shunning weightlifting and offseason conditioning regimens. He was in the purest sense a natural athlete.

Van Pelt won the Maxwell Award in 1972, the first defensive back ever to win the award. That same year he was a consensus All-American. He ended his Spartans career with 256 tackles and 14 interceptions, the second most interceptions in MSU history at the time. The New York Giants selected him in the second round of the 1972 NFL Draft. That didn't stop the St. Louis Cardinals from taking him in the Major League Baseball draft of that same year. The Cleveland Indians and Pittsburgh Pirates would later draft him to no avail. Van Pelt stuck with football where he starred for 14 seasons and made five Pro Bowls. He retired just before the Giants made their first Super Bowl run. But every offseason Van Pelt would return to his hometown of Owosso.

John Pingel

Virtually unknown in high school, John Pingel arrived at MSC with no guarantees. In today's parlance he would be considered a walk-on. But the Mount Clemens High School grad demonstrated quickly that he belonged, impressing coaches in particular with his ability to punt and kick the ball, a key skill in the era of brute force offense and unsophisticated passing attacks, which placed a premium on field position. Pingel was especially adept at the quick kick, an unexpected punt that could pin opponents deep in their own end. Bachman called him, "the best quick kicker I ever coached. His kicks naturally went low, and many of them went 70 yards. Many rolled over the goal line. Usually, there was no return by the safety." In 1938 he set NCAA records that remain to this day for punting yardage (4,138).

Pingel proved to be more than just a master punter. Often referred to as a "triple threat star," he ran the ball and passed it with equal skill and effectiveness. Those close to the program at the time considered the 6'0", long and lean Pingel the finest all-around football player in the history of Spartans football. As a junior in 1937, he amassed 1,146 total yards, including 665 rushing, 481 throwing, and 12 touchdowns. As a senior he rang up 1,127 yards with 556 on the ground and 571 through the air and scored 12 touchdowns again.

Pingel seemed to relish the spotlight, saving his best games for the biggest ones. In 1936 against Michigan, Pingel, then a sophomore, came off the bench to score a touchdown on a 12-yard run to help the Spartans beat their rival 21–7, an unprecedented third straight win against UM. The next year against the Wolverines, Pingel twice brought the Spartans back from deficits—the first time on a 30-yard touchdown pass to Ole Nelson and the second on two consecutive plays that highlighted Pingel's array of skills. Trailing 14–13 late in the game, Pingel threw a laser between a scrum of Wolverines hounding Nelson, who squeezed the ball into his hands at the UM 40-yard line. On the next play, Pingel faded back to avoid pressure, slipped tackles while Nelson made his cut at the 25-yard line, and then released the ball. Nelson jumped, caught it, and then raced into the end zone for the decisive score.

Pingel's finest moment as a Spartans player may have come during one of their darkest stretches. After MSC failed to score an offensive touchdown for two straight weeks in the middle of the 1937 season—including a demoralizing a 3–0 loss to Manhattan—Pingel scored all of MSC's three touchdowns in the Spartans' spirit-boosting 21–7 win against Marquette. One of the scores included a gripping 80-yard run as Pingel directed a wall of Spartans blockers all the way into the end zone.

All these yards, touchdowns, and field-position changing punts helped the Spartans go 20–6–2 in the 28 consecutive games Pingel played, which was highlighted by the 1938 Orange Bowl, the Spartans' first trip to a bowl in their history. After earning second team All-American honors by the AP in 1937, Pingel was elevated to 1938's first team, the first Spartan in history to receive that distinction.

The Spartans' first genuine national star was drafted by the Detroit Lions in the seventh round in 1939. He played only one season but ranked third in the league in punting before entering the army where he earned the Bronze Star and the Purple Heart during World War II. At the end of the war, Pingel settled into a career as an advertising executive in Detroit. He was inducted into the College Football Hall of Fame in 1968 and died in 1999. In 2010 MSU recognized Pingel by making him one of the first Spartans inducted into the Spartan Ring of Fame.

The 1938 Orange Bowl

With another successful season in the books, the 8–1 Spartans passed through Spokane, Washington, in 1937 after a workmanlike 14–0 win at San Francisco. A telephone call at the Spokane train station interrupted the drudgery of the circuitous trip back home. Head coach Charlie Bachman picked up the phone. He heard a distant voice from the other corner of the country. It was an official from Miami, offering the Spartans an invitation to play in the fourth ever Orange Bowl, which they eagerly accepted.

With college football booming and ranking just behind baseball in popularity, Miami and New Orleans (1935), El Paso (1936), and Dallas (1937) created bowl games to compete with the Rose Bowl—the only bowl around for years—on New Year's Day. Considered at the time the greatest honor the football team had ever received, the Orange Bowl invitation leaked back to East Lansing. Student leaders promptly organized a rally to greet the team as it arrived home from the West Coast. To boost attendance at the rally, MSC made classes optional that day. The Spartans traveled in a police-escorted motorcade from the train station to the campus, and the route was lined with hundreds of students and fans waving and applauding. Another 2,000 or so joined the celebration at the gym where fans could cheer again for the men responsible for the momentous achievement.

And there were many. Jack-of-all-tradesman John Pingel was a second team All-American. Tackle Fred Schroeder, end Ole Nelson, and back Gene Ciolek also received postseason honors. Captain Harry Speelman provided stout defense and strong leadership, and Frank Gaines concluded his four years at MSC without ever losing to Michigan.

A few days later, the Spartans learned they would be playing Auburn, who had gone 5–3–2. Jack Meagher, Auburn's coach, was a disciple of Knute Rockne, Bachman's former teammate and friend at Notre Dame. All three men shared many of the same ideas about football.

The Spartans headed to Miami on December 20. The train carried 41 members of the team, the most Spartans ever to travel for a game out of state. The heat coupled with numerous social events disrupted the flow and crispness of the practices. Bachman started to worry especially when Nelson suffered a minor injury to his ankle.

With the game broadcast live on the radio to a national audience, defense ruled the day. The lone score in the 6–0 Auburn victory came on Ralph O'Gwynne's 1-yard touchdown run, the first touchdown scored by a Southern school in the short history of the Orange Bowl. The Spartans defense limited the damage thanks to Harry Speelman and his peers on the defensive line. The offense was about as effective as the early air conditioning units of the 1920s. No matter how much it huffed and puffed, it wasn't able to generate much. Nelson's injury hurt, but Auburn, familiar with the Spartans system, had an answer for everything. "Auburn outplayed MSC all day," wrote the *Lansing State Journal.* "[The] big and fast-charging Auburn line bottled up Spartan running and stifled State's passing."

The Megaphone Trophy

Other than the annual tussle with the Michigan Wolverines, no school on the Spartans schedule roils emotions and boils the blood more than Notre Dame. The Spartans and Irish first played in 1897, a 34–6 Fighting Irish victory. Notre Dame wasn't the program it would become, but it was one of the few colleges participating in the sport at a high level that agreed to play the Aggies. After getting shut out in seven straight games in the series, MAC finally broke through with a 17–0 win in 1910, a landmark victory for the school and one that helped strengthen the college's commitment to football. The Irish won six of the next seven, though George Gauthier, the first Aggie alum to coach MAC, led the Aggies to a 13–7 victory in 1918 against Knute Rockne's first Irish team. The series was suspended after 1921 and resumed in 1948.

Notable Michigan State-Notre Dame Games

1956: Michigan State 47, Notre Dame 14

The Spartans rolled up 494 total yards, scoring on runs of 62, 68, and 65 and putting more points on the Fighting Irish than any Spartans team before or since. The win moved Michigan State into the top spot in most of the polls.

1968: Michigan State 21, Notre Dame 17

On the eve of the game, Duffy Daugherty told everyone who would listen, including several Notre Dame representatives in attendance at the press dinner, that he just might open the game with an onside kick. Laughter turned to disbelief when the Spartans did just that the next day, recovering an onside kick on the opening kickoff, scoring six plays later, and defeating the star-studded Fighting Irish in a huge upset. "As assistant coaches we didn't know anything about that… until gametime," wrote George Perles about the onside kick in his autobiography. "We were kicking off, and I was up in the coaches box hooked up with Henry [Bullough] on the phone downstairs. He said 'You won't believe this: Duffy is going to onside kick.' I thought, *We're nuts. The old man is nuts.*" According to Perles they almost did it again after the first score until Notre Dame moved everyone in position.

1975: Michigan State 10, Notre Dame 3

Without completing a single pass, the Spartans forced five turnovers and upset the No. 8 Irish when Tyrone Wilson busted loose late in the game for a 76-yard run to set up Levi Jackson's four-yard touchdown scamper. It was the Spartans' only win in the rivalry during a 14-year period.

Introduced in 1949 the Megaphone Trophy was created by the Detroit Alumni Clubs of Notre Dame and Michigan State and given to the winning team usually in a quiet presentation in the locker room. Half of the megaphone is painted blue with the ND monogram, and the other side is white with the green MSU logo. Each year the score is painted on the megaphone until the cone is full. The current megaphone is the third incarnation. In the early years of the trophy, the Spartans ruled, winning 11 of the first 14 games. The first of those wins, 36–33 in South Bend, launched

1990: Notre Dame 20, Michigan State 19

In front of the largest Spartan Stadium crowd ever, the No. 1-ranked Irish fell behind 19–7. Still down 19–14 with 1:30 to play in the game, Fighting Irish quarterback Rick Mirer threw a pass from the Spartans 26-yard line to the corner of the front of the end zone. Spartans safety Todd Murray anticipated the throw and stepped in front of it for what should have been an easy interception. Instead the ball bounced off his shoulder pads and floated a yard backward into the hands of Irish receiver Adrian Jarrell, who alertly caught it before being tackled at the two. The Irish scored with 34 seconds left to win the game thanks to—as Irish fans call it—the "Immaculate Deflection."

2000: Michigan State 27, Notre Dame 21

On fourth-and-10, freshman quarterback Jeff Smoker hit Herb Haygood on a slant route. Haygood then split three defenders and ran 68 yards for a touchdown with 1:48 remaining in the game. That made Bobby Williams 4–0 as head coach of the Spartans.

2006: Notre Dame 40, Michigan State 37

A low point in the series for Michigan State, the Spartans squandered a 31–14 halftime lead and allowed 19 unanswered points in the fourth quarter. The go-ahead touchdown came on a Drew Stanton interception returned 27 yards by Terrail Lambert to put the Irish ahead for good. The Spartans' last gasp attempt to salvage the game was foiled once again by Lambert, who made a juggling interception in the waning seconds.

the Spartans into national prominence under Biggie Munn. Duffy Daugherty's Spartans won eight straight against Notre Dame, a stretch in which they outscored the Irish 202–48.

Never were the stakes higher or the buzz greater than in 1966 when the two schools battled to a 10–10 tie in the Game of the Century. After that game Notre Dame seized control of the series for the next 25 years. The Spartans won only three times between 1969 and 1994. Since then the series has been more competitive and featured a little of everything: incomprehensible comebacks, unimaginable blowouts, down-to-the-wire finishes, memorable trick plays, and controversy.

One controversy involved the trophy itself, which over the years had become a forgotten component of the rivalry. Neither Notre Dame nor Michigan State really put much emphasis on it—until 2005 when the Spartans knocked off Notre Dame in South Bend. The 44–41 win in overtime against the Irish probably represented the biggest victory John L. Smith had as head coach of Michigan State. In the postgame celebration, a few exuberant Spartans planted the MSU flag on the turf of Notre Dame Stadium, enraging Irish players and fans. Smith defended the action, saying the Spartans were offended that Notre Dame hadn't presented the Megaphone Trophy to Michigan State on the field immediately after the game. Charlie Weis, Notre Dame's head coach, confessed that he wasn't even aware of the trophy's existence. Both coaches were probably fudging a bit, but the dustup revived interest in the trophy.

The 2010 Final Four

The 2009–2010 Spartans opened the year ranked No. 2 by the AP. Spartans guards Korie Lucious and Kalin Lucas returned from the previous year's runner-up squad. Senior Raymar Morgan, who battled a vexing virus for large swaths of the previous year but was now in full health, wing Durrell Summers, off guard Chris Allen, 6'6" sophomore wing Draymond Green, and the 6'8" defensive-minded postman Delvon Roe filled the other important roles.

The season evolved into a four-act play. The first act underwhelmed. The second act inspired. The third act crashed. And the final act uplifted. In the first act, the Spartans slumbered through a 10–3 preconference schedule. A narrow win at home against Gonzaga represented the only tournament resume builder. Losses to Florida, North Carolina, and Texas caused the usual preconference doubts and handwringing. Through the first 13 games, Morgan had been up and down, Lucas fell in and out of Izzo's doghouse, Summers' jump shot disappeared, and the defense sprang more leaks than a soaker hose. On the plus side, Green began his ascent, grabbing every loose ball, scoring opportunistically, and becoming a co-captain as a sophomore. Somehow the Spartans remained in the Top 15.

The second act calmed everyone's nerves. The Spartans thundered to a 9–0 conference start, MSU's best ever. The highlight occurred in Minnesota where the Spartans trailed the entire game until Lucas hit a three with 1:27 left to give MSU a 65–64 win. Lucas scored 22 while dazzling his coach. "It was the best Lucas has been all year," Tom Izzo said.

Triggered by a stiffening schedule, the third act began 10 days later. MSU suffered its first conference loss, a 67–49 thrashing by Wisconsin. To compound matters Lucas missed most of the second half with a sprained ankle. He missed all of the next game, a 78–73 loss at Illinois. The Spartans kept it close thanks to 17 points and 15 rebounds by Green. "Playing without Lucas, it's no excuse," Izzo said. "Everybody has to play without somebody." Then with Lucas playing on half a wheel, the Spartans tumbled at home to Purdue. "We didn't check anybody in the first half," Izzo said. "We haven't checked in three games, and I don't have an answer for us."

But MSU rescued the season with an unexpected win at Purdue, which pulled them into a second place tie with the Boilermakers. The Spartans shot only 40 percent and committed 23 turnovers. "We're going to enjoy it until we get home on the plane," Izzo said. "And then we've got to figure out that we've got some work to do here. Michigan State's got to get better." A three-game winning streak to end the regular season earned MSU a share of the conference title,

Izzo's sixth. The final scene of the third act ruptured the Spartans' confidence and left many wondering whether they had just witnessed the season's final act. Playing without Chris Allen, whom Izzo had suspended, and with Durrell Summers benched for long stretches because of lackadaisical effort, the Spartans fell in overtime to Minnesota in the first round of the Big Ten tournament.

The fourth act opened in Spokane, Washington. The fifth-seeded Spartans narrowly beat 12th-seeded New Mexico State in the first round of the NCAA tournament. The Aggies, who prompted a weeklong volley of trash talking by asking "Who is Kalin Lucas?" heated up in the second 20 minutes, even overtaking the Spartans midway through the half. MSU managed to hang on though, sneaking by with a 70–67 win thanks to 25 points by that Lucas guy. Morgan iced the game on a controversial free throw with 18 seconds left, a free throw awarded him after an Aggie lane violation had negated a Morgan miss. "I don't want to say I'm glad we had a close game, but I learned something about these guys that I had been looking for this year," Izzo said.

The second round game against Maryland started robustly for the Spartans, who jumped to a nine-point, first-half lead. But tragedy struck with 2:28 remaining in the half. Lucas pulled up lame after hitting a shot near the baseline. He hobbled off the court with an injury and did not return. Nonetheless MSU expanded its lead to 16 in the first nine minutes of the second half. Summers kept hitting threes, Green and Morgan kept pulling down missed shots, and the Spartans swarmed on defense. In the midst of their torrid run, Lucas reappeared on the bench—in a boot. He had torn his Achilles tendon.

When Summers picked up his fourth foul at the 6:19 mark, the Terrapins pounced, speeding up the game and pressuring MSU into a spate of turnovers. Maryland took an 81–80 lead with 31 seconds left. Green responded coolly with an

Draymond Green listens to his mentor, coach Tom Izzo, during Michigan State's 52–50 loss to Butler in the 2010 Final Four.

eight-footer. Maryland's Greivis Vasquez rocketed down the court and hit a runner to put Maryland back in front with six seconds left. Izzo let the Spartans play on. Green hurriedly pushed the ball up the floor. He passed to Lucious, a toss that nearly hit a ducking Roe. Lucious dribbled once and then launched a three from the top of the key. As the ball headed toward the basket, the buzzer sounded. It swished through. Lucious backpedaled down the court, followed feverishly by his teammates, who dogpiled on him. "I had an open look," Lucious said. "Time was running down. I just shot it and it went in." Izzo now had a buzzer beater to add to his memorable March moments. "I told our team when we were up four, up six, whatever, it was, 'We were going to win this game, and it's going to be one of the greatest wins in the history of Michigan State,'" Izzo said.

The game-winning three cannon blasted the Spartans into the Sweet 16 for the third straight year. To advance they would have to play without Lucas, who was finished for the year. That sobering fact was counterbalanced to a lesser degree by what had happened to No. 1 seed Kansas. It had been upset by Northern Iowa, which created an opportunity for the Spartans. They seized it. Behind another sterling performance by Durrell Summers, the Spartans outlasted the Cinderella 59–52. Summers remained on fire, scoring 19 points and leading MSU in rebounding. "I knew it would be just a gut-it-out game," Izzo said.

Another opportunity awaited them in the Elite Eight. No. 6 seed Tennessee had upset No. 2 seed Ohio State to advance to the regional final against MSU. Tennessee missed one of two down the stretch against Michigan State, and Morgan, fouled in the act of shooting with seconds left, buried one to lift MSU to another Final Four. Summers continued his scorching March, shooting 8-of-10, including 4-of-6 from three, for 21 points. He was named the region's Most Outstanding Player.

The march to the Final Four had frayed everyone's nerves. The Spartans had survived the region by winning all of their games by a combined 13 points. They had done it without a healthy Roe or Allen, each of whom played only sporadically. For two full games and half of another, they had soldiered through without their best player. But Lucious had filled in admirably, carrying the team with a dose of swagger, a dash of composure, and a spectacular shot that inspired the team.

The Final Four marked Izzo's sixth, an amazing accomplishment, but the 2010 Final Four failed to match the electricity of the Spartans' road to it. They fell to underdog Butler, an Indianapolis-based mid major playing in Indy, the site of the Final Four. Summers cooled, hitting only one three, and the injuries forced Izzo to play stretches of a Final Four game with two walk-ons, Mike Kebler and Austin Thornton. The Spartans hung tough and had a chance to win it at the end. Down a point Green missed an awkward-looking layup with under 10 seconds left, and the rugged Bulldogs then sealed it at the line. "If I was not playing, I'd be a Butler fan," Izzo said after the game.

74 Spartan Green

The origin of the colors of Michigan State sports are murky at best. What is known is that in 1899 the Athletic Association of MAC decided to officially add a green monogram to all attire worn by Aggie athletes during competition. No explanation exists as to why green was selected. Perhaps the board thought green made sense for a school devoted to teaching agriculture.

Chester Brewer took the declaration seriously when he was hired in 1903, rolling out green and white colored uniforms for the four sports that MAC sponsored: football, basketball, baseball, and track. Brewer coached all four sports.

At the request of new head football coach Charlie Bachman, Michigan State abandoned the green and white football jerseys and replaced them with black and gold ones in the early 1930s. They wore these colors when they beat Michigan four straight times and participated in the school's first bowl, the Orange Bowl. After a decade of mostly forgettable football, MSC hired Biggie Munn in 1947, and he promptly reinstated the green and white colors to the Spartan football uniforms. No one has dared suggest any other color since.

The shade of the green has changed slightly over the years. Today it is a darker hue of green, one that provides more contrast to the natural turf and brings the color scheme closer in line to what it was decades ago. If you want to duplicate it, you can simply look for Pantone Matching System ink color number 567 (known in graphic art circles as PMS 567). You may not find a PMS 567 color chip at your local hardware store, but most paint dealers can help you find the right match if you have the PMS color. So go ahead and spruce up the house with authentic Spartan green.

75 Five Fabulous Receivers

Andre Rison (1985 to 1988)

The Flint native made the most of the few passes that MSU attempted during the George Perles era. Rison could stretch a defense with his scorching speed. But he was more than a burner.

Andre Rison, who ranks second in MSU history with 2,992 receiving yards, is one of the many great receivers to have played at Michigan State. (Getty Images)

Fearless and elusive, he didn't back away from making the difficult catch over the middle. His amalgam of skills helped him turn a meager 39 receptions into 961 yards in 1988. One of Rison's most spectacular catches occurred in the 1988 Rose Bowl when he and quarterback Bobby McAllister hooked up on a 36-yard broken play to keep the game-winning drive alive. Rison had to readjust his route to help McAllister, who had been flushed from the pocket and threw a jump pass at the sideline just before USC drove him out of bounds.

Rison had an even more spectacular day in the 1989 Gator Bowl, his last game as a collegian. "Bad Moon" caught nine passes for 252 yards in a nip-and-tuck game ultimately won by Georgia 34–27. The Spartans kept falling behind, but Rison kept pulling them back into it with scintillating catches. "We weren't able to stop Rison," said Georgia coach Vince Dooley. "He kept them in the game. At times it looked as if we would take control, but because of him, we were never able to." Rison finished his career with 2,992 receiving yards, a record that stood until 2011. He also ranks third in MSU history with 20.5 yards per catch. He was drafted by the Indianapolis Colts and played in five Pro Bowls in a checkered 12-year pro career.

Courtney Hawkins (1988 to 1991)

Despite Perles' general hostility to the forward pass, he still managed to attract the occasional big-time receiver. Hawkins, another Flint standout, caught 60 passes in 1989, which was a school record at the time. He turned those 60 receptions into 1,080 yards, also a school record. "He has speed, the moves, and great hands," said Perles in 1989. Hawkins missed most of the 1990 season with an injury and suffered through an injury-hobbled senior year. But he still ranks in the top five at MSU in career receptions (138) and receiving yards (2,210). The Buccaneers drafted Hawkins in the second round, and he enjoyed a nine-year NFL career. He is now the head coach at his alma mater, Flint Beecher High School.

Plaxico Burress (1998 to 1999)

For two years Burress, a junior college transfer from Virginia, caused many a sleepless night for Big Ten defensive coordinators. Most defensive backs gave up six to seven inches to the 6'6"

Burress, who had the speed to outrun most cornerbacks, the height to reach over the them, and the strength to dominate them while wrestling for the ball. "Plax is the best receiver I ever coached," said Charlie Baggett, MSU's wide receiver coach at that time and the man who had coached Rison and Hawkins. On national television against Michigan in 1999, Burress exploded, noisily showing the country his array of skills. Most opponents double-teamed him. Not Michigan. The Wolverines put David Terrell on Burress in single coverage. He torched Terrell, catching 10 passes for a monster 255 yards. He embarrassed the Michigan cornerback by knocking him on his rear numerous times with relentless, physical blocks. As an encore Burress recovered the onside kick to preserve the 34–31 Spartans win. His 66 receptions in 1999 is tied for sixth all time at MSU. The 65 passes he caught in 1998 ranks eighth. The 252 yards against Michigan are second on the school list. He also became the first MSU receiver to enjoy back-to-back 1,000-yard seasons. Though brash at times, Burress was drafted after his junior year by the Pittsburgh Steelers and had 11-year NFL career, one which included a Super Bowl title with the New York Giants and was later interrupted by a prison sentence for carrying a concealed weapon.

Charles Rogers (2001 to 2002)

One of the most prolific receivers in MSU history, Rogers, the No. 1 recruit in the nation according to some services, sent the hopes of Spartans fans into orbit when he committed to MSU in 2000. The Saginaw, Michigan, native didn't disappoint, even though he had to wait a year before he could take the field because of academic issues. Rogers ran a 4.3 40, freakish ability for someone 6'4". Three times he hooked up with Jeff Smoker to burn opponents for more than 190 receiving yards. In the 2001 Silicon Valley Bowl, MSU's last bowl win for 10 years, Rogers caught 10 passes for a school-record 270 yards. Rogers caught a touchdown pass in 14 consecutive games, an NCAA record. When he left for the NFL after his junior year, Rogers ranked second on the MSU all-time receiving yards list. He remains second on the yards-per-catch list. He is the MSU leader in touchdown receptions and holds the first and second spot in receiving years for a season—1,470 in 2001 and 1,352 in 2002—remarkably accomplished in just two seasons. The Detroit Lions took Rogers No. 2 overall, but he sustained a season-ending injury his rookie year and then had alleged issues with drugs and alcohol.

B.J. Cunningham (2008 to 2011)

Spartans fans didn't throw any parties when Ohio native Cunningham committed to Michigan State in 2008. But they should have. With hands as sticky as maple syrup and sneaky speed, Cunningham shattered the MSU all-time receiving list for most career receptions, receiving yards, and most receptions in a season. For good measure he is also second all time in career touchdowns and third in receiving yards in a season. In his senior year, Cunningham came up big in the Spartans' biggest games, grabbing six passes for 102 yards against Wisconsin and six catches for 120 yards against Northwestern. He turned a juggling grab over the middle into the game winner by taking it the distance with just five minutes left. "He is just a guy that makes plays," Dantonio said. "You can have him covered, and he is still going to make the play. That is the kind of receiver you need out there."

Note that Kirk Gibson would have received mention, but his multi-sport accomplishments were so impressive that he merited his own chapter.

76 Ralph Young

For years if you wanted to give money to Spartans athletics, the university encouraged you to make a donation to something called the Ralph Young Fund. And while that was all well and good, who was this Ralph Young guy? For the uninitiated, Young coached at MAC in the 1920s and then became athletic director for more than 25 years.

Young failed to decorate himself in glory during his brief time as head coach of MAC. In five seasons from 1923 to 1927, the Spartans finished above .500 only once. They suffered five consecutive losses to Michigan: three ugly ones, one that was only a little ugly, and another that almost ended in a tie. Young played college ball at three different schools, including a post-World War I year at Michigan, and mixed in a little professional ball at the same time (a not uncommon practice).

Off the field, however, Young made important contributions to the stability of athletics at MAC, which became MSC in 1925. For starters he helped create the Central Collegiate Conference (CCC) with Knute Rockne from Notre Dame and Con Jennings from Marquette. The conference provided competition in many sports but not football. The CCC grew in prominence, serving as a meaningful alternative source of competition for other Big Ten schools and probably helping Michigan State in its bid for membership in the Big Ten. Also under Young the school built a new football stadium, which opened in 1923 and could seat almost 20,000 spectators.

Young understood the efficacy of good public relations. And few were better practitioners of the art. Garrulous, jovial, and a bit of a bon vivant with the bulging waistline to prove it, he traveled

Mark Hollis: Michigan State's Man in Charge

The current MSU athletic director has ties to MSU sports that extend back to the early 1980s. Mark Hollis served as a student manager for Jud Heathcote during the rocky years immediately following Magic Johnson. Jud could, of course, be cantankerous in the best of times. But Hollis collected towels and jumped when Heathcote said "jump" in years so lean it's a good bet the student manager's job felt even more thankless than usual.

Nonetheless, the gig served Hollis well. He developed a strong relationship with Heathcote that endures and picked up a few pointers on how to best overcome odds that seem stacked against you.

Since becoming MSU's athletic director in 2008, and even before that, Hollis, who roomed with Tom Izzo when Tom was an assistant under Heathcote, has worked seamlessly with the president of MSU, Lou Anna Simon, Izzo, and Mark Dantonio, whom Hollis was instrumental in hiring in 2006, to form the most stable management team MSU has seen since the 1960s.

Innovative, energetic, and wily, Hollis also has engineered numerous glamorous events that have raised MSU's profile regionally and nationally. In 2001 he put together the Cold War, an outdoor hockey game between MSU and Michigan (that ended in a 3–3 tie) at Spartan Stadium that drew more than 74,000 fans, a record for a hockey game at that time. Other signature events he authored: Basketbowl, a 2003 basketball game between MSU and Kentucky at Ford Field (won by Kentucky) that set attendance records for a basketball game at any level (78,129); the Carrier Classic in 2011 between MSU and North Carolina (won by North Carolina) played in front of president Barack Obama on the USS Carl Vinson, an aircraft carrier; and the Armed Forces Classic in 2012 between MSU and Connecticut (won by UConn) played in a hangar on U.S. Ramstein Air Base in Germany.

Locally he swiped powerful and influential radio station WJR away from the University of Michigan, reaching an agreement with the Detroit radio station in 2005 to broadcast all MSU football and basketball games, a deal that was renewed and will now run until at least 2020.

In 2013 Hollis served on the prestigious NCAA Men's Basketball selection committee, a year after being named Athletic Director of the Year by *Street & Smith's Sports Business Daily Journal.*

extensively, spreading his good cheer and news and information about the school in East Lansing.

In 1927 Young stepped down as head coach to become MSC's first athletic director, a job for which he was naturally suited. Under his stewardship MSC hired a string of solid football coaches, each of whom made significant contributions to the development of the program. Basketball and other sports slowly gained in national prominence as well. Young was instrumental in eliciting support and funding for a new basketball facility that finally opened in 1940 under the name Jenison Field House. Through it all he adroitly managed the athletic department's tight finances, which at times required difficult and unpopular decisions such as agreeing to play all Michigan-Michigan State games in Ann Arbor because the payout for the Spartans would be greater. The crowning achievement of his career was the Spartans' admission into the Big Ten. He and president John Hannah worked tirelessly for almost two decades to accomplish this.

Young retired as athletic director in 1954, ending almost four decades of service to Michigan State. When he started the school had a different name, drew fewer than 20,000 fans to football games, and was a pebble in the rock pile of college football. When he called it quits, MSC drew more than 50,000 a game and had established itself as one of the sport's strongest forces.

77 Visit Spartan Stadium

Built in 1923 in response to the increasing popularity of football on campus, Spartan Stadium originally bore the official name MAC Field. Most called it Old College Field. It included stands on the west and east side that could hold 14,000 fans. Bleachers occupied each end zone on the north and south side, which could increase capacity by a few thousand more. The Aggies, the soon-to-be-retired nickname, christened the new field the next season in a game unusual for two reasons. The Wolverines deigned to make an appearance in East Lansing—their first since 1914—and the Aggies managed to keep the rivalry game close, losing only 7–0. Former Aggies head coach John Macklin and Michigan Governor Alex Groesbeck spoke during pregame ceremonies.

MAC Field expanded numerous times in the coming years, usually following an improvement in the football team's fortunes. In 1935 MAC Field changed its name to Macklin Field in honor of Macklin and added 12,000 more seats to the east and west stands. At the dedication ceremonies, MSC president Robert Shaw hailed Macklin for his "achievements as a distinguished athlete, coach, and exponent of the worth of athletic training as preparation for after-college activities."

With the Spartans' football program finding a new gear under Biggie Munn, Macklin Field expanded again. The school added 27,250 seats in 1948 and changed the stadium's name to Macklin Stadium, 9,000 more seats in 1956, and another 15,000 the next year after new head coach Duffy Daugherty triumphed in the Rose Bowl. The final expansion, which ended with a seating capacity of 76,000, included a change as well. In 1957 Macklin Stadium yielded to Spartan Stadium, the name still in use today. A scurrilous rumor circulated in the 1930s, according to Fred Stabley in *The Spartans*, that Michigan State changed the name because it hoped Macklin would bequeath some of his vast fortune to his old school at some point in the future. The fortune belonged to his wife, the daughter of a Pennsylvania coal baron. Macklin died in 1949, leaving nothing to MSC. That prompted his old school, so the cynical theory goes, to dump Macklin's name in favor of Spartan Stadium.

As new technological fads emerged, further enhancements followed suit. Astroturf replaced natural grass before the 1969 season. A modern scoreboard booted the old scoreboard in 1973. A video-equipped scoreboard supplanted that scoreboard in 1991—only to be replaced by a high-definition video scoreboard in 2012. In response to a newfound appreciation for the traditional, Michigan State tore up the Astroturf and restored natural grass to the field in 2002.

The final renovation occurred in 2005 with the appearance of a new press box, 24 luxury suites, and 862 club seats. The current capacity is 75,005, slightly lower than its peak due to a few earlier renovation tweaks. Spartan Stadium attendance has ranked in the Top 25 of college football every year since 1956. The largest crowd ever—80,401—watched, slack jawed as the Spartans fell 20–19 to Notre Dame on September 22, 1990.

Festooned throughout Spartan Stadium are banners saluting members of the Spartan Ring of Fame, which recognize the greatest Spartans of all time.

Next door to Spartan Stadium is the Duffy Daugherty Building/Skandalaris Football Center, which contains coaches' offices and other athletic facilities. Although many areas of the building are not open to the public, the Demmer Family Hall of History is a public museum dedicated to the history of Spartans football. Plaques honoring Spartans greats and title teams make up most of the exhibit, which is downstairs. On your way to the museum, you will pass Perles Plaza in front of the Duffy Daugherty Building. This spot donated by former head coach George Perles provides a pleasant and tranquil place to gather and relax.

Visit Jenison Field House and the Breslin Center

One evokes the sound of squeaky Converse, the sight of satin shorts cut at the thigh, and the smell of old sweats thrown in a pile. It conjures memories of baskets running on Gables hanging overhead, muted lighting, and noise levels so loud one's own thoughts could be drowned out. The second provides comfort, the pulse-quickening sensation of cutting-edge technology, and the sight of baggy shorts. And it launched a period of excellence unmatched in the annals of MSU sports.

Since the beginning of World War II, the Spartans have played basketball in two venues. MSU moved into Jenison Field House in 1940. A state-of-the-art facility, Jenison costs $1.7 million to build. More than 15,000 fans squeezed into Jenison for a game against Kentucky in 1948. The fire marshal, however, deemed that too many, so MSU limited capacity to 12,500. Jenison ultimately ended up holding 10,004 fans.

Named after MAC graduate and insurance millionaire Frederick Cowles Jenison, who donated $315,000 to help build it, Jenison Field House hosted college and high school basketball games and matches in boxing, fencing, gymnastics, handball, swimming, track, volleyball, and wrestling. The Spartans won the very first game played at Jenison, beating Tennessee 29–20 in front of 6,700 fans. In 1970 MSU installed a tartan playing surface and then replaced it with another wood floor in 1979 just in time for Magic Johnson, Greg Kelser, and a national championship.

In its advancing years, the field house became a recruiting liability. Although beloved and a difficult place for opponents to play, Jenison lacked modern facilities and presented numerous practice conflicts as various varsity sports competed for time in the arena.

In 48 seasons there, MSU won 383 games and lost only 189 times, a .670 winning percentage. "Jenison Field House was awful—and super," reflected Jud Heathcote in *Jud*. "It was an awful place to sell recruits and a super place to play for a home-court advantage." You can visit the historic arena, which the volleyball team now calls home.

MSU basketball moved into the Jack Breslin Center November 9, 1989. Named after former MSU football player and longtime administrator Jack Breslin, the Breslin Center seats 14,797 and includes the main gym plus two additional practice gyms. The current floor is the same one on which the Spartans won the 2000 championship. MSU had the floor from the RCA Dome in Indianapolis disassembled and shipped to East Lansing.

Pyrotechnics illuminate the Jack Breslin Center, the setting of one of the best home-court advantages in basketball, during the 2011 Midnight Madness.

Replete with every modern amenity, the arena has proven a tremendous recruiting tool. It also ushered in the greatest era in MSU basketball history. Since the Spartans moved into the Breslin Center in 1989, MSU has gone 277–135 in conference games, the best in the conference by 31 games over second place Purdue. At home MSU is 171–35 in conference games, 15 games better than second place Wisconsin.

Be sure to check out the Wall of Fame while visiting Breslin. Past performers, athletes, musicians, and others have scribbled their autographs on the wall in the corridor.

79 Little Giants and Mousetrap

On the sideline his expression rarely changes. He is stern, unflappable. There is no hint that something daring—even radical—is simmering just beneath that stoic exterior. But it's a surprising part of current MSU head coach Mark Dantonio's DNA. And in 2010 it exploded to the surface in the form of two plays at the most unexpected—and opportune—times.

Both plays became known by the names the MSU coaches had assigned to them, names taken from popular culture. Dantonio cannily offered them up immediately after each game: Little Giants and then Mousetrap. Naming each play ensured that these two seminal moments in MSU history would gain a shelf life well beyond the normal big play in college sports. These two plays have helped define the era of the winningest football coach at MSU since Duffy Daugherty.

Little Giants

Before September 18, 2010, *Little Giants* was merely a movie about a youth football team. By the end of the day, the title had been co-opted by college football. Down three in the first overtime against rival Notre Dame, MSU faced a fourth-and-long at the 29-yard line. The Spartans had come from behind twice to tie the score during the nationally televised night game. The last was a 24-yard touchdown with 7:43 remaining in regulation. Now the Spartans were on the ropes again. Dantonio sent first-year kicker Dan Conroy on to attempt a 46-yard field goal, a conventional move, but it certainly dampened palms throughout Spartan Stadium.

Conroy had never made—let alone attempted—such a high-pressure kick. Dantonio considered the moment. During preparations for Notre Dame, the Spartans had practiced a fake field goal. The coach had been itching all day to use the play, but the right opportunity never presented itself. Dare he attempt it here? As Aaron Bates, the holder and regular punter, ran onto the field, Dantonio gave the go-ahead nod. "I'd rather the pressure be on us—or me" instead of a first-year kicker, Dantonio said afterward.

As Spartans fans crossed their fingers, hoping for another overtime, Bates took the snap, perhaps after the play clock had expired—as Notre Dame would suggest later—then sprang to his feet with the ball, scanning the field for his intended receiver, Le'Veon Bell. The crowd gasped. Caught off guard at first, the Fighting Irish defenders quickly regrouped and moved to cover Bell. With his intended receiver covered, Bates summoned the skills from his days as a high school quarterback and calmly scanned the field for another option. That's when he saw Charlie Gantt open down the seam. He threw a perfect pass to the Spartans tight end. *Please don't drop it*, Gantt said to himself. He didn't it, corralling the ball around the 8-yard line and trotting into the end zone for the winning score.

The Spartans rushed onto the field, dancing and delirious. Dantonio pumped his fist, pleased and relieved. "It took a lot of guts to make the call," Bates said, representing the general sentiment of those who saw it. Running off the field, Dantonio told a reporter that the play was called "Little Giants," named after the movie. There was nothing little about it, however. The Spartans remained undefeated, and Dantonio had revealed an astonishing maverick side.

Mousetrap

A few weeks later, the undefeated Spartans trailed Northwestern by 10 in the fourth quarter. With the ball at the Northwestern 31-yard line and a fourth-and-6 looming, Dantonio sent the offense on the field but then called timeout. He then sent the punting team on the field instead. The Spartans took a delay of game penalty, which moved them back to the 36, 11 yards shy of a first down. Any thought of a trick on the part of the Spartans vanished after this sequence. At least that is what Dantonio wanted the Wildcats to think. Northwestern kept its defensive unit on the field just in case.

Bates, one of the heroes of Little Giants and the punter, stood back waiting for the snap. Bennie Fowler, a seldom-used freshman wideout, lined up wide right across from Northwestern's Jordan Mabin. Mabin had been covering Fowler all day on punts, blocking him for several yards and then cutting to the sidelines to avoid getting hit by the punt. The Spartans coaches had noticed this on film during the week of preparations. Bates took the snap. Just as he had done all day and all season, Mabin chucked Fowler for about 10 to 15 yards and then vacated to the sidelines. But Bates didn't punt the ball. Instead he lofted a pass in the direction of Fowler, who was uncovered and caught the perfectly thrown ball for a 21-yard gain and first down. "It was a mousetrap," Dantonio said.

"We had to get them to take the cheese. We felt like they would drop their receiver after 15 yards and we felt like we could sneak one in there especially with Bates."

On the next play, quarterback Kirk Cousins connected with Mark Dell for a 15-yard touchdown pass to pull the Spartans within three. They scored two more touchdowns in the last 13:12 to complete the rally and win 35–27, keeping intact their undefeated season. Once again Dantonio had outsmarted an opponent with a trick play, though this one called Mousetrap was even more calculated. "I've always been risky," Dantonio said.

Eight Great Defensive Players of the Modern Era

Bill Simpson (1971 to 1973)

A hard-hitting, ornery SOB on the field, Simpson roamed the Spartans defensive backfield alongside All-American Brad Van Pelt from 1971 to 1972 and then anchored new coach Denny Stolz's defense in 1973. Simpson intercepted five passes that year to pace the second best secondary in the country and 12th best overall defense. "We move and we can hit," Stolz said. "We really crack it defensively. We're small, quick, and tough." Simpson had a nose for the ball. He also served as the regular punter and punt returner. In the season opener in 1972, Simpson returned a punt 48 yards for a touchdown and scored on a 20-yard interception return. He also had six picks that season and led the Big Ten in punt return average at 13.6, including a 74-yarder against Georgia Tech. He is ranked seventh on the all-time interception list with 12 picks. Simpson spent eight seasons in the NFL mostly with the Los Angeles Rams. He earned All-Pro honors in 1977 and 1978.

Dan Bass (1976 to 1979)

The 1978 Spartans set a Big Ten record for yards gained and scored points at an absurd pace en route to a share of the Big Ten title. Forgotten in all the scoreboard spinning is the MSU defense, which spent disproportionate time on the field because of the offense's quick scores. One of the leaders of that defense was Bass, a junior linebacker who helped spearhead the third best defensive unit in the Big Ten. Wherever the ball went, Bass followed. He even set an MSU record by returning an interception 99 yards for a touchdown against Wisconsin.

The Spartans suffered 42 injuries in 1979, including 24 to starters and dipped to 5–6. The Bath, Michigan, native, however, played in all 11 games, making it 44 straight during his MSU career and provided one of the few bright spots of the season. He led the Spartans with 160 tackles, including a still-standing school record of 32 in the Spartans' otherwise dismal 42–0 loss to Ohio State. He also registered 24 tackles against Notre Dame. He was a unanimous choice for All-Big Ten first team. Bass is MSU's all-time school leader in tackles with 541. "He has great tools," said his linebacker coach Walt Harris in 1979, "is fun to coach and is good for morale. Dan is like a coach on the field with his leadership." Bass played in the Canadian Football league for 12 seasons and was named the CFL Most Outstanding Defensive Player in 1989.

Carl Banks (1980 to 1983)

Despite never playing on a winning team, Flint native Banks drew attention to himself, earning first team All-American honors. Opponents rarely tested his side of the field especially by his senior year, but Banks nonetheless led MSU with 97 tackles in 1981. A fierce hitter who rang more bells than an altar boy and once—according to legend—dislodged two teeth of an opponent with a massive blow, he provided the total package at linebacker. "[Banks] neutralized big tackles, covered tight ends, and rushed the quarterback," *Sport Illustrated* wrote in 2006 when describing Banks as a collegian and pro. Banks became the first non-kicker at MSU to earn All-Big Ten first team honors for three years. The Giants drafted him third overall. He teamed with Lawrence Taylor to win two Super Bowls in nine seasons and tallied numerous honors. Banks is currently the color analyst for Giants radio broadcasts.

Percy Snow (1986 to 1989)

Another in a long line of stellar linebackers at MSU, the Canton, Ohio, native started for three years and racked up enough hardware to fill an aisle at Home Depot. Snow twice earned first team All-American honors. He became the first player ever to win the Lombardi Trophy and the Butkus Award. He was named the MVP of the 1988 Rose Bowl as a sophomore. Powerfully built, Snow attacked opposing ball carriers like a lumberjack, cutting everything down in sight. "[Snow] could go from Point A to Point B as fast as anybody I'd ever seen," said his coach, George Perles, in his autobiography. "He could accelerate and when he got there he could throw everything into that thrust and not only tackle people but hurt them." Snow was a first round draft pick of the Kansas City Chiefs, but a moped accident ended his career three years later.

Harlon Barnett (1986 to 1989)

"Da Bang Stick" was the nickname given to the Cincinnati native by his brand-conscious father, and Barnett started for three years in the secondary under Perles. As the captain of the 1989 Spartans, he directed a defense ranked No. 1 in the Big Ten and 11th nationally. Just as his father had imagined, Barnett developed into a ferocious hitter. After a seven-year NFL career with the Cleveland Browns,

New England Patriots, and Minnesota Vikings, Barnett returned to MSU in 2006 to coach the defensive backs, a position he still holds.

Julian Peterson (1998 to 1999)

Perhaps Michigan State's most physically gifted defensive player of the last 25 years, Peterson, a junior college transfer from Maryland, made a noisy debut in MSU's 1998 splaying of Notre Dame, picking off a pass at the Fighting Irish 23 and motoring into the end zone untouched. Peterson made an even louder impression in the Spartans' upset of Ohio State later that year. When defensive end Robaire Smith broke his leg in the first quarter, Peterson replaced him and launched a brutal assault on the Buckeyes. He forced three fumbles, recorded four sacks, and made a staggering seven tackles for loss. It was a season's worth of accomplishments in one game. MSU used him at linebacker and defensive end, depending on the situation. Blessed with exceptional closing speed, Peterson won the MVP of the 2000 Citrus Bowl. He set an MSU record with 30 tackles for loss in his senior year, including 15 sacks. Peterson finished his career as the all-time Spartans leader in tackles for loss with 48, which was remarkably achieved in just two years. The No. 16 overall pick by the San Francisco 49ers in the 2000 NFL Draft, Peterson enjoyed an 11-year career that included five Pro Bowl selections.

Greg Jones (2007 to 2010)

An unheralded member of Mark Dantonio's first recruiting class, Jones started at middle linebacker all four years of his MSU career. Committed to Minnesota initially until the Gophers fired their coach, the Cincinnati native made the All-Freshman team in 2007 and never stopped adding hardware after that, winning the National Linebacker of the Year in 2009 and earning a nomination for the Butkus Award in 2010. Jones led the Spartans in tackles for four years, shedding blocks with ease, rarely whiffing on a ball carrier in the open field, and always stationing himself in the proper place. "He's a great pass rusher," Dantonio said. "He'll run well and jump well. But I think he's an instinctive player." In his four years, the Spartans won 33 games, went 6–2 against rivals Notre Dame and Michigan, and played in four bowl games. Jones finished his career as the third leading tackler in MSU history. The Giants drafted him in the sixth round, and he won a Super Bowl with New York.

Jerel Worthy (2009 to 2011)

The Dayton, Ohio, native became a first team All-American. With a quick first step, which referees viewed as too quick at times, the 6'2", 300-pound defensive tackle spent more time in the backfield than a farmer tending to his crops. He also created havoc in the middle of the line, demanding double teams that freed up defensive ends and linebackers to flow unblocked to the ball. It was the kind of work that could go unnoticed by the casual fan but was highly appreciated by coaches, teammates, and those who had to prepare to defeat it. In his junior and final season at MSU, Worthy recorded 30 tackles, 3.5 sacks, and countless quarterback hurries. The Green Bay Packers drafted Worthy in the second round in 2012.

81 The John Benington and Gus Ganakas Years

Right before college basketball started seriously competing for the attention of Spartans fans, the sport trundled along at MSU with two good soldiers as head coaches. Each managed to bring in enough compelling talent that Jenison Field House didn't sit empty. But the period from 1965 to 1976—the just-before-Magic years if you will—was spiced with more memorable individual performers than seasons.

Perhaps the most brilliant of those was Ralph Simpson, a high school superstar with a meddling father from Detroit. He chose MSU because he liked its coach, the eminently likable and self-deprecating John Benington, who replaced Forddy Anderson in 1965. Simpson, who was teammates with Spencer Haywood at Pershing High in Detroit, ranked as the No. 1 high school player in 1968. Simpson, 6'5", 200 pounds, had a game that resembled Oscar Robertson's. He could rebound, pass, handle the ball, and shoot. Simpson led the Spartans in rebounding, jumped center, and averaged 29 points during his sophomore year. Opponents couldn't leave him unchecked—anywhere. The range on his jumper seemed limitless. "One of these days," his new coach Gus Ganakas said, "he's going to shoot before he comes over the half-court line. But he puts those babies in sometimes."

Simpson played just one year for the Spartans, the 1969–1970 season, leaving after his sophomore year for a three-year, $1 million dollar deal with the Denver Rockets of the ABA. Simpson's father had suffered a heart attack, and the family, which included eight children, desperately needed the money. Simpson was a quiet kid, but his father had a reputation for butting in, and occasionally the old man and Ganakas locked horns. Simpson himself could also be recalcitrant from time to time. During halftime of a game in which the Spartans missed a number of free throws, Ganakas, making a point about the importance of the charity stripe, asked the team "Where are more games lost than anywhere else?" Simpson shot back, "Right here at Michigan State." (Some accounts suggest Simpson's father actually said this during a game.) Simpson played six seasons in the ABA, averaging 20 points, and bounced around in the NBA for a number of years after that.

Benington, the man who recruited Simpson, coached the Spartans to back-to-back 10-win conference seasons in 1966 and

1967, a nine-win improvement over the previous two years. The '67 team tied for the title with Indiana but watched the NCAA tournament from home when the Hoosiers were selected as the Big Ten representative. Stan Washington, an undersized forward whose leaping ability and rebounding knack almost rivaled Johnny Green's, and Lee Lafayette, nicknamed "Tree" because of his unyielding presence in the post, provided leadership and key play-making ability over those two years. Tragically Benington never coached Simpson. In the summer of 1969, the popular Benington died of a massive heart attack, leaving behind a wife and nine children.

Munn selected Ganakas, a graduate of MSU, former East Lansing High School head basketball coach, and current MSU assistant, to replace Benington. Ganakas never put together that one incredible season. But he did coach a handful of the finest Spartans to ever wear the Green and White: Simpson, Mike Robinson, Terry Furlow, Bill Kilgore, and Lindsay Hairston. He also recruited superstars Greg Kelser and Bob Chapman—key components of future champions—and did much of the dirty work to attract Earvin Johnson. Ganakas shared many of the same qualities as his predecessor. Compassionate and self-deprecating, he had an underappreciated grasp of the technical aspects of the sport. He also had Robinson.

The 5'11" Robinson always had his detractors growing up. Those critics were rendered mute, however, when the Detroit native won the 1972 Big Ten scoring title in his sophomore and first year. He then repeated as scoring champion in his junior year. In the first four games of Robinson's varsity career, he scored 25, 29, 20, and 32 points, respectively. Named first team All-Big Ten three times, Robinson had a blindingly fast release on his jump shot, dropping his left hand as he let go of the ball with his other hand. "I was on campus two months and thought Mike Robinson never missed a shot," said Chapman in *Magic Moments*. "He'd shoot, and the ball would walk back to him as if it were on a string. His rotation was that good." The Spartans hovered around .500 during Robinson's three-year career, finishing with identical 13–11 records. That's probably why the man who averaged 24.0 points a game—three more than MSU's all-time career scoring leader Shawn Respert—is known today by primarily basketball cognoscenti. His peers certainly appreciated his skills, awarding him the Frances Pomeroy Naismith Award in 1974 for the best college basketball player under six feet.

Furlow shared the court with Robinson for two years, leading the Big Ten in scoring the year Robinson didn't, and adding another scoring title in his senior season after Robinson graduated. Taller and rangier than Robinson, Furlow could score in a number of ways. In one three-game stretch during his senior year, he tallied 50 points against Iowa, 48 three days later against Northwestern, and 42 two days later against Ohio State. "I expected every shot Terry ever attempted to go in," wrote Kelser in *Tales from Michigan State Basketball.*

A Flintstone before that became a thing, Furlow had an out-sized personality that rubbed some the wrong way. It also resulted in a few run-ins with teammates, opponents, and coaches. The controversies—such as the time he sucker punched an Illinois player or assaulted the MSU student trainer—never seemed to linger. He had his staunch supporters on the team, including Kelser and Chapman. "We'd be on the road, and he'd say…'I'm going to turn those boos into oohs.' And in most cases, he did," Chapman said. Drafted in the first round by Philadelphia 76ers, Furlow died in a car crash at the age of 25, denying him a chance at greatness in the NBA.

Kilgore played two years with Robinson, threatening MSU's career rebounding records despite his 6'7" height. The River Rouge, Michigan, native gave up a few inches to nearly every center he defended in the Big Ten, but he always held his own. "Captain

Smooth," as teammates called him, also possessed a quietly effective offensive game, scoring with hooks and finger rolls.

The best team Ganakas had, the one with the second most wins in school history to date, was the 1974–'75 squad led by Hairston. Another undersized big man, the 6'7" Detroit native battled underneath with furor and gumption. Hairston, with a Fu Manchu mustache and an awkward-looking thin frame, shot the ball with his legs spread apart. Hairston could sky well above the rim to grab the ball before it started its descent and swatted many a shot attempt into the stands. He probably would have scored more points, but dunking in the mid-1970s was illegal.

Hairston is often blamed for something else that happened. Before Michigan State's meeting against No. 2-ranked Indiana on January 4, 1975, 10 Spartans walked out of practice the morning before the game. Four of them were starters, and all 10 were black. The details are murky, but at the time it appeared Ganakas' decision to start Jeff Tropf—a white big man from nearby Holt, Michigan, over Tom McGill—sparked the walkout. In a meeting that morning, Ganakas announced his plan to start Tropf. That prompted Hairston to raise his hand and say, "Coach, Jeff can't guard [Steve] Green." Ganakas countered that he was the coach. The players countered by walking out. Ganakas then called up the junior varsity to help take on a great Indiana team.

The players offered no specific reason for why they walked out other than vague grumblings about second-rate facilities, lack of school support for the basketball program, and Ganakas' strategies—particularly his recent decision to start a freshman, white player over a senior, who happened to be black. The Tropf decision may have simply been the final straw.

Just before the tip-off, the players returned to the locker room, planning on suiting up for the game. No apologies followed, so Ganakas suspended them on the spot. The suspended 10 took a seat in the bleachers at Jenison, but when the fans realized what was happening and started to boo, the players ducked out of the building. The 6,000 fans at Jenison cheered the remaining Spartans and junior varsity replacements throughout the game. It didn't matter. The Hoosiers romped 107–55.

When the players apologized to him the next day, Ganakas lifted the suspension. Hairston believes the show of solidarity among the black players helped bring the team together. Victories against Ohio State and Michigan in the next two games and a season total of 17 wins supports Hairston's assertion. Today many of the players involved are contrite. "It was an unfortunate situation when the players got up and walked out on Gus," Chapman reflected in *Magic Moments*. "A lot of things had built up. But it was portrayed as strictly a black-white issue with Jeff. That wasn't it at all."

Ganakas held on to his job for one more year, a forgettable 14–13 season, before MSU decided to fire him. He became fast friends with his replacement, Jud Heathcote, and Ganakas has remained an integral part of the MSU basketball program ever since. He currently serves as the color analyst on Spartans basketball radio broadcasts.

Sleepy Crowley

The 1920s may have been roaring for the country, but for Michigan State College football, which had changed its name from MAC in 1925, the Flapper decade was more of a flop. Coaches came and went, victories shriveled up, and wins against Michigan vanished like the autumn leaves dropping from the maples that dotted the East Lansing campus.

Fed up with a decade of mediocrity, MSC turned to Jim Crowley, one of Knute Rockne's famed Four Horsemen of Notre Dame. Crowley played professionally for three years and then became an assistant at Georgia. MSC hired him in 1929 to re-energize a football program adrift, hoping for a little influx of Irish luck.

Crowley's methods and demeanor proved an instant hit at Michigan State. A natural leader he drove home his points with clarity and wit. He understood human emotions and psychology, using this skill to inspire and critique effectively. "Coach Crowley…was very witty and liked to make puns at every opportunity…He was a great psychologist—able to inspire his teams for each game. He was quick to point out your mistakes in practice and in games. His constructive criticisms were well accepted by the team," said MSC star Bobby Monnett, a crafty, elusive back who scored a school-record 127 points in 1931.

Nicknamed "Sleepy" because he suffered from insomnia, Crowley spent most waking hours in a slouch, giving the impression he wasn't paying attention. Nothing was further from the truth. And despite his fame as an offensive player at Notre Dame, he took a keen interest in defense, viewing it as the key to a successful team.

In his maiden season, the Spartans went 5–3, the school's first winning campaign since 1924. The Spartans improved to 5–1–2 the next year, including a 0–0 tie with Detroit, the reigning national champions. Crowley's emphasis on defense yielded strong results; opponents scored only 32 points. The other tie—against Michigan—represented tremendous movement in the right direction. In the previous 14 games against their rival, the Spartans had lost every one. Even more dispiriting was the combined score of those losses: 390–9.

To fire up his charges before the 1930 Michigan game, Crowley invited former team captain and center Harold Smead, who had been injured in an automobile accident that summer, to fly from Boston to Ann Arbor for the game. Sitting in a wheelchair, Smead ebulliently greeted the Spartans as they came onto the field. That emotional lift helped MSC close the yawning gap between the two schools. The tie was Michigan's only hiccup that year. The Spartans pulled off the same thing the next year, though a monsoon heavily influenced the 0–0 score.

Crowley's finest moment as Spartans head coach also signaled the moment that MSC lost him. Fordham, angling for a national championship in 1932, steamrolled its first three opponents by an average of 50 points. The Spartans traveled to the Polo Grounds, perhaps the nation's most famous sports venue, as a heavy underdog despite their 3–1 record. On the very first play, Monnett scooted through a hole and ran 80 yards for a touchdown. The Polo Grounds crowd hushed, the Rams looked startled, and the Spartans smelled blood. Fullback Bernie McNutt then rumbled 63 yards for another touchdown, and Abe Eliowitz completed the trifecta of oxygen drainers with a 75-yard touchdown run to cap a 19–13 victory. The splashy upset on the East Coast, which was part of the Spartans' 7–1 season and Crowley's 22–8–3 overall record, helped draw national interest in Crowley from colleges looking for the next great coach. One of those colleges happened to be Fordham, who lured Crowley to New York where he would gain immortality by coaching the "Seven Blocks of Granite," which featured Vince Lombardi.

Pete Newell and the Early Years

The decades raced past one after another before Michigan State basketball made a splash on the national scene. Starting in 1899 when MSC fielded its first basketball team, until 1930, few in East

Lansing paid much attention to what happened in the Armory, where the Aggies initially played, and then the IM Circle Complex, where the team moved in 1918. The sport, which still used peach baskets until 1906, had the feel of something one does to occupy the time between what really matters, like a card game during a rain delay. In fact MAC football coaches Charles Denman (who went 11–0 as basketball coach in two seasons against watered down competition), Chester Brewer, John Macklin, and George Gauthier moonlighted as basketball coaches as well.

Perhaps the most recognizable name associated with Michigan State basketball before the program's rise to national prominence in the mid 1950s was Pete Newell, one of basketball's brightest minds. He invented the cross-court pass, the over-the-top pass (to feed the post), and the four corners offense. Known to later generations as the founder of the renowned Pete Newell Big Man camp, Newell is only the third coach in history to win an NIT, NCAA, and Olympic championship. Alas neither the NIT nor the NCAA triumphs came while he was head coach of Michigan State from 1950 to 1954. The Spartans won just a little more than they lost during Newell's four unremarkable years as head coach, proving that all the genius in the world can't overcome a lack of talent or experience.

In those very early years, Chester Brewer enjoyed the most success, winning 70 of 95 games in seven seasons as coach from 1903 to 1910. Brewer failed to beat Michigan in football; basketball proved less daunting. The Aggies first played Michigan in 1909, topping their rival twice that year, the second a solid 45–23 conquest in East Lansing. The reaction on campus fell far short of the hysteria future football wins would generate. There were no national champions in college basketball at the time, and the sport was still rather primitive. Basketballs were brown and not perfectly round, making dribbling difficult. You moved the ball by crisp passing and player motion. The jump shot remained decades away.

In 1927 MSC hired the basketball coach from Ohio Wesleyan. Ben VanAlstyne had posted a .708 winning percentage there and immediately started winning at Michigan State. In 1930–'31, the Spartans went 16–1, still the best winning percentage in school history. The following season included a 14–13 win against Michigan. This victory came two years after the Spartans had toppled Michigan 27–26 with a half-court shot at the buzzer at new Demonstration Hall, which attracted 6,000 fans for the arena's christening. "Gentle Ben" coached the Spartans for 22 seasons, popularizing the pick and roll and emphasizing good shot selection along the way. This often resulted in the Spartans holding the ball for multiple minutes waiting for that shot to materialize. Against Marquette in 1931, MSC held the ball for nine straight minutes while nursing a one-point lead in its 24–21 overtime win. In 1934–'35 he guided the Spartans to a 14–4 record with wins against Stanford, Michigan, and perennial power Kentucky.

Two players stood out during VanAlstyne's reign. A quarterback and outstanding punter on the football team and track-and-field star as well, Roger Grove, a noted long-range shooter, is the one who hit the half-court buzzer beater to beat Michigan in 1930. He was named an All-American in 1930. Chet Aubuchon, only 5'10", became the Spartans' second All-American in 1940. A nifty dribbler in an era when passing dominated, Aubuchon earned the nickname "The Houdini of Hardwood" because of his exceptional ballhandling and passing skills. He could also score, hitting a 75-footer against Notre Dame at the end of the half and leading the Spartans in scoring in his sophomore and senior seasons. (He didn't play his junior year because of a freak injury, which led to a serious blood infection.)

VanAlstyne retired in 1949 with only five losing seasons and 231 wins. His next to last season in 1947–'48 was highlighted by a near victory against Kentucky at Jenison Field House, where the Spartans began playing home games in 1940. Bob Brannum, a

Kentucky transfer still at odds with Wildcats coach Adolph Rupp, paced the Spartans with 23 points in front of the largest crowd ever at Jenison. The teams fought to five ties in the second half before the Spartans fell 47–45 to the eventual national champs.

Alton Kircher replaced VanAlstyne for one disappointing season before Newell, who had coached San Francisco to the NIT championship in 1949, guided the Spartans into the Big Ten where they won their first conference game against Northwestern. Newell never had the horses to win big at MSC, though in December 1952 the Spartans upset No. 2 Kansas State at Jenison, the night after falling by five to John Wooden's UCLA Bruins. Two sophomores from Brooklyn, New York—5'6" Rickey Ayala, the first black basketball player at MSC, and Al Ferrari—keyed the victory. Ferrari scored 22 points in the second half and went on to win team MVP honors three straight seasons. The 1953 Spartans finished third in the conference before slipping to eighth the next year. With an overall record barely above .500, Newell bolted for the California job after that. He would win big there. His successor would do the same at MSC.

The Old Brass Spittoon

The trophy is appropriately named. The Old Brass Spittoon, awarded to the winner of the Michigan State-Indiana game since 1950, dates as far back as circa 1820 when the object was produced for its original purpose. It's doubtful there is another artifact still associated with college football that is almost 200 years old.

The idea of awarding a trophy to the winner of the Michigan State-Indiana game seems absurd today. Although the states of

Michigan and Indiana share a border, no natural rivalry exists between them. Moreover, Hoosiers football in Indiana generates about as much passion as ice hockey in the Sunshine State. That wasn't always the case. A few years prior to Michigan State joining the Big Ten, Indiana had won the Big Ten and gone unbeaten. Bo McMillin led Indiana to eight winning seasons and posted a .561 winning percentage from 1934 to 1947. Before the Spartans joined the Big Ten in 1949, they had played the Hoosiers four times and had never beaten them. For the Spartans, Indiana was no pushover.

MSC had gained admission to the Big Ten by 1950 and had started its rapid ascent under Biggie Munn. In the sixth game of the '50 season, the Spartans upset Notre Dame to move to 5–1. The Spartans' next opponent was 2–2–1 Indiana. Spartans students and fans were concerned about a letdown after the Notre Dame win, which prompted Gene McDermott, the junior class president at Michigan State, to hatch an idea he hoped would manufacture additional enthusiasm for the game.

The year before, the Spartans and Fighting Irish had introduced the Megaphone Trophy, awarded to the winner of the game between the two schools. McDermott thought, *Why not make the game between future Big Ten foe Indiana and the Spartans a trophy game as well?*

McDermott and secretary Virginia O'Brien, exhibiting a wry sense of humor but also an appreciation of history, found a brass spittoon in a local antique shop. A note in the spittoon, which had a few dents, said that the spittoon had been used at a trading post thought to be located on the present site of Michigan State. "We wanted something that held meaning to both schools. There were a lot of trappers from Indiana, and they'd come up to trap and hunt and fish in Michigan. The trading post, Ackley, which is where the university is now, was a big place they'd stop," said McDermott in an interview years later with the *Allentown Morning Call.*

McDermott polished up the spittoon and presented it to Munn and his team. They loved it. Before the game with the Hoosiers, McDermott also walked the spittoon over to the Indiana locker room where the reception was less keen and very quiet. "It felt like a wake in there," McDermott said. The Spartans went on to defeat Indiana 35–0. The score was inscribed on the spittoon, and the Spartans kept it on campus. Eventually the Indiana student council accepted the idea as well, and the Old Brass Spittoon became part of the tradition of all Michigan State-Indiana football games.

Michigan State has dominated the all-time series, going 41–15–2 through 2012. Since the presentation of the Old Brass Spittoon, the series has been even more lopsided, favoring the Spartans 42–12–1, which has given Michigan State frequent possession of a weird prize. "It is kind of funny," said Colin Neely, a Spartans defensive end who played in two Brass Spittoon games, to the *Allentown Morning Call.* "The coaches pass it all around the locker room, and we'd pretend to spit in it. Obviously we didn't."

85

1998 and the Ohio State Upset

In 1997 the Spartans started fast, stumbled in the middle of the season, but finished strong to end 7–4 under third-year coach Nick Saban. A lopsided loss to Washington in the Aloha Bowl didn't dim expectations for the '98 season, especially because so many key parts of the team returned. The offense featured emerging quarterback Bill Burke, All-Big Ten running back Sedrick Irvin, and Plaxico Burress, a promising new wide receiver with incredible gifts. The defense returned All-Big Ten defensive backs Sorie Kanu and Amp Campbell, stalwart defensive linemen Robaire Smith and Robert Newkirk, and capable linebackers T.J. Turner and Courtney Ledyard.

Back-to-back losses to open the season set everyone straight. The Spartans fell to Colorado State at home 23–16, then watched in horror as Oregon embarrassed them on the road 48–14. Adding to the misery, Campbell suffered a mortifying neck injury that put him out for the season.

Fortunes changed swiftly the next week. During a home night game against 10th-ranked Notre Dame, the Spartans pounced on the Fighting Irish early to open a 42–3 lead at half. The first half was highlighted by a blocked punt returned for a touchdown by Richard Newsome and a Burke to Burress 86-yard touchdown completion, the longest ever yielded by the Irish. Things calmed down in the second half, but the Spartans won going away 45–23. "It was a total shock," said Irish defensive back Deke Cooper.

But the rout of Notre Dame failed to carry over. Two more losses in the next five games, including one to Michigan, left the Spartans at 4–4. To move over .500, MSU would need to beat undefeated Ohio State, the No. 1-ranked team in the country that had trounced every opponent by at least 17 points. Vegas made MSU a 28-point road underdog. The mood among Spartans fans was sullen. Many were bitter and had given up on the season. "It's tough, when you're in a situation like us. You're in a foxhole, and no one expects you to win," Burke said.

The first 35 minutes played out as expected. The Spartans trailed 24–9. It hadn't been a bad performance by MSU, whose defense had landed a few punishing hits on Buckeyes quarterback Joe Germaine. Momentum started to change midway through the third quarter when Spartans punter Craig Jarrett had to punt from inside the Michigan State 5-yard line. He kicked the ball low and on a line. It hit the back of a Buckeyes defender turned away from the ball and bounced to the turf at the 50-yard line where an alert Spartan fell on it. With his team rejuvenated, Burke lofted a touchdown pass to Lavaile Richardson, who came out of the end zone to catch it at the 1-yard line before taking a step back for the score, five plays later. Paul Edinger missed the extra point, leaving the score 24–15 in the third quarter. On the Buckeyes' next possession, running back Michael Riley fumbled at the OSU 35-yard line. The Spartans recovered, and Edinger kicked a 49-yard field goal to tie a career long and pull the Spartans to within six.

Down only a score, the Spartans' confidence spiked. They forced the Buckeyes to punt and took over at their own 8-yard line. Two long passes—one to Burress, who used his height advantage to soar over the smaller OSU defensive back—and the other to tight end Chris Baker, a freshman growing up fast, moved the ball inside the Buckeye 10-yard line. On third-and-1 from the 3, Irvin slithered through the OSU defense and into the end zone.

Another Buckeyes fumble caused by Julian Peterson's jarring hit set up Edinger's fifth field goal and put MSU ahead 28–24. Peterson, who had replaced the injured Smith in the first half, had tormented the Buckeyes since entering the game, forcing two earlier fumbles and disrupting OSU's passing game with consistent pressure. Tired of scraping Germaine off the turf, the Buckeyes abandoned their passing game. They ran 11 straight times and picked up 55 yards, taking the ball down to the Spartans 26.

After already picking up one fourth down, Ohio State faced another at the 26. It went for it again. OSU turned to fullback Joe Montgomery, who took two steps to his left and then stopped when MSU's Turner collided with him a yard behind the line of scrimmage. Montgomery's legs churned, but he couldn't move forward. Kanu arrived to help Turner and eventually Montgomery crumpled to the ground. The Spartans regained possession of the ball. "I'm at a loss for words," Turner said after the game. "That's the play I've always dreamed of."

After a 20-yard completion, MSU's drive stalled, and Jarrett once again punted the ball low. Ohio State wide receiver David Boston grabbed it on the run and sprinted to the OSU 48. The Buckeyes had 1:39 to put this nightmare behind them. Two long completions—one of 16 yards and the other of 20—moved the ball to the 15.

Saban called timeout. He accused the defense of playing tentatively as they had down the stretch a couple weeks earlier when Michigan State lost at Minnesota. "Look guys, we have to make the plays," he implored. "We have to make four plays to stop them." The Spartans then blitzed on the next three downs, forcing three incompletions. On fourth down the Spartans brought pressure again. Germaine stepped into the pocket quickly and let go of the ball toward the left side of the end zone probably a half a second before he wanted. Everyone held their breath until Renaldo Hill stepped in front of Buckeyes receiver Dee Miller to snare the ball, juggling it for just a moment then securing it while stumbling out of bounds at the Buckeyes 3. Ohio State's undefeated season, No. 1 ranking, and national championship hopes stumbled out of bounds as well. "This hurts the most," Miller lamented. "We had everything lined up. We just didn't get it done."

The Spartans hadn't beaten a team ranked No. 1 in eight years. "Funny things happen in football when a team plays possessed," Saban said. The Spartans, though, lost two of their next three games to finish 6–6 and without a bowl, adding to the frustrations of a program that found consistent success maddeningly elusive.

86 Biggie Munn's Early Years

As fate would have it, Michigan was Biggie Munn's first foe as head coach. Months after his hire, Munn had blasted the Big Ten, which MSC desperately wanted to join, for paying players under the table. At MSC players were given financial aid, and scholarships were prohibited in the Big Ten. However, Munn, who had spent eight seasons as an assistant at Michigan, knew that Big Ten coaches and boosters had devised clever stratagems to subvert the scholarship rules. Michigan did not appreciate Munn's candor. Furthermore Michigan coach Fritz Crisler was incredulous that Munn would take a job at a rival of Michigan's especially one in the same state. When they met for the first time after Munn's hiring at a banquet, Crisler snorted, "And what are you doing back in the state of Michigan?"

Crisler aimed to embarrass Munn in this first game, a mission his Wolverines accomplished spectacularly. Munn's Spartans fell 55–0. Munn was crushed and convinced that a broken water pipe that had flooded the Spartans locker room at halftime represented a deliberate act of foul play on the part of the Wolverines. Biggie later confided to a reporter at the *Detroit Free Press* that he "didn't even want to show up [in the locker room after the game]. I didn't know what to tell those kids. I felt I had let them down some way. I was low. I was discouraged. And then just as I reached the door, I got mad…at myself. What right did I have to feel so low? How about those players of mine? How were they feeling?"

Munn rallied himself and his team, finishing the 1947 season with a respectable 7–2 record. The only other loss was a close one to Bear Bryant's Kentucky Wildcats. Munn kept tweaking his new

After some tough losses to Michigan to begin his career in East Lansing, Clarence "Biggie" Munn would eventually defeat the Wolverines and guide the Spartans through a 28-game winning streak. (Getty Images)

offense, and his players started to grasp it more and more. Many of them were recruited by the former coach, including running back George "Little Dynamite" Guerre, Lynn Chandnois, Frank "Muddy" Waters, George Smith, and Bob McCurry.

Munn's second season opened against Michigan as had been the tradition for nearly 20 years. A few differences marked the occasion. Crisler, who had never lost to the Spartans, hung up his chalkboard during the offseason to become Michigan's athletic director. The second difference was the venue, an expanded and lavishly renovated Macklin Stadium, the setting for the first game played in East Lansing in the series in 24 years. By the end of the game, another difference asserted itself. The Wolverines won, but the Spartans kept UM in their sights from start to finish, eventually falling 13–7. The gap between the programs, which seemed so unbridgeable just the year before, appeared to be narrowing—and quickly. Munn's Michigan State Multiple offense started bearing fruit immediately after the UM game. The Spartans averaged 39 points a game the rest of the year, finishing 6–2–2 on the season, the only other loss a 26–7 defeat by Notre Dame.

McCurry, a lineman and three-time captain, and Guerre, a pint-sized back who could change speed and direction in a flash, moved on after 1948. The offense still rolled, putting 62 and 75 points on Temple and Arizona, respectively, but MSC slipped to 6–3 in 1949. That included another, albeit narrower, loss to Michigan, the thinnest margin of defeat since 1937.

The gap closed entirely in 1950, accomplished with many fresh faces. Quarterback Al Dorow, running back Sony Grandelius, lineman Dorne Dibble, and end Bob Carey all contributed to the Spartans' 14–7 victory, MSC's first in 14 years against Michigan. LeRoy Crane's seven-yard bulldozer accounted for the winning score. A few MSU supporters in attendance hoisted Grandelius, who scored the first touchdown on a pass from Dorow, and Crane and paraded them in front of a throng of cheering Spartans fans. A week later MSC lost to Maryland 34–7. The Terrapins ran the option, which fooled the Spartans' defense from beginning to end. That irritated Munn, who had brought in a few guest coaches to drill his team on the newfangled offense. Biggie never forgot the drubbing, referring to the loss as the "Maryland fiasco." For the next 28 games, Munn avoided fiascos—or losses of any kind.

87 All-Americans From the Early 1960s

Dave Behrman (1960 to 1962) and Ed Budde (1960 to 1962)
The Spartans finished the 1962 season ranked second nationally in rushing yards. "The B Boys" made it happen. That's what everyone called MSU's offensive line. Four of the linemen's last names began with "B." Behrman, who could play all three offensive line positions, and Budde, who held down the tackle spot, were the best of the "B Boys." Both Behrman and Budde stood 6'4" and moved with agility and speed, which together with their superior strength made them a devastating tandem—and a stark departure from the smaller linemen Duffy Daugherty tutored as an assistant under Munn. Budde was named the captain of the 1963 College All-Stars who defeated the Green Bay Packers. Both lineman were drafted in the first round by the NFL and enjoyed solid pro careers. Behrman spent five seasons with the Buffalo Bills, and Budde played 14 seasons with the Kansas City Chiefs, earning All-Pro honors seven times.

Earl Lattimer (1961 to 1963)

Starting his career as a fullback, Lattimer moved to guard for the 1963 season. The field goal kicker and starting linebacker as well, Lattimer possessed an ebullient personality that made him a favorite of fans and teammates. Oftentimes he broke from the huddle and somersaulted to his position on the line, a flamboyant act that probably earned him a few extra All-American votes. After a 1963 win against Wisconsin, the coaches named Lattimer the Player of Week, calling him a "remarkable morale man." Lattimer had a quick wit and an even quicker first step. The Bills drafted Lattimer in 1964.

Sherman Lewis (1961 to 1963)

Another of Daugherty's southern recruits, Lewis, from Louisville, Kentucky, offered a dynamic game-changing threat at running back, receiver, and defensive back. In 1963 he enjoyed one of the greatest individual seasons in Spartans history. Lewis rushed for 577 yards and caught 11 passes for 303 yards, both team highs. MSU surprised by contending for the Big Ten title that year before falling to Illinois on the final weekend. In a tight win over Northwestern, Lewis scored on an 87-yard run and an 84-yard punt return. "He was the difference," Northwestern coach Ara Parseghian said. "He has been the difference against a lot of people." Later in the season, he stunned Wisconsin with an 87-yard touchdown reception, the second longest touchdown reception in school history at the time. "The minute we take Lewis out of there we seem to get in trouble," Daugherty said.

Lewis finished third in the Heisman Trophy balloting that year, losing to Roger Staubach, the second Spartan to finish that high in the voting. He became an assistant coach at MSU for 14 years then went on to a distinguished career as offensive coordinator for the Green Bay Packers.

George Saimes (1960 to 1962)

Gangly yet deceptively quick and slippery, the fullback scooted his way to 642 rushing yards and nine touchdowns in 1962. Also the captain of the defense, the Ohio native picked off three passes as a defensive back. In a *Time* magazine profile of Saimes in 1961, Daugherty lavishly praised his versatile star. "I've said it before and I'll say it again," his coach said. "George Saimes could play any position on this team—including quarterback and tackle—and I know he would if I asked him to." Lewis called him, the heart and soul of our team."

Saimes ran with his legs wide apart, making it nearly impossible to bring him down with just one leg. "[Saimes] runs like Groucho Marx walks," quipped Michigan line coach Bob Hollaway. In the Spartans' seventh consecutive win against Notre Dame, Saimes scored on runs of 54, 49, and 15 yards en route to 153 total rushing yards during the 1962 game. Saimes enjoyed a stellar professional career with the Buffalo Bills and Denver Broncos and now resides on the AFL All-Time Team.

88 Rebuilding Behind Marcus Taylor, Drew Neitzel, and Draymond Green

One by one, the Flintstones who built the Spartans dynasty used up their four years of eligibility and moved on, heading to the NBA and other points beyond. Tom Izzo had prepared for that. On the other hand, he hadn't prepared for the departure of two key underclassmen: freshman Zach Randoph and sophomore Jason Richardson. Their exit drained most of the experience from the 2001–'02 MSU basketball team and presented Izzo with one of his most daunting challenges. He passed it with flying colors.

The Spartans lost close to 90 percent of their scoring from the year before. Only sophomore Marcus Taylor, who averaged 7.4 as the seventh or eighth man off the bench, had ever been called upon to score. And that was in only a secondary role. Most programs would have slid off the map at least for a year. But in yet one more example of Izzo's magic hand, he forged a team that finished 19–12 overall and an impressive 10–6 in the Big Ten, a mere game behind the three leaders. Three new recruits made essential contributions: Kelvin Torbert, a stocky yet springy McDonald's All-American from Flint; Alan Anderson, a 6'5" wing from Minneapolis; and Chris Hill, a shooting wizard ranked just outside the top 100 from Indiana. Adam Ballinger and Aloysius Anagonye provided upperclassman leadership and enjoyed increased roles from the previous years.

The Marcus Taylor Era

Taylor, however, proved the star, stepping forward to carry the offensive load and elevating his play late in the season to help the Spartans earn a bid to the NCAA Tournament. In the final week of the regular season, he scored 34 points in the Spartans' upset of first place Ohio State in Columbus, Ohio. Four days later he paced MSU with 32 points in a four-point win at home against Iowa. Taylor led the Big Ten in scoring and assists and was named first team All-Big Ten. Alas, MSU lost in the first round of the NCAA Tournament to break a string of three consecutive appearances in the Final Four. The mood soured even more when Marcus Taylor left for the NBA, a more than questionable decision as the Minnesota Timberwolves cut him in training camp.

After that early departure, Izzo had to rebuild again. But the coach added 6'11" McDonald's All-American Paul Davis, top-50 wing Maurice Ager, and intriguing foreign import and post player Erazem Lorbeck. They joined rising and improving sophomores Torbert, Anderson, and Hill, along with seniors Anagonye and

Ballinger, to bolster hopes for the season. When walk-on Tim Bograkas nailed a three-pointer to beat Kentucky in the final seconds at Lexington, Kentucky, it appeared all was well again. But the Spartans struggled on the road in conference, losing six games away from home and finished 22–13 overall and 10–6 in the conference. A surprising run to the Elite Eight—where MSU lost to No. 1 seed Texas—helped the Spartans redeem their season and spiked hopes for 2003–'04.

Another McDonald's All-American joined MSU that year, Shannon Brown, an off-guard with swagger and tremendous leaping ability. Lorbeck, however, headed back to Europe, leaving an unexpected hole in the post. Then a brutal non-conference schedule sapped the Spartans' confidence. They lost to Kansas, Duke, Oklahoma, Kentucky, and UCLA. MSU rallied during Big Ten play, falling short of a Big Ten title by losing to Wisconsin at home in the final regular season game. At 18–12 overall and 12–4 in the Big Ten, the Spartans lost to Nevada after blowing a 16-point lead in the first round of the NCAA tournament.

The Drew Neitzel Era

Michigan State made the Final Four the next year, and that 2004–'05 season marked the beginning of Neitzel's career. Two seasons later, Neitzel did his best Taylor impression, helping the Spartans keep their NCAA tournament streak alive at 10 years by scrapping together a 23–12 overall and 8–8 conference record. A November upset of Texas on a Neitzel floater in the closing seconds of the game, and a 64–55 upset of No. 1 Wisconsin at home provided the highlights. Neitzel burned the Badgers for 28 with many coming off of hard cuts followed by quick-release threes. He averaged 18 points a game and shot 41 percent from three to earn second team All-American honors. The Spartans topped Marquette in the first round of the NCAA Tournament and then led No.1 seed North

Carolina in the final 10 minutes before losing 81–67 in the round of 32. During the 2007–'08 season, Neitzel led the Spartans to a 27–9 overall mark and fourth-place finish in the Big Ten with a 12–6 conference record.

The Draymond Green Era

Though the only Izzo team to win the Big Ten and fail to reach the Final Four, the 2011–'12 Spartans enjoyed a great and surprising season. Picked to finish in the middle of the conference, the Spartans stunned college basketball by winning a share of the Big Ten, winning the Big Ten Tournament, and earning a No. 1 seed. The heart and soul of the team was Green, one of the most engaging figures and natural leaders in Spartans sports history. Green led the Spartans in nearly every important category and willed them to many of their 29 victories, the fourth most in school history. Highlights included: a win against 23rd-ranked Gonzaga on the road, MSU's first non-conference road win against a ranked team since 2002; a 15-game winning streak; a defeat of No. 3-ranked Ohio State on the road; and a thrilling comeback win against Minnesota when the Spartans erased a six point deficit in the final 3:23. The Spartans advanced to the Sweet 16 in the NCAA Tournament before falling to Louisville.

Green left an incredible legacy. Driven and bursting with personality, he delighted both his coach and the media. The Saginaw, Michigan, native improved each year, eventually making himself into a consensus first team All-American. Green finished his career at MSU as the school's all-time rebounding leader (1,096). He became only the third player in MSU history to record 1,000 points and rebounds.

Among his many accolades and awards was the Big Ten Jesse Owens Male Athlete of the Year, rewarding the most outstanding Big Ten athlete regardless of sport. He became just the fifth basketball player to win the award and only the second athlete from MSU. (Ice hockey's Ryan Miller was the other.) "He's been a great ambassador for Spartan basketball, Michigan State University, college basketball, and the Big Ten Conference," Izzo said. "He's all about other people and making others better and being a good teammate."

89 Tailgate Before—or After—the Game

The penultimate college football fan experience, tailgating is the yin to the actual football game's yang. Before and—sometimes—after the game, tailgating often serves as the highlight of the gameday experience. Fans in the United States have been gathering together and eating and drinking before sporting events since at least the 1860s when institutional sports began in earnest. The tradition at Michigan State became a popular mainstay in the 1950s and 1960s.

Every tailgater on MSU's campus must abide by a few rules:

- No kegs, large communal beverage containers, and drinking game paraphernalia
- Open alcohol is permitted during tailgating except at Munn Field, pedestrian areas adjacent to Spartan Stadium, and public areas of campus buildings
- Tents must be smaller than 10' x 10'
- No furniture, including couches
- No trailers or roasters
- RVs must park in RV lots
- No underage drinking
- Dispose of all trash in nearby receptacles

At most games the MSU Alumni Association hosts a tailgate party near the northeast corner of Spartan Stadium. It includes live music, contests, and face painting for kids. The MSU cheerleaders, Sparty, and Zeke the Wonder Dog make appearances. The event commences more than two hours before kickoff. Off-campus tailgating tends to attract students and younger fans. On campus is the preferred choice for alumni and older adults.

Below are a few favorite spots to pick up supplies and ready-to-eat goodies:

- **Backyard Bar-B-Q (2329 Jolly Road)** It makes the best barbeque sandwich in town and also offers a large BBQ platter.
- **Stateside Deli (313 East Grand River)** Call ahead and the best deli in the area can put together a large tray of corned beef, pastrami, turkey, and other delicacies.
- **Lansing City Market (325 City Market Drive)** It has the best fresh produce and organic meats in mid-Michigan.
- **Westlund's Apple Market (2301 E. Grand River)** Renowned for its fried chicken and freshly made brats, it is an excellent place for a large party tray of assorted meats and other picnic essentials.
- **Big Ten Party Stores (1108 E. Grand River)** Come here for beer, wine, liquor, simple sandwiches, subs, burritos, and desserts.
- **Spartan Spirits (221 Ann Street)** The name says it all.
- If you would like to cater your tailgate, two superior choices are: **Troppo (111 E. Michigan)** or **Spartan Sports Hall of Fame (1601 W. Lake Lansing Road)**.

Before or after the game, head over to the MSU Dairy Store. A school originally founded to promote the science of agriculture knows something about dairy products. That's why the best ice cream in the mid-Michigan area can be found at the MSU Dairy. It's where you can taste ice cream and cheese made on campus and get a tour of the cheese-making facility. The two locations are at Anthony Hall and MSU Union.

John L. Smith's Wild Ride

He ran with the Bulls in Pamplona, flew a jet fighter, and skydived. He planned on climbing Mount Kilimanjaro. Head coach John L. Smith was an odd duck.

Born and raised in Idaho, Smith cut his teeth coaching on the West Coast. By the time he caught the eye of Michigan State, he had become head coach of Louisville where he employed the spread offense, a pressuring defense, and edgy special teams play. Louisville won big, which enticed MSU officials. Michigan State hired him in 2003 to replace Bobby Williams, whose three-year stint as head coach had ended in disarray and embarrassment.

Returning from a drug suspension, quarterback Jeff Smoker helped Smith finish 8–5 in his first year, the most wins ever for a first-year head coach at Michigan State. Smith's peculiarities surfaced immediately. In the postgame press conference after his first game—a win against Western Michigan—Smith gave a quick slap to a surprised Jeff Smoker, sitting next to him. The coach joked that Smoker "likes it. Our guys are into pain."

In the ensuing years, losses piled up like falling leaves. Smith's unorthodox behavior, however, continued unabated. In the same motion as if he were spiking a football, he threw down a soft drink in the postgame press conference after a 2004 win against No. 4-ranked Wisconsin, one of only two wins against ranked opponents he enjoyed at MSU. At Columbus, Ohio, he complained bitterly to a sideline reporter after Ohio State had blocked a field goal attempt and scored to cut what should have been a 20–7 Spartans halftime lead to 17–14. Confusion beset the field goal unit before the snap. "That's a dang coaching mistake. The kids are playing their tails off, and the coaches are screwing it up," he said.

The final straw likely for the continually slap-happy coach arrived after the 2006 homecoming loss to Illinois, who hadn't won a Big Ten game in two years. A reporter asked Smith about a comment from Charlie Weis, the Notre Dame coach. Weis claimed he had been slapped by a Spartans player the week before in the Irish's 40–37 victory. Smith, attempting to mock Weis, slapped himself repeatedly. Many fans and media mocked Smith instead.

Smith's teams aped his wild and unpredictable personality. Running a spread/read option offense, the Spartans—with the brilliant but erratic Drew Stanton under center—chewed up yardage left and right, moving the ball almost effortlessly until they entered the red zone. At that point the goal line seemed to move back 10 yards. The defense, the unit Smith coached throughout his career, was scattered, soft, and couldn't stop a racing cart going uphill. The Spartans allowed at least 30 points in more than half of their games each season under Smith except for during 2003.

The embarrassing loss at home to Illinois, followed by poor efforts against Michigan and Ohio State, ramped up the calls for Smith's dismissal. Then Northwestern jumped to a 38–3 lead early in the third quarter of the next game. You couldn't blame MSU fans for googling for names of potential head coaching replacements. While those browsers searched, the Spartans scored. On their next possession, they scored again. Garbage points, everyone assumed. Heading into the fourth quarter, MSU still trailed 38–17. Northwestern lined up for another punt, and Devin Thomas blocked it. Ashton Henderson grabbed the ball and returned it 33 yards for a touchdown, making it 38-24. "I think the blocked punt is when people really started to believe," Stanton said.

Winning still seemed a long shot but not an impossibility. The suddenly competent Spartans defense forced another Wildcats punt. Casting off a season-long problem of imploding in the red zone, Stanton finished another drive with a 12-yard run to make it a one-touchdown, 38–31 game. Then more insanity ensued. The defense stopped the Wildcats cold again, and the Spartans took over inside six minutes. The runaway locomotive scored again as Stanton marched the Spartans 58 yards, a drive capped by a nine-yard touchdown pass to T.J. Williams with 3:43 on the clock to tie the game at 38.

Northwestern's Nightmare on Central Street continued. On the Wildcats' next and final possession, C.J. Bacher threw a pick deep in Northwestern territory. "We knew anything was possible," said Travis Key, who made the interception.

The Spartans nursed the ball for a couple of minutes. Brett Swenson then trotted on and kicked the 28-yard game winner with 13 seconds left. "I am proudest that nobody gave up on each other," reflected linebacker Kaleb Thornhill. "Hopefully this can be a turning point in our season," Stanton said. Center Kyle Cook declared unambiguously, "We saved our season."

The win evened the Spartans record at 4–4. It gave them their first conference victory. It also made history. No team in big time college football had ever come back from a 35-point deficit to win. "They continued to fight and they pulled together and deserved everything they got today," Smith said about the historic comeback.

Alas, the wild finish and comeback against the Wildcats represented nothing but the last gasp of a terminal patient. Lowly Indiana ripped the Spartans 46–21 the next week. That ended Smith's reign. The Spartans closed out the season with three more losses, ending a disappointing but never dull four-year period.

Smith would encounter further adversity, serving as the Arkansas head coach for just one turbulent season in 2012, a year when he declared bankruptcy because of real estate debts.

91 Visit the Campus Plaques and Murals

Scattered throughout the Michigan State campus are a few memorials relevant to Spartans football and basketball.

Ralph Young Stone Marker

Just west of Spartan Stadium and north of Ralph Young Field, where the field hockey team plays, is located this stone memorial. It reads:

> Dedicated to Ralph Young
> Coach and Director of Athletics
> Michigan State
> 1923–1954
> Devoted Friend of Track and Field

Young coached Spartans football for five years with only modest success before becoming Michigan State's first athletic director in 1927, a position he performed ably until 1954.

Varsity Club Stone Marker

To honor the varsity club members from MAC who died in World War I, this marker was created after the Great War. It reads:

> In memory of the members of the MAC Varsity
> Club who gave their lives in the Great War:
> E.E. Peterson '15
> I.F. Lankey '16
> F.M. Stewart '17
> O.N. Hinkle '19

The marker can be found west of Spartan Stadium just on the north side of Red Cedar Road.

"S" Marker

Greeting all who enter the John Hannah Administration Building is a bronze block "S," representing the "S" in State. That letter is built into the sidewalk just outside the entrance. The Class of 1978 donated it.

Jenison Field House Murals

Adorning the halls of Jenison Field House are plaques and murals recognizing pivotal figures and moments in MSU sports history. Among the most prominent include:

- Plaque honoring the 1952 NCAA National Champions in football
- Painting of Frederick Cowles Jenison, which bears the inscription "an ardent sportsman"
- Painting of the 1954 Rose Bowl and Big Ten champion team
- Life-sized mural of football player John Pingel, the first consensus All-American in Michigan State history

Spartan Stadium Plaques

On the southwest facade of the stadium stand three bronze plaques, honoring great Spartans teams from the following years: 1953–'54, 1955–'56, 1965–'66, 1978, 1987–'88, 1990, and 2010.

Jack Breslin Plaque

Hanging from the center of the Jack Breslin Student Events Center is a bronze plaque, honoring the man for whom the basketball facility was named. Donated by the Kellogg Company in Battle Creek and the Calhoun County Alumni Club, the plaque praises Breslin for his years of devotion to Michigan State where he played football, basketball, baseball and later became a longtime administrator and eventually vice president for state relations.

John Hannah Statue

In front of the MSU administration building, overlooking the lovely plaza, stands a handsome, seven-foot bronze statue of Hannah, the legendary president of Michigan State from 1941 to 1969 and an unshakeable advocate of intercollegiate athletics. The statue shows Hannah in mid stride, walking with purpose, likely heading to his next pivotal meeting.

92 All-Americans From the Late 1960s and Early 1970s

Eric Allen (1969 to 1971)

Eric "the Flea" Allen starred during the wilderness years, the seasons of Daugherty marked by relentless mediocrity. That consigned Allen to the dustbin of great players on forgotten teams. Allen, the cutting, darting, slippery, fast 5'9" halfback, pulverized the Big Ten record book in 1971. Named the Big Ten's MVP that year, Allen rushed for 1,494 yards, becoming only the second MSU back to surpass 1,000 yards and setting the single-season school record for rushing yards in a season. In Big Ten play only, he amassed 1,283 yards. He also scored 110 points. Both were Big Ten records at the time. He rushed for 100 yards seven times and scored 18 touchdowns, also a Big Ten and school record.

One game, however, eclipsed in greatness his season totals. Playing at Purdue, Allen unfurled touchdown runs of 24, 59, 30, and 24 yards en route to collecting 350 rushing yards on just 29 carries. The 350 yards represented an NCAA record, which stood until 1978. Allen finished his MSU career as the all-time leader in rushing attempts (521) and yards (2,654). Daugherty once quipped about Allen, "He changes direction so fast that he's only a blur in the films." Drafted by the Baltimore Colts, Allen later signed with the Toronto Argonauts and spent four seasons there.

Allen Brenner (1966 to 1968)

By the late 1960s, the two-way player in college football had suffered the same fate as the steam locomotive—rarely found and usually as a curiosity. Brenner, however, played both offense and defense and not as a gimmick. He went full bore on both sides. The Niles, Michigan, native averaged 50 minutes a game in 1968, starting at both split end and safety. Moreover, he returned punts and excelled in the classroom, carrying a 3.77 grade average. One of only two sophomore starters on the great 1966 team, Brenner returned a punt 95 yards against Illinois that year, an MSU record that still stands. He earned team MVP honors in 1968 while making 63 tackles and catching 25 passes. For his career he caught 73 passes (second most in school history at that time) for 1,232 yards. "[Brenner's] got the sixth sense," said Cal Stoll, his position coach. "He'll start out doing one thing but adjust for a better pattern if he's cornered. You don't have to tell Brenner anything more than once." Brenner played two years in the NFL with the New York Giants and seven years in the CFL with the Hamilton Tiger Cats. He died in 2012.

Ron Curl (1968 to 1969, 1971)

The defensive tackle from Chicago disrupted things everywhere on field. He knocked down passes, harassed quarterbacks, and stopped running backs in their tracks. In 1971 Curl collected a team-leading seven tackles for loss and 89 tackles total. He picked up 10 tackles in the Spartans' upset of Ohio State that year. In his sophomore year of 1969, he blocked four punts and an extra point. His ability to drum up mayhem behind the line of scrimmage resulted in 25 career tackles for loss, a school record. Overall he made 204 career tackles. It would be almost 40 years before another MSU defensive tackle earned first team All-American honors. Curl was drafted by the Pittsburgh Steelers but never played a minute in the NFL.

Joe DeLamielleure (1970 to 1972)

The Center Line, Michigan, native was a bulwark at offensive guard for three seasons. As a senior he anchored the line of the second best rushing unit in the conference, one that pounded the 1972 Buckeyes for 334 rushing yards and a massive upset.

In the trenches when Allen swept his way to 350 record-breaking rushing yards against Purdue in 1971, DeLamielleure played 13 seasons in the NFL for the Buffalo Bills and Cleveland Browns, making key blocks to spring Buffalo's O.J. Simpson for 273 yards against the Lions. He's probably the only offensive lineman to block for two backs who set single-game rushing marks (Allen at MSU and Simpson at Buffalo). He was named to the Pro Football Hall of Fame in 2003, one of only two Spartans in Canton, Ohio. "His work ethic was second to none," said former MSU offensive line coach Joe Carruthers. "Joe never slacked off in practice. He was the first guy out on the practice field and the last guy to leave it. I'm not so sure Joe didn't invent the pancake block because the pro scouts said they had never seen anything like that before on film. It appeared that he was superglued to his opponent. Joe wouldn't quit blocking until he had his man on the ground."

Billy Joe DuPree (1970 to 1972)
Tall, rangy, and with hands the size of goalie gloves, the Louisiana native set the standard for tight ends at Michigan State. He led the Spartans, which ran the Wishbone, in receptions and receiving yards in his junior and senior years, the last tight end to lead the Spartans in receptions. Against USC in 1972, he grabbed eight passes, which tied him for the second most in Spartans history at the time. Particularly adept at catching the overthrown pass, DuPree's 69 career receptions ranked third on the all-time Spartans list at the time. He also played on the basketball team and won the intramural fencing championship at MSU. DuPree blossomed in the NFL, playing 10 seasons for the Dallas Cowboys and earning Pro Bowl honors three times. DuPree started a highly successful construction business.

93 Marvel at Zeke the Wonder Dog

As the popularity of Frisbee-catching dogs started to creep into the mainstream during the 1970s, word spread around campus about a local Golden Labrador racking up several awards and championships in dog disc tournaments. Zeke the dog had started catching

Frisbees when his owner, MSU student Gary Eisenberg, would toss him the plastic disc to pass the time during his achingly boring night job at a gas station. MSU officials got wind of it and invited the dog to perform at the stadium.

Zeke the Wonder Dog made his first appearance at Spartan Stadium in September of 1977. Performing at halftime Zeke, dressed in a green bib sporting the MSU logo, raced furiously after the Frisbees Eisenberg floated in the air. Each toss was longer than the last, but Zeke, almost without fail, ran the Frisbee down, leaping in the air to capture it with his mouth. The crowd stood spellbound, breaking into wild applause whenever Zeke snatched the disc.

For seven years Zeke and Eisenberg entertained the Spartan Stadium crowd to the chants of "Zeke, Zeke, Zeke." Darryl Rogers, the Spartans head coach, cracked that Zeke was the best receiver in the Big Ten and awarded him a varsity letter. By 1982 Zeke started losing a step, so Eisenberg added another dog, Keze. Unfortunately Keze was killed in a car accident two years later, and Zeke had to hang up his bib due to old age. The tradition ended with them, at least until the new millennium when Spartans assistant athletic director Mark Hollis decided the tradition needed to be revived.

University officials searched for a new Zeke, eventually settling on Dexter, a Black Labrador owned by Spartans fans Jim and Terri Foley, who had been performing at local sports events in Holland, Michigan. Dexter, adopting the stage name Zeke II, was an instant hit with old fans, who remembered the original Zeke, and new ones, who appreciated the act.

"We had two weeks to get ready for the first game [in 2002], and it was a whirlwind," Jim Foley told the *State News*, Michigan State's student newspaper, in 2012. "I walked out on that field and I had an instant anxiety attack." His wife cried the first time Dexter, aka Zeke II, performed at Spartan Stadium. "They did a

Zeke the Wonder Dog, a halftime favorite of Michigan State fans, jumps over the back of his owner, Jim Foley, during a 2005 game against Indiana.

video of the original Zeke and gave a little history about who Zeke was, so that people, who didn't necessarily know the Zeke tradition, could join in and become part of that tradition," Terri Foley said in the same article. "I'll never forget how much the crowd was cheering and I walked along the side. The tears were just running down my face."

Zeke II retired in 2007 after his vision started faltering and died in 2012, triggering an outpouring of grief among Spartans fans. But Zeke III, whom the Foleys started training before Dexter retired, has carried on the tradition and can be found running after Frisbees during Spartans football home games.

Fire and Ice

Jud Heathcote cranked out great guards as if he had a patent on them: Magic Johnson, Sam Vincent, Scott Skiles, Steve Smith. He even reshaped and coached up those a notch below the pantheon until they could play at a high level in the always competitive Big Ten. Guards such as Mike Brkovich, Darryl Johnson, Kirk Manns, and Mark Montgomery all benefited from Heathcote's tough love and acumen on the nuances of playing guard at the major college level. The last two guards to play for Heathcote arrived in East Lansing as unfinished products and departed as members of Heathcote's great guard club.

Fire and Ice as they became known were Shawn Respert (Fire) and Eric Snow (Ice). Like many of Heathcote's success stories, Respert and Snow came to MSU as unheralded recruits. Respert enrolled at MSU in 1990 from Bishop Borgess High School in Harper Woods, Michigan, where he excelled on defense and only occasionally flashed the shooting skills that would flower at MSU. Heathcote liked his hand quickness and acceleration and respected his high school coach, who thought Respert had great potential. Tom Izzo and Stan Joplin were lukewarm about him.

Snow, Respert's partner in the backcourt at MSU, came from a family well known to Spartans fans. Snow's brother is Percy, the All-American linebacker who had graduated in 1989. Eric, 6'3", played small forward at Canton McKinley in Ohio and dominated the competition because of his superior athletic ability. As a shooter, however, he made for a good decoy. Izzo and Joplin overlooked his flaws, focusing instead on how his team always won. Heathcote fretted that Snow's shooting range ended three feet from the basket. But Heathcote's assistants won him over on

Snow, and Heathcote won over Izzo and Joplin on Respert. The give and take of the coaching staff seemed to transfer to Respert and Snow, who eventually developed a strong relationship both on and off the court.

Respert sat out all but one game his freshman year due to an ACL injury he suffered his senior year of high school. He mended quickly and spent the season playing on the scout team. Heathcote took the time to work with Respert on his shooting, refining his release and stressing the importance of using his legs. The last month of the season, he found his stride, lighting up his teammates in practice. Word leaked around East Lansing that the Spartans had unearthed a lethal new weapon.

Snow arrived the next year. Heathcote immediately moved him to point guard where he struggled to find his footing. In high school, like many great athletes, he treated defense indifferently, going through the motions until the obligation mercifully ended. But in college especially early in his career, defense became his refuge, the one part of the game at which he thrived. Offense tormented him. His outside shot brought groans and grimaces. His real nemesis, however, was at the free throw line where he produced more clangs than a rusty old furnace. He rarely saw the court in his freshman year as he adjusted to life as a point guard.

With Snow snowed under by the demands of learning a new position, Respert started proving the recruitniks wrong—before the first snowfall. In the 1991 Maui Classic in November, he scored 25 points in his collegiate debut. In the championship game of the tournament against No. 2-ranked Arkansas, Respert burned the Razorbacks for 22 points. He earned MVP of the tournament, which the Spartans won. Respert's name soon cropped up in national conversations about college basketball. He led the Spartans in scoring that year and helped MSU rebound to a 22–8 record and reach the second round of the NCAA tournament.

The next three years, Respert continued to refine and improve on his game. "Shawn was a gym rat, always working on his game," said his teammate Dwayne Stephens in *Magic Moments*. "He would come in before practice and shoot, then stick around, and work some more." In his sophomore year, Respert averaged 20.1 points a game, but the Spartans sunk to 15–13, missing out on the tournament.

Snow made his debut in 1991 as well. At times it was ugly. He shot 20 percent from the free throw line and averaged only a point a game. But he also revealed new dimensions to his gradually improving ability as a guard. Passing, a dormant skill in high school, became a strength. So did pushing the ball on the counter break, a staple of Heathcote's offense. His scoring average inched up a bit in 1992–'93, and his ability to run the break and the half-court offense started paying dividends especially for Respert. Snow's defense proved an incredible asset. "We may have lost a couple of games that year because Eric missed free throws," Heathcote said. "But we won some games because of him [his defense], too."

The next two years gave birth to Fire and Ice. The Spartans won 42 games during that time, competing for the Big Ten title in 1995 and making two NCAA tournament appearances. Snow led the Big Ten in assists in both seasons, setting a league record in 1995. He also led the Spartans in steals and assists three times each. He improved at the free throw line as well and eventually made himself a scoring threat from 15 feet and in. "The thing with Eric is that he improved every year," said his coach in reference to his free throw shooting, which had made him a target of fan abuse for years.

Respert, benefitting from Snow's improving play at the point, increased his scoring average to 24.3 as a junior and then 25.6 as a senior. He led the Spartans in scoring in 29 of his team's 32 games in 1994. An assassin behind the arc, Respert set a Big Ten record for threes in a season. "Everything about [Respert's] jump shot was perfect—the release, the arc, the follow through—just magnificent," noted former Spartan and TV analyst Greg Kelser. In a losing cause, he scored 43 points against Minnesota, earning generous praise from Clem Haskins, the Gophers' head coach. It was the first time since MSU's Scott Skiles in 1986 that anyone in the Big Ten had scored 40 in a game. Then two weeks later in an upset of Indiana in Bloomington, Indiana, he reached that threshold again, putting 40 on the Hoosiers. Respert almost left for the pros after his junior year when he earned third team All-American honors. But a loss to Duke in the second round of the NCAA tournament, a game in which he watched Grant Hill dominate from start to finish, convinced him to return for his senior year.

"Shawn and Eric weren't that close their first two years," wrote Heathcote in *Jud*. "But once they started playing together, they developed something special. They were roommates on the road. They had tremendous respect for each other…It was the same thing Earvin and Gregory had." Fire and Ice fell just short of a Big Ten title in 1995, finishing 14–4.

Occasionally Respert shot the ball too indiscriminately, causing his field goal percentages to dip and the Spartans' fortunes to sag. But those times were rare especially during his senior year. During a nationally televised game against Michigan, he scored 30 points in the second half despite playing on an ankle he had sprained just before halftime. The two-point win came in the midst of the national worship of Michigan's Fab Five and provided a huge emotional lift for the Spartans. A No. 3 seed entering the tournament, MSU lost in the first round to Weber State. "We were out of gas," Respert said.

As seniors Respert and Snow earned a bushel of honors. Respert was a first team All-American, and the *Sporting News* selected him National Player of the Year. He finished his career as the all-time

MSU leader in points scored. For his part Snow was named Big Ten Defensive Player of the Year. "The Fire and Ice theme was good for us and good for the school," said Snow in *Magic Moments.* "It got national attention and helped sell tickets." On the final day of the regular season—a 97–72 pasting of Wisconsin—Michigan State honored Respert and Snow. In a gesture repeated by nearly every Spartans senior since, Respert kneeled down and kissed the floor at center court of the Breslin. "[The kiss] is part of history now," said Respert in 2012.

Both Respert and Snow enjoyed NBA careers. Snow lasted 13 years in the league, carving out a reputation as a defensive stopper and playmaker. During that time he was honored twice with NBA sportsmanship awards. He also raised his free throw shooting percentage to higher than 75 percent. Hampered by stomach cancer that he concealed from his family and many friends, Respert spent four seasons in the NBA. Since retiring as an active player, Respert moved into NBA player development and is currently the player development coach of the Minnesota Timberwolves.

Camp Out for Seats in the Izzone

If you're an upperclassman at MSU and want to sit in the Breslin Center's lower bowl, an area cleverly named the "Izzone," you need to attend the Izzone Campout. If you graduated years ago and just need a fix of college life, well, why not join the nearly 3,000 MSU students who attend the event every September?

Since 1996 the 24-hour event has been held on Munn Field during the early fall, starting on Saturday and ending Sunday.

Just about everyone pitches tents in order to secure a spot in the lower bowl. Priority is based on seniority, faithful attendance of past games, and verifiable presence at the Campout. Campers have to check in at regular intervals throughout the event. The eligibility requirements for obtaining upper bowl Izzone tickets are considerably less rigid since the demand for those tickets is not as competitive.

The Campout festivities often start with a broadcast of a road Spartans football game, which these days is aired in the Munn Ice Arena. (The games used to be broadcast inside the Breslin Center.) After a close loss to Wisconsin one year, Izzo led the students at the Campout to the Duffy Daugherty building where they cheered and consoled the football team as it arrived home.

Other activities are plentiful, including video game tournaments, basketball shooting contests, bouncy games, ice skating, and football and Frisbee tossing. The event reaches its crescendo Saturday evening when Izzo and his team show up to mingle with the crowd. The players hang around and challenge students to video games and more.

One tip: Chat up somebody working the event. They can give you the skinny on the check-in times, so you can leave for a while—and maybe even catch a quick nap at home. Many consider attending the event a labor of love. "It's my third time camping out, and it's just a really good time," an MSU student told the *State News*, Michigan State's independent newspaper, in 2012. "There are always a lot of really cool events going on, and it gets me really pumped for the basketball season."

Spartans Famous Family Trees

Jay and Sam Vincent

The Vincents grew up in Lansing. Jay, the older brother, attended Eastern High School at the same time Earvin Johnson starred at Everett High School on the other side of town. Overshadowed throughout his career by Magic, Jay was a heck of a basketball player, too. Four years younger than Jay, Sam enjoyed all the accolades during high school that eluded his brother. Between the two of them, they scored 3,765 points at MSU and led the Spartans in scoring four times from 1977 to 1985.

The taller, thicker Jay provided a steady presence in the post during Magic's two sublime years at MSU. One of the few times he upstaged Johnson was in their very first collegiate game, against Central Michigan. Magic started but struggled, shooting 3-of-11 and looking unsure of himself. Jay didn't start but came off the bench to score 25 points and rescue the Spartans from an upset. A stress fracture in his foot, however, severely limited his minutes during the Spartans' 1979 tournament run. In his final two years, Jay became the focal point of sub .500 teams, leading the league in scoring both years. "As a junior and senior people saw how good he could be—the second-best player ever from Lansing," his coach Jud Heathcote said in *Magic Moments.* "Jay had the softest hands of anyone I ever coached—just great, great hands."

Heathcote also coached Sam, who after almost choosing Michigan, followed Jay to MSU. The guard possessed a nearly unstoppable hanging jumper that helped him lead the Big Ten in scoring at 23.7 in 1985. After watching Vincent score 31 against his Hoosiers, Indiana coach Bob Knight called him one of the best guards he'd ever seen in the league. That same year Vincent torched Purdue for 39 and Baylor for 32, the latter in a losing cause in the NCAA tournament. Sam earned first team All-American honors in 1985. Both Vincents enjoyed lengthy NBA careers.

The Ducketts

A father, two sons, and three of the most compelling football players in Spartans history. All three made sizable contributions to the football program over their careers. All three were present in different decades at games that became part of MSU football folklore. And all three figured prominently in helping to ensure those games are remembered today.

Ellis, the father, played in the 1954 Rose Bowl against UCLA. He blocked a punt and scored a touchdown that reversed momentum in favor of the Spartans, who had trailed deep into the first half. Tico, the oldest son, played in the 1990 rivalry game against Michigan. He scored the difference-making touchdown late in the game in the Spartans' memorable upset of the Wolverines. T.J., the second son, caught the pass on the final play of the game that sunk Michigan in the Spartans' controversial upset of the Wolverines in 2001. Three epic games. Three key plays. One family.

Ellis, an All-American receiver during his sophomore year, specialized in the big play, averaging 32.5 yards a reception in 1952. His sons did their damage on the ground. They had different styles. The total package, Tico possessed excellent vision, straight-ahead speed, and cutting ability. T.J., who came to MSU as one of the top recruits in the nation at linebacker, had broad shoulders and a tackle-breaking, north-and-south style. Together they ran for 7,555 yards at Michigan State and are third (Tico) and fifth (T.J.) in career rushing yards at MSU.

The Bulloughs

Three Bulloughs have played linebacker at Michigan State. The only Bullough who didn't play the position at Michigan State is the guy responsible for starting it all, Hank.

Hank Bullough was a lineman on Biggie Munn's 1952 national championship team, 1953 Big Ten and Rose Bowl champion team, and on Daugherty's first team in 1954. His greatest fame came as a coach, however, first as an assistant defensive coach under Daugherty, including the memorable defenses of 1965 and 1966, and then as coordinator for the New England Patriots, Cincinnati Bengals, Green Bay Packers, and Detroit Lions.

He passed his football acumen on to his sons, Shane and Chuck, both of whom played linebacker at MSU under George Perles. The All-Big Ten performers were heady, hard-nosed players like their father. Shane's son, Max, starting in 2010, plays linebacker at MSU as well. He may be the best of the bunch. The Bulloughs are the first three-generation family at Michigan State. They are only the fifth in the Big Ten. "It really is something special," said Chuck Bullough in an interview in the *Lansing State Journal.* "I'd like to think that nobody in America has more admiration, respect, loyalty, die-hard feelings for his university than my dad has for Michigan State. To him Michigan State helped his family move up a class, allowed his kids to get educations. He's indebted. Michigan State helped us get where we are, so there's a special bond there."

Ron and Rich Saul

Photographers were keen to shoot Ron and Rich Saul together when they played at MSU. Rich had a chipped tooth, which prompted Coach Daugherty to say he needed the identical twins to smile before he could call their names.

Ron earned All-American honors as a senior guard in 1969. He also was named an Academic All-American that year. So was

Rich. That had never happened before—two brothers being named Academic All-Americans. Ron had more success on the field where he earned the nickname "Hercules" because of his almost supernatural strength. Rich injured his knee against Ohio State in 1968, and many thought his career was over. "The best player I ever coached was Rich Saul," said Dave Smith, Saul's MSU line coach, in an interview with Spartan Nation. "He was a great linebacker. Unfortunately...he had total knee construction. He rehabbed his knee and was bound and determined to play his senior year and graduate with his brother." Remarkably Rich returned to play defensive tackle in 1969, and both Sauls played 12 seasons in the NFL.

The Thornhills

Charles Thornhill came to Michigan State from Roanoke, Virginia, part of Daugherty's Southern pipeline. A vicious hitter, "Mad Dog" was nicknamed that by an MSU assistant after Thornhill told him to take his hands off of him during a practice. Mad Dog began his career in 1964 as a fullback. Daugherty moved him to linebacker in the middle of that season, and a week later he skied over three Purdue defenders to block a punt that teammate Harold Lucas returned for a touchdown. Thornhill started 25 consecutive games with most of those coming during the thick of MSU's greatest defensive run. George Webster, Bubba Smith, and Thornhill embodied the best attributes of those 1965–1966 defenses: orneriness, intimidation, and incomparable athletic skill. Thornhill could keep pace with most wide receivers and move side to side as well as most backs. But he hit with the force of a tidal wave. "Mad Dog is one of the hardest hitting guys I've ever come across," said teammate Dwight Lee in 1966.

Injuries derailed his NFL career, so he moved back to Lansing and worked for General Motors and then the state. He also had two sons, Kaleb and Josh. Sharing similar builds and attitudes as their father, they both played and started at linebacker at MSU. Josh was first team All-Big Ten in his junior and senior years (2000 to 2001) and ended up in the Top Ten in career tackles and tackles for loss.

Robaire and Antonio Smith

Flint natives Robaire and Antonio played different sports. One earned All-American honors; the other made sure America took notice of Michigan State. The older one, Robaire, bludgeoned quarterbacks with pressure off the edge of the defensive line. Despite almost constant double teams, Smith led the Spartans in tackles-for-loss in 1998. He also contributed 54 tackles and was named first team All-American. Drafted by the Tennessee Titans, Robaire, who left after his junior year, spent 11 seasons in the NFL. Often compared to Bubba Smith and not because of their shared surname, Robaire's contributions sometimes went unnoticed in the stat sheet.

Brother Antonio rarely went unnoticed. He committed to MSU basketball coach Tom Izzo when no one else would. But his decision to say yes to Izzo triggered an avalanche of commitments from other talented Michigan basketball players—most notably Morris Peterson and Mateen Cleaves, two of the four Flintstones. Antonio had been toughened up by his football-playing brothers growing up. Perhaps that's why he became the locker room enforcer during the formative years of Tom Izzo's budding dynasty. Usually a man of few words, Smith made sure everyone rowed in the same direction and gave the utmost effort. When he sensed trouble, he pounced as he did after a 20-point loss to Michigan in 1997. Bothered by what he considered a subpar effort from Jon Garavaglia, a former big-time recruit, he slammed Garavaglia against the wall and then threw him a few feet. "You many not care if we win or not, but I do…Play harder," he warned. Smith posed little threat from eight feet and out, doing most of his damage on put-backs and a little jumper. As a rebounder he had few peers, finishing his career as the third (now fourth) most prolific rebounder in Spartans history. "I could have signed five McDonald's All-Americans, and I'd rather had Antonio as my first recruit than any of them," said Izzo in *Green Glory*. To honor Smith, Izzo created the Antonio Smith Glue and Guts Award.

97 The Land Grant Trophy

Michigan State (February 12) and Penn State (February 22) were founded 10 days apart in 1855, the first land grant schools in the nation. Created by their respective state legislatures, each college was charged with the same mission: teach agriculture and the mechanic arts together with the traditional liberal arts to the state's farmers. They predated the Morrill Act, which set aside land throughout the country for other states to follow the model established by Michigan State and Penn State. To celebrate the school's historical bond, Michigan State and Penn State created the Land Grant Trophy when Penn State joined the Big Ten in 1993 and agreed to play each other every year and in the last game of the season. (Because of Big Ten expansion, the two schools had to stop playing each other annually, starting in 2011.) Michigan State's George Perles led the design of the trophy, which includes one iconic structure from each school: Beaumont Tower from Michigan State and Old Main from Penn State. It's an awkward-looking piece, and fans of both schools were slow to warm to the idea of the rivalry, which many felt had been manufactured out of incredibly thin fabric. Over the years, however, the games have

Notable Land Grant Trophy Games

1993: Penn State 38, Michigan State 37

The first and perhaps still most thrilling game in the series, Penn State rallied from a 20-point deficit to beat the Spartans. Jim Miller and Mill Coleman connected on two long passes, including a touchdown, to help the Spartans take a 37–17 lead early in the third quarter. After plugging up the Big Ten's No. 1 rush offense in the first half, the Spartans couldn't stop Penn State's passing attack in the second half as Kerry Collins threw for 352 yards and three touchdowns to lead the comeback.

1997: Michigan State 49, Penn State 14

Looking to end a season of peaks and valleys on a high, the Spartans oiled up the running game and pounded Penn State into the Spartan Stadium turf. Michigan State amassed 452 yards on the ground and scored the second most points ever allowed by Joe Paterno's Nittany Lions. Two Spartans rushed for more than 200 yards, Sedrick Irvin (238) and Mark Renaud (203), the most combined yards in NCAA history by two rushers with at least 200 yards each.

1999: Michigan State 35, Penn State 28

A victory meant nine regular season wins, a milestone with heavy significance. The Spartans started fast and led 28–7 after 30 minutes. The Nittany Lions evened the score in the second half on a deluge of passes. Then it became MSU freshman T.J. Duckett's coming out party as he rumbled through multiple would-be tacklers for an 11-yard touchdown run with 2:38 left in the game. The win turned out to be Nick Saban's last as head coach of the Spartans.

2007: Michigan State 35, Penn State 31

The Spartans outscored the Nittany Lions 28–7 in the last 25 minutes of the game to overcome a 24–7 deficit. Brian Hoyer, who was 16-of-21 for 257 yards, engineered the comeback with seven passes of 20 yards or more in the second half. The win clinched a winning season for first-year head coach Mark Dantonio and sent the Spartans to their first bowl game since 2003.

been entertaining more times than not, and the series and trophy are slowly earning the respect of both universities.

The schools didn't play each other until 1914, a game won 6–3 by MAC. They played 10 times over 79 years with the Spartans posting an 8–1–1 record. Many of the wins were blowouts. With the start of the Land Grant Trophy, the series advantage shifted to Penn State, which holds a 13–5 edge. The games have generally contained boatloads of offensive fireworks and stat-stuffing feats.

Ten Top Kickers and Punters

They are the unsung heroes of football especially in today's game of high specialization. Asked to bail their team out of a possession that ended short of its goal, they usually only appear after disappointment. Field goals and punts, however, can be the difference between winning and losing.

Always looking for an edge, Duffy Daugherty experimented with kickers of all types, including barefooted ones, soccer style ones, and even some who had never played football. A disproportionate number of great kickers and punters in the Big Ten over the last half century have come from Michigan State. Below are some of the most noteworthy in MSU history (* indicates All-American).

Dick Kenney (1964 to 1966)
Kenney was one of 11 players Daugherty recruited from the Hawaiian Islands. He was also one of the first in the college game to kick barefooted. Kenney kicked a 47-yarder in the Game of the Century and surprised Ohio State in the Spartans' pivotal 11–8 win

that same year with a fake extra-point and pass to holder Charlie Wedemeyer, another Hawaiian, for a two-point conversion. "He'd take that shoe off, snow, rain, 0-degree weather. The fans loved him," Bob Apisa, the third Hawaiian on the 1966 Spartans, told the *Honolulu Star-Bulletin* after Kenney's death in 2005.

Borys Shlapak (1970 to 1971)

The first soccer-style kicker at MSU, Shlapak booted three field goals of 54 yards and one of 53 yards in 1970–'71. Those are four of the longest field goals in MSU history. In fact he's the only kicker to have four kicks ranked among the 16 longest in school history. His 54-yarder against Northwestern in 1970 set the then-record for longest field goal in Spartans history.

Dirk Kryt (1972 to 1973)

Daugherty elevated Kryt, an exchange student from the Netherlands who played soccer, from the junior varsity days before the Spartans were to face fifth-ranked Ohio State in 1972. Kryt, wearing blue soccer shorts, kicked four field goals, one a 40-yarder, to help MSU upset Ohio State 19–12. The loss so enraged OSU coach Woody Hayes that he shoved a camera into a photographer's face after the game. Kryt admitted afterward that he knew little about football and barely understood the rules, which helped remove a lot of pressure. Later in the season, Kryt was suspended for smoking in the locker room, something he'd actually been doing since being put on the team.

Morten Andersen (1978 to 1981)*

Andersen owns three of the longest field goals in MSU history, including the longest, which is also the Big Ten record. Against Ohio State in 1981, Andersen surprised the Buckeyes just by lining up for a 63-yard attempt. He nailed it, though, and put his name in the record book. "The 63-yarder against Ohio State was pretty cool," Andersen said in 2011 in the wake of his induction into the MSU Hall of Fame. "The crazy thing about it was I had a pretty good wind behind me. It probably would have gone through from 73. I kicked it a long ways."

In his career Andersen also converted on field goals of 57 and 54 yards, giving him three of the five longest three-pointers in MSU history. Andersen, who only played football for one year in high school after coming over from Denmark in 1977 as an exchange student, made seven field goals of 50-yards or more. He finished his career at MSU as the Big Ten all-time leader in field goals made (45) and represented one of the few Spartans bright spots during his upperclassmen years of 1980 to 1981. He went on to star in the NFL primarily with the New Orleans Saints.

Ray Stachowicz (1976 to 1980)*

For a couple of seasons, Stachowicz saw as much action as a pool cleaner in Alberta. He still made first team All-Big Ten as a punter in 1977 and 1978. In his junior year, Stachowicz's workload increased, but his effectiveness did not falter. He led the Big Ten in punting in 1979 and 1980 to earn first team All-Big Ten honors again each year, making him the first player ever to earn four first team All-Big Ten honors. His 46.2 yards a punt in his senior year set a Big Ten record. When he finished his career at MSU, he held the record for the four longest punts in school history.

Rolf Mojsiejenko (1981 to 1984)*

Perhaps the greatest all-around kicker and punter of the last 70 years at MSU, Mojsiejenko was a key weapon for George Perles from 1983 to 1984. Emphasizing defense and field position, Perles needed a sound kicking game. Mojsiejenko provided both, punting for an average of 43.8 yards, third on the all-time MSU list, and offering a long distance field goal threat. He owns three of the six longest field goals in Spartans history: 61, 59, and 54. He punted

77 times in 1982, the most since 1938; 76 times in 1984; and 74 times in 1983, accounting for three of the five highest total number of punts in a season in MSU history. He enjoyed a long career in the NFL mostly with the San Diego Chargers.

Greg Montgomery (1985 to 1987)*

Distance and consistency were the hallmarks of Montgomery, who helped Perles execute his field-position strategy effectively from 1985 to 1987. Montgomery recorded at least one 50-yard punt in 33 of his 35 games and averaged 45.2 yards a punt over the course of his career, which is best all time at MSU and second all time in the Big Ten. In 1986 he averaged 47.8 per punt, then a school record, and banged one 86 yards against Michigan in 1986, the longest punt in MSU history.

Paul Edinger (1996 to 1999)*

One of most accurate kickers in MSU history, Edinger kicked his way into Spartans bowl lore by booting the game winner against Florida in the 2000 Citrus Bowl. In 1998 he converted on 22-of-26 field goal attempts, a single-season MSU record for makes. From beyond 40 yards, he made 8-of-9 that year. In 1999 he booted kicks of 54 and 55 yards. He still shares the MSU record for field goals in a game, five, which he did twice, once to help upset No. 1 Ohio State. Edinger also shared the MSU record for field goals in a season with 22.

Brandon Fields (2003 to 2006)*

Fields regularly rocketed the ball 50 or more yards, giving the Spartans defense, which from 2003 to 2006 suffered from numerous talent and scheme issues, much-needed help. When Fields wasn't booming punts, he was downing them inside the 20-yard line. Fields led the nation in punting at 47.9 yards in 2004, still a Spartans single-season record. That average included 23 punts of

50 yards or more and 13 downed inside the 20. His career punting average of 45 yards a punt ranks second all time at MSU and third all time in the Big Ten.

Bret Swenson (2006 to 2009)

Dependable if not spectacular, Swenson attempted more field goals than any Spartan in history (91). He also made more field goals than any Spartan (71). He shares with two other kickers the school record for most field goals in the season, 22, which he accomplished in 2008. And he is the all-time points leader in MSU history with 377. In 2009 Swenson was named team MVP, the only kicker in school history to win the award.

Have a Drink at Coral Gables

In its heyday from the 1940s to the 1960s, Coral Gables, a roadhouse, teemed with athletes from the football and basketball team. And why not? Nearly every Michigan State student from that era headed to the restaurant and bar for a little R & R.

Coral Gables, located on East Grand River just outside the dry corridor of East Lansing, has been a little a bit of everything over the years. Opened in the 1920s as Fleur-de-Lis (flower of the lily) Inn, it started as a high-end supper club and then morphed in the 1930s into a square dance hall under a new name, Green Gables, which also included an ice-rink. It remade itself as a concert venue in the 1940s called Coral Gables Ballroom, hosting big band acts. Its popularity among MSC students started climbing during this era. Duke Ellington, Tommy Dorsey, Woody Herman, and all the big acts came through Coral Gables.

In 1957 Coral Gables burned down, which triggered the establishment's fourth act: a casual restaurant and bar that featured local rock-and-roll bands such as the Sunliners, Me and Dem Guys, and the Kingtones. Occasionally a national band appeared, but the Gables' bread-and-butter consisted of bands from the area whose music encouraged dancing. Created by owner Tom Johnson, the new format and atmosphere proved a colossal hit with MSU students, who packed the Gables well over capacity on weekends. The food was plain but cheap, the beer poured frequently, and the ear-splitting music was loud and constant.

Many MSU students of the late 1950s and 60s enjoyed their first legal drink at Coral Gables. Those celebrating their 21st birthday at the Gables received a free drink and a small pizza. When the place wasn't rocking, it hosted literary readings from heroes of the Beat and hippie generation. Allen Ginsberg and Timothy Leary, according to some sources, were welcomed at the Gables after MSU officials booted them from an on-campus reading. Many MSU clubs, including the sailing and ski clubs, hosted their meetings at Coral Gables as well.

Johnson, who was recruited by Charlie Bachman but suffered a career-ending injury before ever putting on a Spartans uniform, had an excellent relationship with the football program. He regularly hired athletes to serve as bouncers, a tough job in a college town where so many potential patrons were underage. Ron Curl, "Mad Dog" Charles Thornhill, and Robert Viney were just a few of the prominent MSU athletes who handled the job. After the football games on Saturday, the Gables often swarmed with girdiron players, dancing or simply relaxing after the afternoon's 60 minutes of mental and physical stress.

Coral Gables, which had only male servers until the 1970s, started to lose its grip as top nightlife dog in 1970 when East Lansing changed its liquor laws to permit drinking closer to campus. MSU students began opting for the new bars and restaurants that were more nearby. But you can still get a meal and a drink at Coral Gables, which sits where it has since the 1920s. Mementoes from it heyday adorn the walls.

100 The World According to Duffy

Duffy Daugherty coached great teams. He recruited and mentored men of sublime talent and will. And boy, could he handle a room of reporters, fat cat donors, alumni, fans—you name it. Below are some stories, one-liners, quips, and jokes from Daugherty, a man known for his sense of humor as much as coaching success.

"You can credit me for getting Biggie [Munn] into the Hall of Fame. After six years of my coaching, they appreciate what a great coach he really was."

In reference to a letter he allegedly received from an unhappy alumnus: "Remember, Duffy, we're with you win or tie."

To an excited group of supporters during an alumni gathering: "The trouble with you people is that you get carried away by my enthusiasm."

"A football coach's main problem is that he is responsible to irresponsible people."

After learning that he had received a threat on his life before a game against Marquette: "I told Bob Devaney, who sits on the bench

Michigan State coach Duffy Daugherty, who marches off the field after defeating Michigan 23–12 in 1969, was known for his wit and amusing one-liners.

with me, that I thought it would be a good idea if he wore the 'Head Coach' in large letters on the back."

"I could have been a Rhodes Scholar except for my grades."

In a ragged 0–0 game against Notre Dame, Daugherty sent in a play that called for the quarterback, Dean Look, to hand the ball off to halfback Herb Adderley, who was to follow a trio of linemen pulling to the left. This was a staple play, and Daugherty really liked its chances in this situation. Look called the play, but instead of handing the ball off to Adderley, he kept it himself, fooling everyone, including his own team. He was hit behind the line of scrimmage but managed to escape the Notre Dame defender and run for 40 yards down to the 7-yard line. Though pleased with the result, Daugherty was also upset that Look had defied him. He yanked his quarterback, who had a huge grin on his face, out of the game, grabbed him, and yelled, "Dean, we don't even have a play like that." Look never stopped grinning and said, "Duff, you ought to. It's a dandy."

"I like those goal-line stands of ours, but I wish they'd make them up around the 50-yard line where I can see them better."

"I have a couple of big freshmen preparing for a special job next fall. At the end of each game—win or lose—they are to hoist me to their shoulders and carry me off the field. Then fans in the stands will say, 'Look, there goes old Duffy again. He might not be much of a coach, but his players sure love him.'"

When a reporter asked him before the 1965 season whom he was happy to have back, he replied, "Me."

"My only feeling about superstition is that it's unlucky to be behind at the end of a game."

After the famous 10–10 tie with Notre Dame in 1966: "A tie is like kissing your sister."

Referring to his married players on his team: "They all agreed to move into dormitories for the first two weeks of fall practice. Of course, I helped their decision a little; I made it a rule."

After center Walt Forman, whose grade point average was 3.89 out of a possible 4.0, quit the team to enter medical school: "We've learned our lesson. We won't recruit anybody that intelligent again."

"Football is not a contact sport; it's a collision sport. Dancing is a contact sport."

After a day at Santa Anita Race Track: "The only place where windows clean people."

When a reporter asked him why he didn't do what Woody Hayes did at Ohio State by leading his team on the field while singing the Ohio State fight song, Daugherty quipped, "That's fine, but I don't even know Ohio State's fight song."

On fourth-and-1 at a key point late in a game, the Spartans quarterback looked to the sidelines for some guidance from Daugherty on what to do next—punt or go for it. Daugherty just stood there, arms folded, and let the quarterback decide. Asked after the game why he didn't help the quarterback, Duffy said: "That kid has a four-year scholarship. My contract is a one-year deal. Let him make his own decision."

In a game the Spartans were winning big, Daugherty emptied the bench all the way down to the scout team quarterback, Bobby Popp. The coaches told him to call straight ahead running plays. Instead he called a 21 reverse, which went for a touchdown, the last thing Daugherty wanted. On the sidelines Daugherty asked him why he called that play against his coach's wishes. Popp responded: "Well, Coach, I'll tell you. My number is 13. You had John in at wingback, and his number is 9. Since the two of us are roommates, I just took the 13 and the 9, added them up, and figured it'd be nice to call the 21 reverse." Flabbergasted, Daugherty pointed out the obvious to Popp. "Bobby," he said, "13 and 9 add up to 22—not 21." "Coach, if I were as smart as you, we wouldn't have scored," Popp stated matter of factly.

After beating Notre Dame handily in 1956: "I wasn't worried about getting our boys up for this one. They were so high this week that we had to shake the trees around the field to get them down for practice."

"To be a great football player and a great person, you have to have three bones in your body: a wishbone, a backbone, and a funny bone."

Sources

The author gratefully acknowledges the following sources used in researching and writing this book with a special shout-out to Fred Stabley's essential book on the first 75 years of Spartans football history, *The Spartans*, and Jack Ebling's numerous invaluable contributions to the history of MSU sports.

Books

Grinczel, Steve. *Michigan State Football: They Are Spartans.* Charleston, South Carolina: Arcadia Press. 2003

Rexrode, Joe. *Stadium Stories: Michigan State Spartans: Great Moments in Team History.* Guilford, Connecticut: Morris Publishing LLC. 2006

Heathcote, Jud with Ebling, Jack. *Jud: A Magical Journey.* Champaign, Illinois: Sagamore Publishing. 1995

Ann Arbor News and Lansing State Journal. *Backyard Brawl: The Storied Rivalry of Michigan-Michigan State Football.* Birmingham, Alabama: Epic Sports. 2000

Stabley, Fred Jr. and Staudt, Tim. *Tales of the Magical Spartans: A Collection of a Stories From the 1979 Michigan State NCAA Basketball Champions.* Champaign, Illinois: Sports Publishing. 2003

Celizic, Mike. *The Biggest Game of Them All: Notre Dame, Michigan State, and the Fall of 66.* New York: Simon & Shuster. 1992

Stanford, Linda O and Dewhurst, Kurt C. *MSU Campus: Buildings, Places, Spaces.* East Lansing, Michigan: Michigan State University Press. 2002

Young, David, M.D. *Arrogance and Scheming in the Big Ten: Michigan State's Quest for Membership and Michigan's Powerful Opposition.* DJY Publishing. 2011

Sports Illustrated. *Champs: Michigan State Spartans: 1999–2000 National Champions. A Special Collector's Edition.* New York, New York: Time Inc. 2000

Ebling, Jack. *Heart of a Spartan: The Story of Michigan State Football Renaissance.* Lansing: Sports Community Publishing. 2012

Ebling, Jack and Farina, John. *Magic Moments: A Century of Spartan Basketball.* Chelsea, Michigan: Sleeping Bear Press. 1998

Ebling, Jack & Lewandowski, John. *Green Glory: Champions of the Hardwood 1998–2001.* Gametime Sports and Entertainment LLC. 2001

Stabley, Fred W. *The Spartans: Michigan State Football.* Huntsville, Alabama: The Strode Publishers. Inc. 1975

Perles, George with Gregorian, Vahe. *George Perles: The Ride* of a Lifetime. Champaign, Illinois: Sagamore Publishing. 1995

Daugherty, Duffy with Diles, Dave. *Duffy: An Autobiography.* Garden City, New York: Doubleday & Company, Inc. 1974

Daugherty, Duffy and Wilson, Clifford B. *1ˢᵗ and Ten.* Dubuque, Iowa: WM C Brown Company Publishers. 1961

Davis, Seth. *When March Went Mad: The Game that Transformed Basketball.* New York, New York: Times Books Henry Company LLC. 2009

Kelser, Gregory with Grinczel, Steve. *Tales from Michigan State Basketball.* Champaign, Illinois: Sports Publishing LLC. 2006

Henning, Lynn. *Spartan Seasons II: More Triumph and Turmoil of Michigan State Sports.* Bloomfield Hills, Michigan: Sports Seasons Publishing. 2006

Gibson, Kirk with Henning, Lynn. *Bottom of the Ninth.* Chelsea, Michigan: Sleeping Bear Press. 1997

Periodicals

Lansing State Journal
Detroit Free Press
The Detroit News
USA Today
Wisconsin State Journal
The Toledo Blade
The State News
The New York Times
The Morning Call
Ann Arbor News
Chicago Tribune
The Daily Herald
Orlando Sentinel
Time magazine
Honolulu Star Bulletin
The Christian Science Monitor
Star Tribune
Journal of Sport History

Digital Media

www.sportsillustrated.cnn.com/vault
www.mlive.com
www.msuspartans.com
www.theonlycolors.com (SB Nation Network)
www.msu.edu
www.examiner.com
www.spartannation.com
www.espn.go.com
www.profootballresearcher.org (Coffin Corner)
www.aolnews.com

www.cbssports.com
www.spartanband.net
www.alumni.msu.edu
www.tourntheten.com
www.newspaperarchive.com
www.collegefootball.org